S0-FDR-343

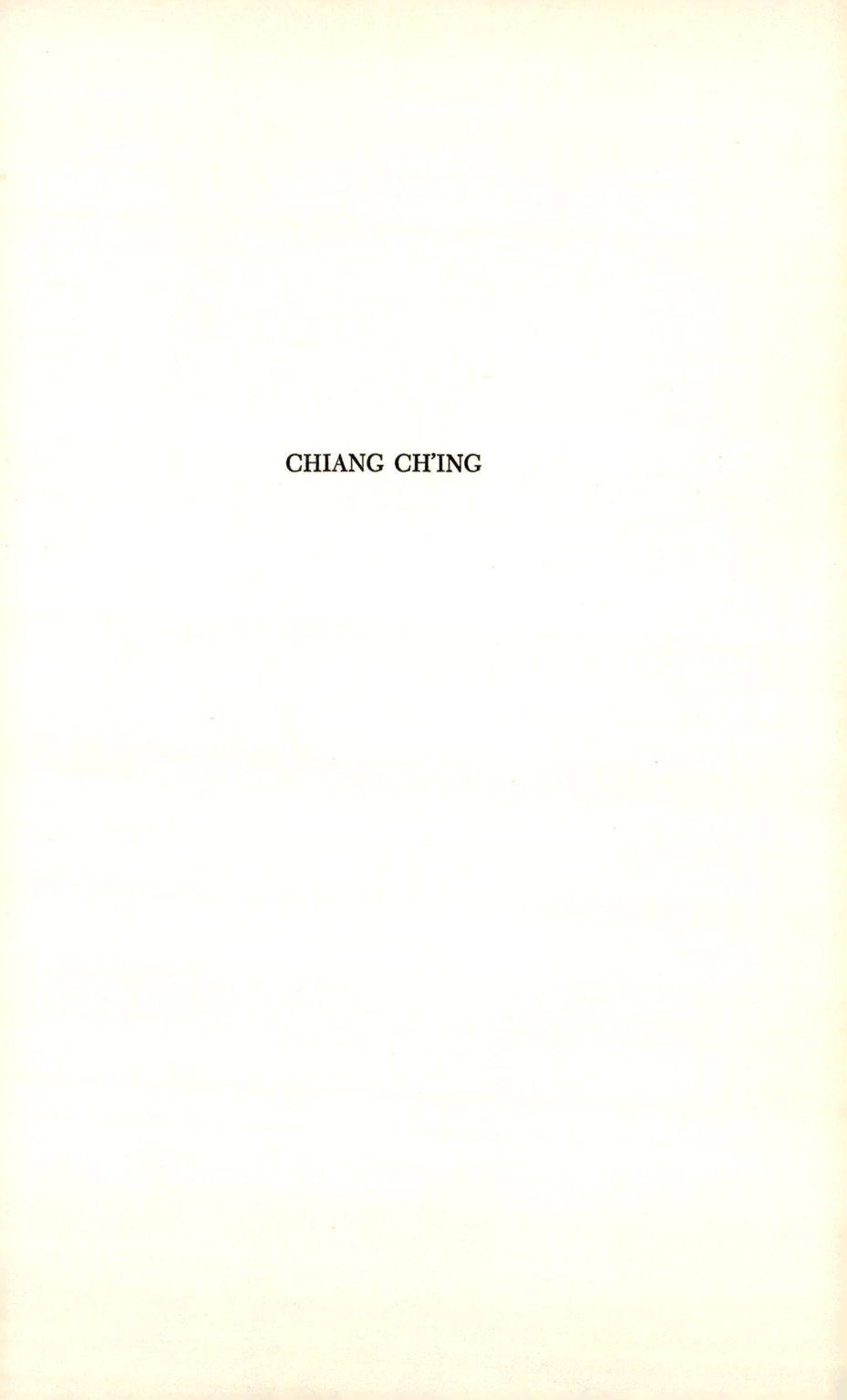

CHIANG CH'ING

CHIANG CH'ING

*The Emergence of a Revolutionary
Political Leader*

Dwan L. Tai, Ph.D.

An Exposition-University Book

Exposition Press   Hicksville, New York

Acknowledgment is hereby given to reprint material from the book CHINA RETURNS by Klaus Mehnert. Trans. from the German. Eng. trans. copyright © 1972 by E. P. Dutton & Co., Inc., publishers, and used with their permission.

Library of Congress Cataloging in Publication Data
Tai, Dwan Liang, 1941—
    Chiang Ch'ing: the emergence of a revolutionary political leader.

(An Exposition-university book)
Bibliography: pp. 199-213
1. Chiang Ch'ing. 2. China—Politics and government —1949—
DS778.C5374T34   951.05'092'4 [B]   74-10618
ISBN 0-682-48060-6

FIRST EDITION

© 1974 by Dwan Liang Tai

All rights reserved, including the right of reproduction in whole or in part, in any form or by any means, electronic or mechanical, including photocopying, recording, or by any information storage and retrieval system, without permission in writing from the Publisher. Inquiries should be addressed to Exposition Press, Inc. 900 South Oyster Bay Road, Hicksville, N.Y. 11801

ISBN 0-682-48060-6

Printed in the United States of America

TO MY DEAR SISTERS
AND BROTHERS

Contents

PREFACE ix
    Historical Setting x
    Acknowledgments xiv
INTRODUCTION xvii
    Framework of Analysis xviii
    Format: Approach, Scope, Structure, Viewpoint
    and Sources xxiii

Part One
THE CHINESE COMMUNIST PARTY AND CHIANG CH'ING

1. Chiang Ch'ing's Membership and Early Party Work   3
2. Major Party Policies and Chiang Ch'ing's Participation   9
3. The Ninth Party Congress and After   20

Part Two
CHIANG CH'ING IN GOVERNMENT AND OFFICIAL CIRCLES

4. Party, Government, and the National Leadership   27
5. Chiang Ch'ing on the National Scene   32
6. Chiang Ch'ing in International Affairs   36

Part Three
THE CHINESE ARMED FORCES AND CHIANG CH'ING

7. Chiang Ch'ing's Relationship with the People's Liberation Army   51
8. Chiang Ch'ing as "Adviser" of the Armed Forces   55
9. Chiang Ch'ing, the People's Liberation Army, and the Red Guards   61

10.	Chiang Ch'ing and the Military Leadership	66
11.	Military Problems and Chiang Ch'ing	68
12.	Chiang Ch'ing and Military Conferences and Receptions	73
13.	Cultural Workers within the Chinese Armed Forces	78

Part Four
CHIANG CH'ING IN THE IDEOLOGICAL AND CULTURAL SPHERES

14.	The Maoist Line on Literature and Art	87
15.	Early Ideological and Cultural Struggles	90
16.	Reform Movement in Peking Opera, Ballet and Symphony	96
17.	Chiang Ch'ing and the Mass Media of Communication	106

Part Five
CHIANG CH'ING'S ROLE IN THE GREAT PROLETARIAN CULTURAL REVOLUTION

18.	Planning and Launching of the Great Proletarian Cultural Revolution	113
19.	Red Guards and Mass Rallies	123
20.	Chiang Ch'ing and the Development of the Great Proletarian Cultural Revolution	127
21.	Chiang Ch'ing and China's Youth	140

Part Six
CHIANG CH'ING'S WORKS AND CONTRIBUTIONS

22.	Maoist Thought and Chiang Ch'ing's Contributions	145
23.	Chiang Ch'ing's "Revolutionary" Works: A Digest	149
24.	Popular Response and Impact	165

Part Seven
SUMMARY AND CONCLUSION

Summary and Conclusion	173
REFERENCE NOTES	178
SELECTED BIBLIOGRAPHY	199
INDEX	215

Preface

"The week that changed the world," as President Nixon characterized his February 1972 visit to the People's Republic of China, has become the phrase which has served to designate the milestone of a new era in international politics and in the relations between the United States and China.

About the same time, many Americans began to readjust their perceptions about China—a country with a continuous civilization that has flourished for five thousand years, which has undertaken in this century one of the most far-reaching social, economic, and political revolutions in history.

Since 1972 people of all walks of life have visited mainland China, and numerous books and countless articles have been written on a wide range of Chinese subjects. These developments are in response to the public need for more extensive information on China.

For the past half century, a very intensive revolutionary movement has been surging in a nation whose population constitutes one-quarter of mankind, living in an area of 3.7 million square miles (slightly more than the 3.6 million square miles comprising the United States). In terms of the length of time involved, the number of people affected, and the size of the land area engulfed, as well as the impact of resulting socio-economic changes, the Chinese Communist Revolution has eclipsed the American, French, and Russian revolutions.

It is essential now more than ever to understand and evaluate the Party that carried out this Revolution, the individuals who led the cause forward, and their motivations and perspectives.

The present work is a political case study of one of the leaders of this movement—Chiang Ch'ing, the most powerful woman in the history of modern China and the wife of Chairman Mao Tse-tung. Evaluation of Chiang Ch'ing's role as a leading political figure in China's history begins with this query: Will Chiang Ch'ing simply fade away after Mao's passing, or will she remain a member of the top Chinese Communist leadership as a political force in her own right? This study attempts to analyze in systematic fashion the hypothesis that Chiang Ch'ing's power, while initially derived from Mao Tse-tung's, has become increasingly independent, self-sustaining, and most likely to endure even beyond Mao's life span.

In order to place the study in proper historical perspective, a brief review of the rise of the Chinese Communist Party (CCP) from 1921 to 1949 is appropriate.

HISTORICAL SETTING

China, known to some historians as the "Middle Kingdom," had from time immemorial been regarded by its people as the center of civilization. This conception was shattered in the nineteenth century by a series of foreign invasions and defeats beginning with the Opium War (1839-1842). Finally, the revolution of 1911 succeeded in overthrowing the Ch'ing Dynasty, which for centuries had ruled China, but economic difficulties and continued outside pressures from Japan and the West kept the country in bondage.

Having witnessed the failure of the existing form of government to solve China's problems and political instability, a group of intellectuals in China began turning to Marxism as a possible solution to her difficulties. On July 1, 1921, twelve Communist delegates, including Mao Tse-tung, Tung Pi-wu, Chen Tan-chiu, and Ho Shu-heng, gathered in Shanghai to hold the First National Congress of the Communist Party of China. With the assistance of representatives from the Comintern (Communist International), they drew up and adopted the first Constitution of the Communist Party of China.

Inasmuch as the Communist International had embarked

upon a policy of cooperation between Communists and other parties in movements for national liberation at its second Moscow congress in 1920, Comintern agents contacted Dr. Sun Yat-sen, who was then endeavoring to wipe out the corrupt northern warlords and unite China. Anxious to accept Soviet aid, he issued a joint statement with Soviet Minister Adolf Joffe on January 26, 1923, announcing Soviet support of China's unification. In June 1923, submitting to Comintern pressure, members of the Chinese Communist Party joined the Kuomintang Party (KMT) nominally as individual members, and in January of the following year the Kuomintang's First Congress adopted a new national program for China.

Working closely with Michael Borodin, the chief Soviet agent in China, Sun began an active political and military campaign against the northern warlords. Chiang Kai-shek, Sun's military aide, was sent to Moscow to observe and learn about the organization of the Soviet military forces. On Chiang's return, he was appointed head of the Whampoa Military Academy and later commander in chief of the Kuomintang (also known as Nationalist) Army.

While the Kuomintang continued to augment its military power under Chiang, the Communists moved into key positions which enabled them to concentrate on propaganda and organization of workers and peasants, hoping ultimately to capture the Kuomintang from within. But after Sun Yat-sen died, on March 12, 1925, Chiang Kai-shek took control even though Wang Ching-wei, leader of the nominal left wing of the KMT, succeeded Sun in a civil capacity. During the next year, the long-awaited Northern Expedition to smash the warlords was initiated; military success was phenomenal, and by the end of 1926, the Kuomintang had captured the Wuhan cities (Hankow, Wuch'ang and Hanyang) in Central China.

However, as the expedition continued, a split developed between the left KMT-Communist forces in Central China and right KMT forces under Chiang Kai-shek along the eastern coast. Finally, in April 1927, Chiang instituted a bloody purge to stamp out Communists and left Kuomintang elements in

Shanghai. An anti-Communist campaign soon spread throughout the nation, and by the autumn of 1927, Borodin and other Russian advisers had fled the country. In quick succession the scattered military forces loyal to the Communist Party were suppressed. The Communist leaders Mao Tse-tung and Chu Teh managed to escape to south-central China and during the spring of 1928 started their underground movement anew on the Hunan-Kiangsi border, which evolved into the major Communist guerrilla area in China.

From 1928 on, a new dimension was added to the unfolding internal turmoil. Military clashes with the Japanese aroused increasingly strong anti-Japanese sentiment among the people. Although Chiang Kai-shek was concerned with national defense, he was more determined to annihilate the Communists and mounted five extermination campaigns against them between December 1930 and October 1933. Finally, in October 1934, the Kuomintang forces encircled the Red Army base in southern Kiangsi. The Communists, on the verge of defeat, managed to slip away from them and began the famous Long March north, with other Red Army units gradually withdrawing from their bases and joining them along the way. After traveling about 6,000 miles, they reached the northern province of Shensi one year later; there they established their revolutionary center at Yenan. The hardships and setbacks of the trip had reduced their ranks from 300,000 men to less than 20,000.

During the Long March, notwithstanding the fact that the Communists were involved in their most difficult and intricate struggle to survive, there were clashes within the Communist leadership. It was at this time, while out of contact with Moscow, that Mao began to emerge as preeminent, and at a meeting of Party leaders at Tsunyi, his leadership, at least for the duration of the Long March, was formally acknowledged.

As the Red Army settled down in Yenan, the war against Japan continued to intensify while Chinese nationalism increased proportionally. In May 1936, responding to Comintern demands and his own Party's needs, Mao called for a second united front against Japan, but Chiang nevertheless continued to concentrate his attacks on the Red Army until he was seized in Shensi while reviewing Chiang Hsüeh-liang's troops. There he was forced to agree that he would end the civil war, reorganize the government, and form a united front against Japan.

In 1937 full-scale war finally broke out between Japan and China. The Sino-Japanese War remained undeclared even after December 8, 1941, when it then merged into the worldwide conflagration known as World War II.

While in Yenan, the Communist Party began to grow in strength and size. It was during this period of Mao Tse-tung's rise and the Party's rebirth that Chiang Ch'ing, a long-time social agitator and dedicated Party underground worker (since 1931), arrived in Yenan from Shanghai and began to work at Mao's headquarters.

With Chiang Ch'ing as his aide and counsel, encouraging him to assert his thoughts and helping him to crystallize and implement new concepts, Mao launched his first Party rectification campaign, and mapped out his strategy for the Chinese Communist Revolution. During the so-called Yenan period, many innovative techniques were developed and applied on a large scale, including, among others, the "mass line," "criticism and self-criticism," "survey" and "investigation" teams, "study groups," "unity-criticism-unity," "struggle-criticism-transformation," and "hsia-fang" ("down-to-the-countryside") movements. Mao's objective was to build a strong Party and army; develop self-sufficient, strategically located, and armed territorial bases; and implement political and economic programs to gain mass support. These programs were to be carried out by three methods: (1) by relying on poor peasants and farm laborers as the base of the Communist Party, uniting with middle peasants, restricting the rich peasants, protecting the medium and small industrialists and businessmen, and abolishing the landlord class; (2) by using the Red Army for propaganda, aid and organization of the countryside into small Red bases; and (3) by utilizing guerrilla or mobile warfare as the main form of fighting, with the Red Army scattering during ordinary times to aid and educate peasants, and at times of battle concentrating its forces to encircle and annihilate the enemy swiftly and decisively.

The result was that during the prolonged Japanese invasion of China, the Communists were particularly successful in using guerrilla tactics to resist the Japanese aggressors. They moved into vast rural areas behind Japanese lines, organized villagers, created local governments, and established goodwill between the people and the armed forces, a relationship that had always been strained in China. Gradually, their armed forces expanded from less than 50,000 men in 1937 to more than 500,000 in 1945 (a tenfold increase), while Party membership increased from 40,000 to more than 1,210,000, according to their own figures.

Following the end of World War II, the United States sent General George C. Marshall to China in 1946 to reestablish Chinese unity, but the Marshall mission failed and the civil war continued. The Communist forces, equipped with captured Japanese arms, shifted from guerrilla warfare to large-scale offensive campaigns. In 1948 they defeated the Nationalist Armies in Manchuria. One year later they captured Nanking, the Nationalist capital, and finally, on December 6, 1949, Chiang Kai-shek fled to Taiwan.

On October 1, 1949, the People's Republic of China was formally proclaimed in Peking. Chiang Ch'ing, who had been working within the Party since 1931 and had been helping Mao since 1939, was one of the old-timers who had the great satisfaction of partaking in the Communist triumph.

ACKNOWLEDGMENTS

As the manuscript of this book goes to press, I feel a deep sense of gratitude to all those who helped make it possible.

Over the past fourteen years of study and research at the University of Hawaii, Columbia University, New York, and the George Washington University, Washington, D.C., I have been most fortunate to have studied economics, political science, and

Preface

international relations under leading and renowned scholars, especially: Professors Arthur F. Burns, Robert M. Dunn, Jr., Harold C. Hinton, William Reid Johnson, A. Kisselgoff, Donald W. Klopf, Ilse Mintz, Benjamin Nimer, Ronald M. Schneider, Charles Shami, George C. Y. Wang, Stephen J. Wayne, and Richard Y. C. Yin. Their teachings remain vivid in my remembrance and undoubtedly have had an impact on this work. Particularly is this true of Professors Johnson and Hinton, who like Professor Parris H. Chang, Dr. David Albright, and Dr. Theodore R. Giuttari, so generously contributed their time and thoughts to provide me with valuable suggestions.

I am also indebted to Dr. Lloyd H. Elliott, Dean Arthur E. Burns, Dean William F. E. Long, and Dean Aaron W. Warner for their guidance and inspiration. This book is based on research done in partial fulfillment of the Doctor of Philosophy degree at the George Washington University. For reviewing and commenting on this study. I would like to express my appreciation to Professors King Chen, Lee Houchins, Young Kim, John B. Tsu, and Hsing-nung Yao.

For much-needed encouragement and advice I wish to express my gratitude to the Honorable Gerald R. Ford, Vice-President of the United States; Senators Hiram L. Fong and Robert Dole; Congressmen John Brademas, Joseph P. Addabbo, Barber B. Conable, Jr., and Lester L. Wolff, and former Congressman Seymour Halpern.

I wish also to thank my friends for their concern and assistance during the period of my travels and research: Mr. and Mrs. Robert Albert, Admiral and Mrs. Irwin Chase, Jr., Frank M. C. Chen, Mr. and Mrs. Clarence Ching, T. Faillace, S. Fu, Reed Hanson, Mr. and Mrs. Louis F. S. Hong, E. Houshmand, Virginia Lackey, Mr. and Mrs. C. Y. Lee, Mr. and Mrs. Kingchau Mui, Dr. Vera Radcliffe, Mr. and Mrs. Francis Sen, General and Mrs. W. T. Tsai, T. Wong, and others in Hong Kong, Taiwan, New York, and London—particularly those who have recently visited mainland China and have provided me with materials that have been useful in documenting my analysis. My special thanks are extended to Alfred Hsi Liu for his many contributions, including the design of the jacket, and to my sister Lala for her invaluable assistance in preparing the manuscript for publication.

All the advice, opinions and materials collected for this book were evaluated, selected, and interpreted by the author. The book presents the writer's views and personal conclusions; should there be any errors or shortcomings, they are the author's responsibility.

D. L. T.

Introduction

There are many approaches to the study of politics. The prevailing concern of early American political scientists was with the legal aspects of government and politics. However, the discipline gradually became increasingly interested in the description and analysis of the dynamic aspects of government in contrast with its legal organization and formal functions. This emphasis led in turn to a broader spectrum, a view of politics as encompassing "forces" as well as "institutions," "organizations" as well as "individuals."

Individual case studies have become an important approach to the study of politics and history, one that is growing in attraction and advancing in methodological sophistication. These case studies have examined the personal characteristics, beliefs, and value systems of individuals, together with their methods and style, environmental envelopes, and their achievements and failures as political figures who possess influence and authority. Some of the case studies have greatly illuminated the dynamics of government and politics.

With the emergence of mainland China as a world power in recent times, political scientists and scholars have studied the doctrines, policies, economic and political structures, and other facets of the Chinese Communist movement with renewed interest. Since little information is available on nearly all prominent figures of modern China, individual studies have not often been attempted. Nevertheless, the concentration of power and the general nature of the Chinese Communist political system, its major developments and events, cannot be fully understood without examining also the perceptions, values and power of the few individuals who are primarily responsible for them.

FRAMEWORK OF ANALYSIS

Since the role of leaders in the development of modern China—and of nearly any society structured on authoritarian lines—is vital if not determinative of that development, it is appropriate to examine the qualities inherent in the concept of political leadership and apply them to China and Chiang Ch'ing particularly. In short, the question that arises most frequently is what makes a leader strong or weak. In political science, leadership power can be defined as an individual's capacity to influence the conduct of persons who make and carry out public policy and/or affect the thinking and behavior of the masses. The individual's impact is viewed as a measure of his leadership. To evaluate Chiang Ch'ing's leadership power in China, it would be useful to follow this approach and consider power in its components, examining the interrelationships among them, and their relationship to her effectiveness. These elements may be best understood in terms of basic questions:

1. What does Chiang Ch'ing stand for (i.e., her philosophy, principles and beliefs), what are her values and commitments, with what policies has she identified herself, what is her concept of "right", what cause and ideas does she symbolize, and are they gaining or losing in force over the long run? (Think of this as the Authority of Ideas.)
2. What are her formal powers, what is her official position, what is her formal relationship to the crucial institutions of political power in China, what is her effective power in these subsystems, how much organizational and political experience has she had and how much practical knowledge does she seem to have, how do other leaders view her and respond to her? (What is her Formal and Effective Authority?)
3. Does she have leadership qualities, initiative, timing, courage, patience, determination and stamina; does she have a talent for strategic planning and political maneuvering, what is the degree of her appreciation of power, does she have the capacity to inspire loyalty, does she have the ability to

employ people to the best advantage, what are her typical methods of operation, what is her age, what is the condition of her health, does she have the ability to mobilize large numbers of people and communicate effectively with them, does she have an effective leadership style and "charisma"? (These questions relate to her Authority of Confidence.)
4. Does she have widely disseminated literary or artistic works of a nature which will attract many followers? (The Authority of Prestige.)
5. Does she have special assets, such as useful personal relationships? (The Authority of Special Assets.)

The following treatment will help show how each of these five elements enters into the evaluation of a political leader's overall power of endurance.

The Authority of Ideas

The first element of leadership power is identification with a cause that fulfills felt needs and aspirations of the masses. People, organizations and governments, at home and abroad, who share a leader's convictions and wish to endorse or promote that cause, are potential supporters of that leadership. If they associate him with ideas and values that are relevant to the historical setting and time, and specific policies appropriate to a given situation, then, because of the intrinsic force of his ideas, they will support his policies or solutions, and over a period of time they become accustomed to following his leadership. When a leader is inseparably identified with a cause and is its most authoritative spokesman, the leader acquires ideological leadership. If the cause is moving with the general current of social development, it will gain increasing numbers of supporters and he will be carried by its momentum, gaining greater and greater support and power.

How can we determine what a person stands for? Clues can be found in his early activities, his words or his actions, his friends, the type of people with whom he chooses to identify, in his decisions, and finally, in the responses of others to his actions. Indications can also be had in his past performances, the policies and causes he has endorsed, and the effort he has expended to implement them. The depth and sincerity of his conviction is likewise important, and although difficult to ascertain, analysis of the sacrifices he has made for his cause may provide valuable insights into such convictions.

Formal and Effective Authority

The second element of leadership power is the formal powers that an individual derives from his official position and rank in the party or government. In Communist countries, this power could be formidable, extending to every aspect of an individual's life. A position in the Chinese Communist Party Politburo and other departments, for example, gives a leader formal power to participate in policy-making and shaping of directives, and the potential power to reward or punish people in many ways, such as by removal from office. If he has effective personal influence, he may gain access to certain information within different organizations, or access to resources and other people to carry out his ideas, build up his public image, help his followers, and consolidate his power. By utilizing the official channels of communication within the organization and to the public, it is possible for the leader to reach people with great effectiveness. Furthermore, he may be able to legitimize his gains by changes in the Party Constitution or in the "rules of the game."

In China, the crucial institutions of political power are the Party, the government, the army, the mass organizations (especially literary and art organizations), and the mass media. The Party and government concededly make and implement policies; the army is an armed and disciplined mass organization that carries out political tasks which are assigned to it by the Party Politburo; the literary, art, and educational organizations are sources of new literary and art creations and publications; and the mass media are important as tools for disseminating information, educating people on desired ideals, shaping their

Introduction

opinions, and persuading them. They are the most effective tools available for reaching the masses and gaining supporters. In conjunction with other factors, they can help a leader change his public image and gain popular support through conditioning over a period of time.

If a person has a high position or rank within an organization, he has indeed formal authority, but the problem is to assess his authority in terms of effectiveness. Clues may be found in the history of his association with the organization, such as his activities, his work record, the length of time he has spent in each position, and his effectiveness during his tenure. What type of functions has he performed and what have been the nature, the variety, and complexity of his experience? What contacts and friends has he made in these spheres and what have been his common experiences with other members of these spheres? What are his attitudes toward these organizations and their members—and more importantly, their attitudes toward him and his actions? What they think of him is likely to be affected by the experience they have had with him and by his professional and general reputation.

The Authority of Confidence

The third element of leadership power consists of the impressions people retain as the result of observing the leader's personal style—general performance and real or imagined attributes. Since others will be motivated to follow his guidance and support him in part by their respect and confidence in him, they must be convinced that he has leadership qualities, political knowledge and skill, ambition and the will to win, time, physical and mental strength, and the overall endurance to carry through his policies to the end. If he has a reputation for using his special assets and opportunities to good advantage, people will be even more inclined to follow him. Certain personal and leadership qualities stir public imagination and have mass appeal; others may not.

How is the authority of confidence assessed? Basically, through assessing the leadership style. His expression of himself, his ability to project an impression of competence, his conduct, his responses, his handling of crises, his decisiveness, his tenacity and perseverance during difficult times—all tend to enter into such an assessment. It is also possible to judge whether he has credibility and charisma from the public's response to him, what is said about him generally, and what is published and broadcast about him in the mass media.

The Authority of Prestige

An important aspect of the fourth element of leadership power is whether or not a leader has literary or art works in readily available form. In China, certain literary and art works add depth and another dimension to a leader's stature, especially if those works are widely disseminated. In the Chinese mind, this lends additional prestige and authority to the leader and his views. They are a means by which a leader can assert his authority. By having a body of works that people can study in order to determine what a leader represents, the leader has greater potential for acquiring supporters and more popular acclaim, especially if the works justify the needs and desires of the people, in which case the author comes to be identified with popular aspirations. This wide dissemination is in itself a sign of effective influence at the top and at the same time increases the leader's support from below. A leader's works can provide the most effective means of reaching the masses directly and of making the masses feel that he is less remote. Works lend legitimacy to a leader's ideas and leadership, and provide a focus for loyalty. By studying a leader's works, the public is automatically conditioned to respect the authority of his ideas and accept his leadership.

In an overall evaluation, it is necessary to determine what works a leader has produced, the extent of their influence, the nature and form of these works, and the extent to which and channels through which they are disseminated. Widespread acceptance and familiarity certainly lend legitimacy to the

Introduction xxiii

leadership and add to the leader's national and international stature. These works, therefore, have the potential to enhance his standing, reinforce the authority of confidence, and promote his cause.

The Authority of Special Assets

The fifth element of leadership power is derived from an individual's background and from relationships with associates who enjoy goodwill and standing. A person living in a special environment may have had the opportunity to come in contact with certain people, may have gained advantageous learning experiences, and may have acquired special knowledge in certain fields.

For example, in Chiang Ch'ing's case, as the wife of Mao Tse-tung, and also as his adviser, representative, confidante, and aide, she obviously has a special relationship with him and has been in a special environment which could lend authority to her ideological position, since she is the one who can credibly claim to know best Mao's intentions, his ideals, and his goals. To assess her potential as a possible successor to Mao, it is necessary to determine whether she has made the best use of this special relationship and capitalized on it, and whether she has the potential, based on a combination of factors—including this special asset—to claim special authority. If so, she has the potential to strengthen her existing power and authority.

FORMAT: APPROACH, SCOPE, STRUCTURE, VIEWPOINT AND SOURCES

The purpose of this work is to explain what Chiang Ch'ing's actions have actually been over the years, to analyze the effects of her actions on the sources of leadership influence (already discussed), and to assess the implications. Chiang Ch'ing's rise to power in the crucial spheres of political power in China will be examined in detail: her rise in the Party, the government, the armed forces, the mass media, and in ideological and cultural circles. Her sources of leadership power, her activities, her relationships with people in these spheres, and other aspects of her career will be explored. This work assumes a basic knowledge of the Chinese Communist movement and its recent developments.[1]

Part One of this study is limited to a review of Chiang Ch'ing's early life and her rise to power in the Party hierarchy, analyzing, among other things, her use of personal influence and the consolidation of her gains.

Part Two deals with the distribution of power in the Chinese political system and explores Chiang Ch'ing's relationships to other key members of the national leadership. Her activities and participation in international affairs are also examined.

Part Three explores her relationship to the military establishment; her status and rise within it; and her role in bringing about leadership, organizational, educational, and cultural changes within the armed forces.

Part Four presents a detailed explanation of the Maoist line on literature and art, and analyzes Chiang Ch'ing's efforts to implement it. Her efforts to revolutionize literature and art and to create her eight model works are illustrated and documented.

Because of the magnitude of the Great Proletarian Cultural Revolution and the leadership vacuum it created, and other reasons stated earlier, Part Five describes Chiang Ch'ing's role in that major event in China's history. It analyzes the planning, launching, and implementation of the Revolution and attempts to assess the effects of her actions.

Part Six studies Chiang Ch'ing's revolutionary works, the public response to them, and the impact they have had on the country and on Chiang Ch'ing's leadership power.

An effort is made in this study to ascertain the responses of average Chinese citizens living in China, which are undoubtedly different from those of people with different cultural backgrounds, given the Chinese tradition of authoritarian government and political culture, their history of war and disorder, and the reality of their limited material resources and huge population. In order to understand the environmental influences which have

Introduction

been most powerful in shaping their feelings and attitudes, a review is made of the themes which have been most frequently repeated in speeches, wall posters, published materials, and the mass media. Whether truthful or not, these themes have been endorsed by the most authoritative and prestigious of China's leaders and have presumably exerted profound influence on the masses. Therefore, it is important, for an understanding of the dynamics of Chinese politics, to be aware of these systemic influences.

This analysis is based on a careful examination of voluminous primary and secondary sources, including a variety of materials and publications from Taiwan, Hong Kong, Japan, Great Britain, France, and the Soviet Union; Chinese Communist official sources; Red Guard sources; intelligence sources; and eyewitness reports. The materials were difficult to locate since they were widely scattered in different parts of the world. It has taken more than two years to collect them, read them, make notes on them, verify them, and classify them. In view of the importance of the Great Proletarian Cultural Revolution, both as an episode in Chiang Ch'ing's career and as a period when much documentation on contemporary and earlier Chinese political developments was produced, a high proportion of the sources cited necessarily date from that period. Because of the unique atmosphere surrounding the Cultural Revolution, sources from that period require even more critical evaluation than normal in the case of Chinese Communist documents. The writer has therefore checked the information derived from such sources very extensively, and as far as possible, against other sources. These include, in addition to published writings cited in the notes and bibliography, interviews in Hong Kong, Taiwan, and the United States, with individuals, including officials, who have first-hand or expert knowledge of some of the events and persons treated in this work but who prefer to remain anonymous. Where anonymity of the source must be preserved, there obviously can be no citation to a source for a statement made in the text. In order to retain the tone and flavor of the original source yet avoid unnecessary, repetitious or ritual expressions, there are a number of ellipses in quotations cited.

Chiang Ch'ing's career, including her early life, has appeared to some to have been the object of a myth-making process since 1966. Even such myth-making, however, does not affect the validity of the analysis presented here because it is grounded on historical evidence. The possible existence of a myth-making process is significant in itself, since it is normally applied only to important individuals.

In preparing this study no effort was made to gather and encompass every minute detail concerning Chiang Ch'ing's private life. The thrust of the study was to explore her sociopolitical role and contributions in the Revolution, and to the extent that personal matters do not relate to her status and influence as a leader, they have not been included. This omission however, should not detract from an objective description of Chiang Ch'ing's revolutionary and political activities, and, to the contrary, may make an impartial evaluation all the more possible. Although it is concededly difficult to distinguish between relevant and irrelevant personal details when discussing the role of public and political figures, it is hoped that the standards used to eliminate irrelevant facets are, in the last analysis, complementary to the achievement of the basic purpose of this study, which is to focus on the political image and role of Chiang Ch'ing.

Since news of Chiang Ch'ing's activities was, for the most part, not available to the general public before 1962, rumors circulated outside China to the effect that she had been restricted in her Party activities for twenty years by Party officials as a condition of her marriage to Mao. No confirmation for this rumor has been found, and the writer considers it as implausible. Other explanations considered more plausible are: (1) a personal preference on her part not to dilute Mao's prestige and authority; (2) a deliberate attempt by her opposition to suppress as much information about her activities as possible; (3) the lack of communication with the outside world; (4) the normal secrecy about movements and activities of Chinese Communist policy-makers; and (5) the particularly secret nature of the process of intelligence collection, analysis, and policy formulation, which was Chiang Ch'ing's primary task before 1962. Intelligence sources suggest that Chiang Ch'ing was continuously active over the years. Chiang Ch'ing's post-1962 efforts to revolutionize China's political culture and arts and to implement the Socialist Education Movement and the Great Proletarian Cultural Revolution were inevitably more obvious, and therefore more information about them is known to outside observers.

The research underlying this study covers Chiang Ch'ing's activities in the Party, the government, the armed forces, in ideological and cultural circles, in the Great Proletarian Cultural Revolution, and in political socialization, as well as her revolutionary works. This approach in studying Chiang Ch'ing and her leadership role is basically an original experiment which may lay the groundwork for developing a more "scientific" and comparative approach to the study of other political leaders in general in Chinese and other Communist systems. From the framework of analysis or political model proposed here, quantifiable measures may be developed for subsequent studies, and vast documentary resources and computer techniques can be utilized for purposes of political science research.

The organization and structure adopted in this study also make possible the consolidation of facts relevant to a given topic in a single chapter so that the reader can arrive at his own conclusions on the subjects discussed in each part. Since the study attempts to discuss the topics on the basis of evidence available over the span of Chiang Ch'ing's entire career up to the present, certain related facts and themes are referred to in more than one section for the sake of emphasis and to bring out more clearly their impact and significance. One of the advantages of this method of organization is that the reader may be able to study a given topic directly and exclusively without having to start at the beginning of the work or review other topics. Hopefully, this topical approach will be more useful than a strictly chronological approach for such purposes as assessing a leader's power and making predictions.

To date, there has been no comprehensive, scholarly, and systematic research presented on Chiang Ch'ing, and no documentary analysis attempted on her political role, even though she is an important member of the top leadership. An effort is made to give a general interpretation that will best explain all the available facts. It is hoped that by thus bringing Chiang Ch'ing into the focus of critical attention, it will be possible to shed some light on the obscure aspects of major movements in mainland China and in this fashion contribute to a better understanding of contemporary Chinese political processes and the environment in which they operate.

Part One

THE CHINESE COMMUNIST PARTY (CCP) AND CHIANG CH'ING

Chapter 1

Chiang Ch'ing's Membership and Early Party Work

Chiang Ch'ing was born about 1915 in Chucheng in Shantung, a dry and not too fertile province on the northeast coast of China.[1] This area had produced many ancient traditions and was the birth place of Confucius and Mencius. Because of its poor economy and bitter weather, the natives are rugged and hard working, physically tall and strong, and characteristically persevering and straightforward.

Chiang Ch'ing was born at a time when the country was going through a chaotic period, politically and economically. Her father had died when she was eight, and her mother was required to work as a domestic to support the family. A year later they moved in with her maternal grandfather in Tsinan, the provincial capital. When Chiang Ch'ing was about twelve, her mother died, leaving her with no inheritance of any kind. From that time on she was on her own and managed to support herself by enrolling at the Shantung Experimental Drama Academy, where students received their livelihood and free training in Peking Opera and Soochow and Mandarin stage plays in exchange for public performances on Saturdays and Sundays.

The Shantung Drama Academy, headed by Chou T'ai-mo, a dramatist educated in the United States, started a progressive program in the performing arts, introducing to the Chinese theater Western plays and techniques. Chiang Ch'ing was deeply impressed by the heroine of Ibsen's play *A Doll's House*.[2] In the play, Nora breaks away from her social slavery and through her own efforts becomes strong and independent. Three years later, in Shanghai, Chiang Ch'ing played Nora with considerable success. The Chinese translation of the play was considered a symbol of Chinese women's liberation, and she was able to lend support to a movement which encouraged women to participate more actively in public affairs.

In early 1930, Chou T'ai-mo was appointed as the dean of Tsingtao University in Tsingtao, a seaport east of Tsinan. Having been on her own at an early age, Chiang Ch'ing had experienced many hardships and observed the tragic injustices that the masses, especially women, had to endure in their struggle for survival. She became more and more outraged by existing conditions and began to yearn for social change. Hearing of the liberal political activities of the Tsingtao students, Chiang Ch'ing left for the university. There she prevailed upon Chou T'ai-mo to grant her a job in the university library, where she was able to study on her own, avidly reading books on socialism and revolution.

Tsingtao University was known for its intellectual and literary atmosphere; many students and faculty members were actively involved in underground revolutionary activities. Chou En-lai, Ch'en Po-ta, K'ang Sheng, Li Ta-chang and others have reported that Chiang Ch'ing joined the Chinese Communist Party (CCP) and participated in the Revolution at this time. In addition to attending Marxist-Leninist study classes and workshops, she joined a left-wing group whose discussions were geared to further the revolutionary cause through propaganda films. She also received training as an underground Communist and was assigned to do Party propaganda film work in Shanghai.

In Shanghai, Chiang Ch'ing worked for a motion picture company which specialized in making leftist films. These films were designed to mobilize the illiterate masses by revealing to them the imminent threat of Japanese conquest and the deplorable conditions that existed at the time. The company was under the direction of Ch'u Ch'iu-pai, one of the founding members of the Chinese Communist Party. The well-known Communist film director Ssu-t'u Hui-min had already recruited many noted writers and leading actors who were not only engaged in filmmaking but were also writing and editing newspaper supplements. Soon, however, government authorities closed the film company, and some of the members joined the reorganized Lien Wah Film Company.

Between 1935 and 1937, Chiang Ch'ing was featured in three films under her stage name, Lan P'ing. In *Blood Flowing on Lang Shan,* she played the role of a courageous peasant woman who fought off a pack of wolves to save her son in a story symbolic of the struggle against the Japanese aggression. It was one of the early Communist films made with strong symbolic undertones.

In her next film, *Wang Lao Wu,* she played a young girl who made a living by mending people's clothes. In the story she married Bachelor Wang and the two lived in unabashed poverty. It was a comedy supported by the two well-known comedians, Han and Yen, the Chinese Laurel and Hardy. The film was extremely popular, and through it Chiang Ch'ing was recognized as an exceptionally talented actress. Her natural ability, combined with her training in speech, body control, expression and discipline, made it possible for her to interpret materials to their best advantage. It was obvious that she had the ability to communicate a message and sway an audience. Because of the film's popularity, Chinese still refer to bachelors as Wang Lao Wu.

In her third film, *Twenty Cents,* she starred opposite Yen, the fat comedian. Although praised by critics, she was unhappy with the material. She turned down roles in similar films that had insufficient social and political significance, though they probably would have established her as an important star. Unlike most other actresses, who were interested primarily in personal fame, her main interest was to advance the national cause by enlightening illiterate peasants and increasing their political awareness.

As she became more convinced of the importance and righteousness of her cause, she spoke her mind at private gatherings and public meetings with increasing frequency. When a noted Japanese writer visited Shanghai in the summer of 1937, Chiang Ch'ing boldly handed her a note at the farewell party which read: "Please take back from the Chinese film workers and the Chinese public a request that Japanese producers refrain from making films that insult Chinese people." In her personal life Chiang Ch'ing was often considered a loner; she dressed plainly and poorly in contrast to the many other contemporary actresses whose taste for luxury and good living repulsed her.

On August 13, 1937, Japan launched an all-out attack and Shanghai was in turmoil. Under the direction of the Shanghai Cultural National Salvation Association (a Communist Party front), those working for left-wing film companies were organized into thirteen National Salvation Theatrical Troupes which immediately traveled to the interior of China to propagate the war of resistance against Japanese aggression. Chiang Ch'ing joined one of the groups which went to Nanking and later settled in Chungking, where she made *Sons and Daughters of China,* a film composed of four episodes. She played the part of a peasant wife who was tortured and murdered by Japanese invaders.[3] During her one-year stay in Chungking she agreed to act in only one film, *The Awakening of a Farmer.* She was anxious to make more revolutionary dramas, but she was unhappy with most of the pictures that were being made. The films were still exposing social injustices, but no solutions were being presented to encourage the poor to act in their own behalf and improve their conditions. She decided that it was imperative for her to go right to the heart of revolutionary thought and activity, the Communist Party's central headquarters in Yenan. Even though she knew that the journey would be long, uncomfortable, and dangerous, and not knowing what actual conditions would be there, she nevertheless, made the difficult decision to go to Yenan.

At this time the Red Army Group office was expanding its ranks and was enlisting young intellectuals for their propaganda war against Japan. With her record of serving the cause since 1931, she was readily accepted by army recruiters and traveled with the army to Yenan. There she reported to the chief of the Communist Intelligence Bureau, K'ang Sheng, who was a native of Shantung. He assigned her to Lu Hsun Academy of Arts, where she wrote propaganda plays for soldiers and peasants. She also starred in a stage play, *The Downtrodden People.* It was in this play that Mao Tse-tung first saw her and was deeply impressed by her performance.

Later, when Mao went to the academy to give a speech,

Chiang Ch'ing, sitting in the front row, exchanged ideas with him after his lecture. Mao was again impressed by her opinions and thoughts and a friendship soon developed. Subsequently, Chiang Ch'ing served as Mao's aide and counsel, and in 1940 she married him. During all the years, she helped him with his writing and shared her ideas with him.

Chiang Ch'ing believed that literature and art should serve the Communist cause by enlightening and educating the masses, implanting in them the seminal desire to change their condition, and giving them hope for success. It should serve the needs of the overwhelming majority of the people by featuring their problems and solutions, instead of merely entertaining the privileged few. Literature and art should exist for the people, but it should also be by the people, either created by illiterate peasants, soldiers, and laborers who would dictate scenes or stories to Party scribes, or by professional writers and artists who lived among them, experiencing their tribulations and vicissitudes, and writing honestly and vividly about their emotions, their problems, and their success in solving them. Through truthful portrayal of existing conditions and the stirring struggles of ordinary people, the purpose of drama should be to inspire the masses to revolution and to raise the fighting spirit of army men. Chiang Ch'ing also felt that literary works should foster positive morality, presenting examples of virtuous, self-sacrificing individuals who steadfastly fought for positive goals. Introspective heroes who rationalized or analyzed their own character or motives filled the audiences with self-doubt and caused them to vacillate instead of steadily pursuing their goals with confidence and optimism.

In May 1942 Mao presented his famous lecture "Talks at the Yenan Forum on Literature and Art,"[4] which embodied her ideas as well as his own. Immediately Chiang Ch'ing began to make efforts to implement their new policy in the arts, the ideological basis of which was derived in part from earlier Chinese Communist thought and Communist theory. The most difficult fortress to reform was the Peking Opera (P'ing Chü). She wrote and staged an opera in line with the new policy, *P'inghsing*

Pass,[5] which was received with mixed emotions by Party members. Chairman Mao was enthusiastic, and in a letter to the Yenan Peking Opera Theatre, he wrote: "History is made by the people, yet the old opera (and all the old literature and art, which are divorced from the people) presents the people as though they were dirt, and the stage is dominated by lords and ladies and their pampered sons and daughters. Now you have reversed this reversal of history and restored historical truth, and thus a new life is opening up for the old opera. That is why this merits congratulations. The initiative you have taken marks an epoch-making beginning in the revolutionization of the old opera. I am very happy at the thought of this. I hope you will write more plays and give more performances, and so help make this practice a common one which will prevail throughout the country."[6]

Chou En-lai also praised Chiang Ch'ing's writings. He said on one occasion: "If someone read Comrade Chiang Ch'ing's writings at that time, he would find them to be Red writings.... Her writings are fighting works that deserve our study."[7]

But resistance to her work had already risen among other factions within the Party. The playwright T'ien Han, as late as 1956, still brooding about these early efforts in Yenan, stated: "In the old liberated areas, some people in Yenan made an inappropriate attempt. This is a strange thing. For instance, Peking Opera performed during the struggle against Japan had dramatized the Japanese and the common Chinese folk.... It was of course wrong on the stage to raise a big knife to attack the Japanese. This must be negated."[8] This resistance, however, did not discourage Chiang Ch'ing from continued efforts to "revolutionize" the arts.

When Yenan was attacked by Nationalist General Hu Tsung-nan in the spring of 1947, Chiang Ch'ing and Mao were among the last group to evacuate the Communist wartime headquarters. She continued to work with him throughout that critical time.[9] When the period ultimately ended in Communist triumph, Chiang Ch'ing had the satisfaction of witnessing the culmination of many years of unflagging effort.

Chapter 2

Major Party Policies and Chiang Ch'ing's Participation

In 1949 the Chinese Communists triumphed militarily and politically, settling ultimately in Peking to begin the enormous task of putting the war-torn country in order. Chiang Ch'ing arrived in a position to influence public opinion since she worked in various capacities in the propaganda and cultural organs of the Party and government. A scriptwriter and director who worked in the film bureau at that time later observed: "Comrade Chiang Ch'ing looked over our outline and film material and studied with us the theme and display of it, giving us great help."[1]

The propaganda and cultural organs in which Chiang Ch'ing was active throughout the rehabilitation period were primarily responsible for censorship and determining the content, substance, themes, and interpretations utilized by all mass media. Their policies were implemented by all channels of communication, both formal and informal, including newspapers, books, radio, television, theater, films, community meetings, adult education classes, public rallies, discussion clubs, displays, posters, documents and circulars, amateur talent shows, speakers and their materials, demonstrations, and parades.

Because of the thoroughness and pervasiveness of the propaganda and cultural organs' influence throughout the country, especially on the illiterate masses, Chiang Ch'ing believed that the Party could not afford to circulate negative thoughts that were self-defeating and would hinder national development. She felt that it was vital to present the purest form of Maoist Thought and the best models for the people to emulate.

Since she had worked closely with Mao during the formulation of his Thoughts and was therefore knowledgeable of their basic tenets, she campaigned vigorously against important decisions by her colleagues which she felt violated Mao's intentions. Unlike the traditional demure, submissive women of ancient China, Chiang Ch'ing leaped into the arena when she disagreed with someone and energetically scolded or launched full-scale ideological attacks. Some of her cases became national causes, among them her criticism of Mei Lan-fang, the leading Peking Opera star, who resisted her efforts to change the Peking Opera into an organ for disseminating revolutionary ideals.[2] In 1950 she led the repudiation of *Inside Story of the Ch'ing Court*, a film which she, and later Mao, described as a national betrayal for encouraging passive acceptance of foreign aggression. In 1951 she set off another nationwide controversy in literature and cultural circles when she pointed out that the film *Life of Wu Hsun* advocated begging and capitulation, and therefore had to be repudiated.

However, many of Chiang Ch'ing's colleagues in the propaganda and cultural departments enjoyed the old-fashioned films that glorified the aristocracy and considered them harmless. They were able to exert enough influence to stifle most of her attempts to publish her views. After she had met with continued resistance, Mao finally wrote an editorial criticizing the Wu Hsun film, stating: ". . . the praise lavished on Wu Hsun and the film show the degree of ideological confusion reached in our country's cultural circles."[3]

By this time it became obvious that if the revolutionary line was to be advanced, the intellectuals would have to experience the workers' problems in order to empathize with them and present a true reflection of their lives. A program of ideological reform, political education, and physical labor "aimed at replacing the wrong picture of laboring people and their struggle" was accelerated. Writers who were hopelessly intransigent were removed from positions of influence.

In 1952 Chiang Ch'ing prepared and supervised the writing of a model opera with a revolutionary theme, *Sung Ching-chih*. She tried to promote its production, but it was blocked by those in the Ministry of Culture who were against her.

In June 1950 Mao delivered an address entitled "Fight for a Basic Improvement in the Financial and Economic Conditions of Our State," in which he pointed out that of the three basic requirements that were vital to the improvement of China's conditions, "the fulfillment of agrarian reform" was foremost. Liu Shao-chi, however, reportedly opposed Mao's view and expressed the opinion that "China still cannot carry out socialism today."[4] By 1953 the agrarian reform still had not progressed substantially, and Mao and Chiang Ch'ing shared the fear that private ownership would become entrenched if the country did not move steadily toward socialism. Chiang Ch'ing left her position in government and began to work intensively with Mao. Some foreign observers noted that Mao appeared to be "an old man in a hurry."

Throughout their marriage, whenever Mao traveled, Chiang Ch'ing was nearly always with him, contributing her observations and exchanging thoughts with him to help shape his ideas and conclusions. They had always shared the same values, aims, and hopes, and obviously worked well together. After many inspection tours of the countryside and having personally assessed the conditions of the peasantry, they came to the conclusion that China was ready for an accelerated agrarian revolution. Bypassing the Party center, Mao met with provincial leaders, and on July 31, 1955, at a conference of provincial, municipal, and district Party secretaries, he launched the co-operativization movement in which individuals began to pool their land and resources throughout the country.

During this time, the split between Mao's policy of co-operativize first and then mechanize, and Liu's policy of mechanize first and then cooperativize, continued to grow. Liu, "taking advantage of Mao's absence from Peking, . . . formulated the . . . policy of 'suspension,' 'compression,' and 'reorganization' and personally approved the plan for chopping away agricultural cooperatives on a large scale. Over the period of more than two months, 200,000 agricultural cooperatives were eliminated throughout the country."[5]

Mao's and Chiang Ch'ing's own field investigations led them

to conclude that "the high tide of social reformation in the countryside, the high tide of cooperation, has already reached some places and will soon sweep over the whole country."[6] They noted: "Please take a look at this township in Kunshun County, Kiangsu Province. Here, the whole township has gone cooperative not in three years but in two." Thus despite some comrades who were "tottering along like a woman with bound feet and constantly complaining, 'You're going too fast,'" Mao, with Chiang Ch'ing's encouragement and assistance, was intent on moving the nation firmly toward socialism.

In February 1956 a dramatic occurrence took place in the Communist world when Khrushchev delivered his de-Stalinization speech before the Soviet Twentieth Party Congress. This speech, delivered unexpectedly and without prior warning to Mao, precipitated a period of crisis for the Maoists. The opposition began to undermine Mao's leadership and reduced the role of Mao's thoughts by eliminating them from the new Party Constitution adopted at the Eighth Party Congress. Even though Mao, in his keynote speech, urged the assemblage to "fight for building a great socialist China,"[7] the opposition was able to write into the Constitution: "the question of who will win in the struggle between socialism and capitalism has now been basically resolved."[8]

At the same Congress, Secretary-General Teng Hsiao-p'ing announced that additional central organs were being set up in the Central Committee because of "the pressure of Party work." In effect this meant that much of Mao's political power was turned over to Teng as head of the Secretariat in charge of the daily work of the Central Committee, and to Liu Shao-chi as the senior vice-chairman of the newly established Standing Committee of the Politburo.

The Soviet challenge and domestic developments made it necessary at this time for China's leaders to make a decision as to which direction China would move: whether to break away from Soviet influence in spite of the enormous problems involved and sacrifices that would be necessary, or to accept the Soviet terms and run the risk of becoming its satellite. At this critical turning point in China's history, Chiang Ch'ing emphatically urged Mao to reject "unreasonable" Soviet demands, and not to "follow the foreigners to death. . . . We must tread our own path. It doesn't matter if we make mistakes. If we fall down, we can rise again." After considerable discussion and deliberations with Chiang Ch'ing, Mao responded to the Soviet challenge with a series of major initiatives beginning with the Hundred Flowers Movement, and followed by the Great Leap Forward, the commune movement, the Socialist Education Movement, and the Great Proletarian Cultural Revolution.

The Hundred Flowers Movement, a program designed to "promote freedom and independent thinking, freedom of debate, freedom of creation and criticism, freedom of expressing one's own views," epitomized one of Chiang Ch'ing's basic commitments to the people of China. But continued opposition to their program convinced them to work out a more theoretical and persuasive elaboration of their ideas and beliefs. At the Supreme State Conference on February 27, 1957, Mao presented their ideas in a major speech explaining that problems exist even during the period of building socialism and that they should be handled properly according to the nature of each problem. In a speech entitled "On the Correct Handling of Contradictions Among the People," Mao laid the theoretical foundation for the subsequent Great Proletarian Cultural Revolution and also provided the rationale for the Great Leap Forward which was launched in February 1958.[9] In this speech Mao reiterated the advisability of developing agriculture and light industry along with heavy industry. He observed: "If we can achieve an even growth in our agriculture and thus induce a correspondingly greater development of light industry . . . heavy industry, assured of its market and funds, will grow faster."[10]

When Mao and Chiang Ch'ing made an inspection tour of the Honan, Hopei, and Shantung countrysides in August 1958, they decided that the time had come to communize the cooperatives. Mao commented: "The establishment of people's communes is a good thing," and accordingly, by the end of the year, the entire mainland had been organized into 26,500 communes. According to Anna Louise Strong, who traveled in China and visited representative communes, she was told by one peasant: "When Chairman Mao said: 'People's communes are good' and that they should include all those things we wanted, we said at once: 'Then why wait?' "[11]

At the Lushan Conference, convened in August 1959, the opposition violently criticized the commune movement. They called it "left-deviation adventurism," "feverish," "premature," and "making a mess of things." According to official Communist sources, Defense Minister P'eng Te-huai led the attacks.[12] Mao pointed out that the lines had finally been drawn sharply between the two opposing factions within the Party. "The appearance of this struggle at Lushan is a class struggle between the two antagonistic classes of the bourgeoisie and the proletariat in the course of the Socialist revolution over the past ten years."[13]

In September, P'eng Te-huai advocated a strictly military organization in direct opposition to the concept of a people's army serving the masses, which Mao and Chiang Ch'ing had always advocated and had spent long years building. During his tenure as head of the PLA, P'eng Te-huai had practically abolished programs of political education, the army's work with the masses, public works projects, and had tried also to disband the local militia and armed forces.[14] P'eng Te-huai was eventually replaced by Lin Piao, with whom Chiang Ch'ing had worked at the Party's Military Commission in the 1930s. Lin immediately began to reverse P'eng's emphasis, reinstating political and cultural education within the army and the army's service to the masses.

Disagreement over the Soviet Union continued to be another source of dispute between the Maoists and Liu Shao-chi's forces. The Maoists were in favor of an independent stance, whereas the opposition contended that China could not develop without Soviet cover and cooperation. Mao nevertheless stood firmly against compromise, and in 1961 the Soviet Union terminated all economic and technical assistance ties with China.

From 1960 through 1962, partly because of natural calamities and problems encountered in the readjustment of the economy after Soviet withdrawal, China suffered a series of economic difficulties. Liu's people dubbed the Great Leap Forward "immature," characterized by "thoughtlessness," and a "great leap backward."[15] The communes were abandoned in all but name and the peasants were given material incentives. Agricultural production rose gradually.

Even though natural conditions had improved and undoubtedly contributed to the rise in production, Mao and Chiang Ch'ing surmised that part of the cause was also attributed to the people's increased efforts as the result of greater material incentives. They decided that a more intensive program of ideological education was necessary before socialism could successfully compete with private ownership in the countryside. In September 1962, at the Tenth Plenum of the Eighth CCP Central Committee, the Socialist Education Movement was launched.

In keeping with their plans for increased ideological education, Chiang Ch'ing rapidly decided that one of the most effective tools for indoctrinating the illiterate masses and providing inspiration and proper values for the youth of the country was theatrical productions presenting model heroes and model behavior for them to emulate. After intensively studying existing productions, she became convinced that the most effective form and far-reaching in its influence was the Peking Opera. Selecting some materials already in existence, she began to rewrite and reshape them until they met her standards. From the very beginning she met resistance from the opposition faction, but in spite of sabotage, hostility, and ridicule, Chiang Ch'ing persisted, and managed to complete eight model works: five operas, two ballets, and a symphony.[16]

At the same time, open opposition to Maoist ideals and thinly veiled ridicule of Mao himself began to increase and spread. Wu Han, the vice-mayor of Peking and a historian, wrote a play, *Hai Jui Dismissed from Office,* which was a blatant criticism of Mao's dismissal of P'eng Te-huai. The "Three-Family Village," a group of three writers, including Wu Han, who wrote under pen names, published over 150 satires ridiculing Mao and Mao's Thought. One of them, Teng T'o, was later accused of "pointing at the mulberry while actually reviling the locust tree . . ."[17] T'ien Han, a playwright and chairman of the Union of Chinese Drama Workers, criticized socialism as useless.[18] A Forum on Short Novels, summoned in August 1962 and presided over by Chou Yang, devoted most of its time to attacks on the Great Leap Forward.[19]

During this time, Chiang Ch'ing was holding informal discussion with students and young intellectuals at Wanchow Shan, on the outskirts of Peking.[20] Through her meetings with them, she was able to ascertain the emotional and political climate on the campuses. Her findings led her to believe that the young people of the country, idealistic, energetic, and nurtured all their lives in Maoist Thought, were convinced that the Party had been taken over by a small, elite, and privileged group of so-called revisionists. She also came to the conclusion that the young idealists would not only quickly answer the call to defend their beliefs but would benefit from learning by revolutionary experience; they would form themselves into a strong Maoist force. Chiang Ch'ing discussed her findings with Mao: the hostility she had encountered while trying to produce her model operas, the savage criticism and ridicule of Mao within the literary field, the need for the masses to increase their ideological consciousness, and the necessity for the youth to participate in a government which implemented its own ideology. As a result of their talks, Mao and Chiang Ch'ing decided to launch the Great Proletarian Cultural Revolution.

In November 1965, Chiang Ch'ing went to Shanghai, taking an article she had been working on for many months. She enlisted the aid of Yao Wen-yüan to review the final draft, and then exerted pressure on a Shanghai newspaper to publish it. The article, "On the New Historical Play, *Hai Jui Dismissed from Office*" revealed the irreparable split within the Party and was the opening shot of the Great Proletarian Cultural Revolution.[21] Using the revolution within literature and the arts as a smoke screen, on February 2, 1966, Chiang Ch'ing called the military leaders to a Forum on Literature and Art in the Armed Forces and placed the People's Liberation Army (PLA) firmly under Maoist control, with Chiang Ch'ing serving as an "adviser" in charge of the entire organization.[22]

By utilizing her friends on the campuses, Chiang Ch'ing encouraged the formation of youth pressure groups who demonstrated and brought about the removal of anti-Maoists in the educational hierarchy, the press, the Party, and the government. Through control of several publication channels, Chiang Ch'ing was able to publish articles that reaffirmed and interpreted Maoist ideals, in addition to instructing the revolutionaries on how to carry out their movement.

By the spring of 1967, difficulties had developed among the revolutionary youth forces. Opposition from anti-Maoists, internecine disagreements, and armed attacks by opposing local groups caused severe disruptions and, in some cases, even bloodshed. However, the youthful revolutionaries with military support continued their pressure on the entrenched revisionists, and one by one the anti-Maoists were removed from office. As soon as the offices fell vacant, Chiang Ch'ing began the task of reconstituting the Party and government with her own Maoist supporters.

By issuing authoritative directives in the name of the Cultural Revolution Group and the All-PLA Cultural Revolution Committee, she attempted to establish her own links with the provinces by placing loyal Maoists in leadership positions in the army, government, mass media, and literary and arts circles. Chang Ch'un-ch'iao and Yao Wen-yüan, for example, were appointed first and second secretaries of the Shanghai Revolutionary Committee, and Li Teh-sheng, in addition to being made director of the PLA's General Political Department, was placed in the position of first secretary of the Anhwei Revolutionary Committee. Tan Fu-ying, a young actor who had tried to introduce contemporary themes to Peking Opera as early as 1958 and had supported Chiang Ch'ing's efforts and worked with her on her model operas, was appointed to serve on the Peking Revolutionary Committee when it was formed.[23]

During the meetings, receptions, and rallies that followed, Chiang Ch'ing made many new friends and acquired many more followers by lending her support to loyal Maoist factions and deciding in their favor during provincial disputes.[24] In the Ipin case, for example, Chiang Ch'ing investigated the circumstances and the people involved, made a decision, and in the name of the Central Cultural Revolution Group assigned the proper people to establish the new Szechuan Revolutionary Committee. According to the duly installed members who came to Peking for the meetings and instruction, "All this greatly supported and encouraged us."[25]

During the establishment of the Revolutionary Committees, Chiang Ch'ing performed many functions: she greeted new committees, met with members for discussions, helped them resolve problems, gave speeches laying down the guidelines for the Cultural Revolution and the formation of the new Revolutionary Committees, held receptions, and accompanied committee members to see her model operas. Evidence presently available suggests that she was deeply involved in the formation of the Revolutionary Committees in Shanghai, Canton, Tsinghai, Szechuan, Shansi, Kweichow, Heilungkiang, Shantung, Peking, Honan, Hupei, Kwangtung, Kwangsi, Chekiang, Hunan, and Kiangsu, among others.[26]

Some of the important achievements of the Cultural Revolution and the formation of new Revolutionary Committees have been a relative decentralization of government, a gain in upward mobility for aspiring local leaders, and an increase in the number of political positions locally available. Encouraged by the Maoist emphasis on equality of opportunity for women and their liberation since the Cultural Revolution, many women are actually becoming more active and participating more effectively in the economy and in government. One example is "Wang Yin-o, a young woman cadre . . . praised as a people's good servant, "who was elected to the Shansi Provincial Revolutionary Committee. "This young woman is also a deputy-instructor of a militia battalion in Chi village."[27]

Prior to the Cultural Revolution, despite professed support

The Chinese Communist Party

for a classless society, the revisionists had effectively resisted efforts to implement Communist ideals about women. Only recently is there evidence of real changes on the local scene. A commune in Kiangsi Province led the way in making women's pay equal to that of men for the same job. When the proposal was first made at the Liuchung commune, someone quickly opposed it, declaring: ". . . women's ability was not even half that of men." But "after reviewing women's past achievements in the great revolutionary movements, cadres and members of the production team realized that their judgment was wrong and one-sided."[28]

The Maoist line has long advocated the emancipation of women and their active participation in Socialist society. "In order to build a great Socialist society, it is of the utmost importance to arouse the broad masses of women to join in productive activity."[29] "The day of the rising up of women throughout the country is also the day of the victory of the Chinese Revolution." All the major Maoist policies have encouraged women to participate on an equal footing with men. The Great Leap Forward and commune movement provided mess halls, nursery schools, and child-care centers to free women from household drudgery. In fighting for these major policies, Chiang Ch'ing has, without fanfare, firmly and steadily promoted women's rights. More than any of the outspoken feminists, she has improved women's conditions, and by doing so quietly, she has avoided provoking united opposition to her stand. In all of Chiang Ch'ing's model works, women play an important role, displaying courage, intelligence, initiative, and dignity. Through these model works she has endeavored to change the "old feudal and bourgeois"[30] attitudes of both men and women, and to develop women's political consciousness. As documented in chapters 17 and 24 of this study, these model works have been widely disseminated, to the point of saturation. Consequently, women are becoming more aware of their potential, and of Chiang Ch'ing's great contributions to their cause. Undoubtedly, she has been gaining a formidable block of support for her policies and her leadership.

Chapter 3

The Ninth Party Congress and After

After the enormous difficulties the Maoists, the PLA, and Chiang Ch'ing had in dismantling the old Party and government apparatuses, it was decided to reconstruct them more carefully along Maoist lines. The future of China, and Chiang Ch'ing's own political future, depended on her careful screening of loyal supporters for key positions and the inclusion of important Maoist features in the new Constitution. As early as November 1967, she helped prepare a "Notification Concerning the Inquiry into Opinions on the Convening of the Ninth Congress" and sent it out to thousands of Party members under the name of the Central Cultural Revolution Group and the CCP Central Committee.[1] As she had stated to an enlarged meeting of the Military Commission of the CCP Central Committee on April 12, 1967, "I am now also the secretary of the Standing Committee. As a matter of fact, the entire Central Cultural Revolution Group is nothing but a Secretariat for the committee."[2] The circular proposed that the "central authorities should set up draft committees for the new Party program and Party Constitution" and that these drafts should be issued to the committee members "and revolutionary masses for discussion, before convening the Ninth Congress."[3]

During the ensuing months, Chiang Ch'ing held repeated conferences with the new members of the provincial committees, carefully judging rival factions from various areas, interviewing loyal supporters of the Maoist line for various key posts, and discussing the new Party program and draft of the new Constitution.[4] As she had pointed out in the circular, she felt that it was the Party's "most fundamental task" to "hold aloft the great red flag of Mao Tse-tung's Thought . . . elect a Central Committee infinitely loyal to Chairman Mao . . . and loyal to Chairman Mao's proletarian revolutionary line."[5] The preparation for the Ninth Party Congress and selection of delegates proved to be an enormous task, with 1,512 delegates finally attending. During the year and four months that Chiang Ch'ing worked on its problems, she came to know many of the delegates intimately, having investigated them thoroughly and met with them repeatedly for discussions. Evidently her preparations were successful, for of the 176 members elected to the Presidium, many new members were model workers and Maoist activists who had participated in the Cultural Revolution.[6] Of the twenty-nine Revolutionary Committee chairmen nominated, twenty-five were elected to regular membership on the Central Committee and the other four were elected to alternate membership.

On April 1, 1969, Chiang Ch'ing attended the opening of the Ninth Party Congress and was shown on television dressed in an army uniform.[7] During the day's business, she was elected to the Presidium.[8] On April 14 she was reportedly seated on the rostrum at the plenary session;[9] on April 24 she was elected a full member of the Central Committee[10] and was seen on the rostrum during the closing of the Congress; and on April 28 she attended the First Plenary Session of the Ninth CCP Central Committee and was elected to full membership in the Politburo.[11] Her two deputies, Chang Ch'un-ch'iao and Yao Wen-yüan were also elected to full Politburo membership.[12]

A clause in the Constitution adopted at the Ninth Party Congress guaranteed the right of all Party members to "criticize Party organizations and leading members at all levels and make proposals to them."[13] If a Party member holds different views, he "is allowed to reserve his views and has the right to bypass the immediate leadership and report directly to higher levels, up to and including the Central Committee and the Chairman of the Central Committee."[14] This is a significant new feature which makes direct appeals to Chiang Ch'ing and Mao an accepted official practice, prevents blockage of communication, and enables Chiang Ch'ing to deal directly with Party cadres at all levels and bypass anyone she wishes, especially unsympathetic Party officers. This practice increases her capacity to influence the conduct of the millions of Party cadres who perform the actual task of running the country and provides her with substantial new grass-roots support.

The Constitution also emphasized the importance of consulting the masses and listening to the opinions of the masses "both inside and outside the Party" and accepting their "supervision." During the course of the Ninth Party Congress, the youth of the country were urged to remain ready to launch another cultural revolution if "revisionism" were to develop again.[15]

The government had been decentralized during the Cultural Revolution and power was delegated to a network of provincial committees designed to promote mass participation in decision-making at lower levels. One of the important clauses in the new Constitution authorized the setting up of "a number of necessary organs, which are compact and efficient . . . [to] attend to the day-to-day work of the Party, the government and the army in a centralized way."[16] This clause in effect justified reorganization of Party and government, and authorized the formation of some new departments at the Party center: one to reply to and handle appeals made to Chiang Ch'ing and to Chairman Mao; another to supervise and keep check on the actions of Party branches and members; and a third to continue the functions of the Secretariat which had been performed by her Central Cultural Revolution Group since 1966. Chiang Ch'ing is now in an excellent position to consolidate and strengthen her independent power base by being a critical link between the Central Committee and provincial leaders. It should be remembered that Teng Hsiao-p'ing, while serving in this capacity, had created an "independent kingdom" for himself, and Stalin concededly owed his position of power to his control of the Soviet Party Secretariat.

Since the Ninth Party Congress, Chiang Ch'ing has been very active in helping to restructure Party and government organs.

Her duties include supervision of some of the "necessary" departments at the center; reconstruction of the Party apparatus; and building grass-roots support among the youth, new Party members, and the masses. She is also to "carry out the Revolution," formulate revisions and additions to the Party Constitution after the purge of Lin Piao, prepare for the Tenth Party Congress, determine national and international policy as an influential member of the Politburo, and train and bring up revolutionary successors "to carry on the cause of the proletarian revolution." At the Tenth Party Congress held in August 1973, she was again elected to the Presidium, the Party Central Committee, and its Politburo.[17] Her past performances, coupled with her devotion to the cause, her appreciation of power, and her tenacity, suggest that she will probably continue to play a most active revolutionary role and will continue to exert an important influence over the masses and the critical organs of power in China: the Party, the government, the armed forces, the mass media, and mass organizations.

Part Two

CHIANG CH'ING IN GOVERNMENT AND OFFICIAL CIRCLES

Chapter 4

Party, Government, and The National Leadership

In China, the Party acts as the sole policy-making body for the country, whereas the government, the armed forces, mass organizations and other hierarchies all function under close Party direction, administering Party policies, applying Party directives, and performing the tasks assigned to them by the Party. No provision is made for a distribution of power among legislative, executive, and judicial branches of government. Power is organized in a system of overlapping and interlocking organs which make mobilization of resources and effective direction from the center possible.

At the Ninth Party Congress in April 1969, Chiang Ch'ing was elected to the Central Committee and to the Politburo of the Party.[1] Almost continuously since that time, the primary responsibility for national policy-making and authoritative decision-making in the government, as well as in the Party, has been with a nucleus of seven people, one of whom is Chiang Ch'ing. The others are her husband, Mao Tse-tung; her long-time friend, Premier Chou En-lai; her protégés Chang Ch'un-ch'iao and Yao Wen-yüan; and two long-time associates, Yeh Chien-ying, and Li Hsien-nien.

As Mao's wife, Chiang Ch'ing holds a unique position, having worked diligently over the years to raise his thoughts to the level of canon and his image to that of a near deity. With his Thought firmly established as the supreme authority in China and with her emergence as the most authoritative interpreter of his Thought, Chiang Ch'ing has been in a position of enormous influence. She has frequently acted as his representative and spokesman at state functions and private political meetings.

Over the years Mao has repeatedly indicated his support for her views and endeavors. As early as the 1930s, while still in Yenan, he voiced his approval of a model opera she had written which utilized a revolutionary theme (see chapter 15 for details and documentation). Later, in the 1950s, when she aroused national controversy over her stand on certain films, Mao took time from his pressing schedule to write newspaper editorials supporting her views and even called the matter to the attention of Politburo members. He also lent support to her efforts to produce model theatrical works, attended performances of all her works, and voiced his satisfaction and approval with the results.

Throughout their marriage, Chiang Ch'ing has traveled with Mao, shared her views with him, helped him crystallize new ideas, encouraged him to assert his thoughts, supported his decisions, and has contributed her youth and energy to carrying on his work at various times, especially when Mao's health was frail. Some Chinese sources published in Taiwan and Hong Kong have suggested that it was Chiang Ch'ing who convinced Mao of the necessity for the Cultural Revolution.

Her experiences while living with Mao have undoubtedly taught her many lessons that have been valuable to her political career and will continue to be so in the future. She has learned how best to maintain power through, among other things, careful restructuring of the Party and government so as to concentrate power in "necessary organs" under her leadership at the center, as well as through decentralization at the lower levels, through checks on the actions of Party branches and members, through more careful selection of personnel for key positions, and through the establishment and utilization of direct access for Mao and herself to Party members at all levels.

As Mao has grown older, he has relied more and more on Chiang Ch'ing to implement his ideas and carry out his thoughts. From the favorable reports on Chiang Ch'ing and the steady flow of praise in the mass media, it appears that she has been regarded as a member of a collective leadership expected to succeed Mao, and that the public has been conditioned to support her.

In Government and Official Circles

Ranked second to Mao in national leadership (since the fall of Lin Piao in 1971) is Premier Chou En-lai, who has been a colleague of Chiang Ch'ing's since Yenan days. She pointed out that "when we first entered the cities [i.e., in 1949], I was given a few assignments by the Premier,"[2] indicating his confidence in her ability and trust in their friendship. They appear to work well together. "Comrade Chiang spoke to the Capital's literary and art circles on the twelfth," Chou stated in one of his speeches. "You people should study her recorded speech well."[3] On another occasion, after Chou had spoken to a crowd, Chiang Ch'ing told them, "Premier Chou has mentioned all that I wish to say."[4] Chou En-lai has frequently voiced his admiration for Chiang Ch'ing. "You must know that Comrade Chiang Ch'ing has passed many fighting years. During the thirties . . . even at that time, when she was very young, she had the tough-boned courage of Lu Hsun and hit back at those who . . . falsely accused her. . . . Even in the preparatory stage of the Great Proletarian Cultural Revolution, we could already see Comrade Chiang Ch'ing's ability."[5] During the Cultural Revolution, when the Red Guards were fired with revolutionary zeal and wanted to denounce almost everyone in authority, Chiang Ch'ing restrained them from attacking Chou.

This is not to say consequently that conflicts between the two are impossible in a different set of circumstances, but their longstanding friendship and their mutual respect and appreciation for each other's support seem to provide a basis for mutual accommodation. Chou has a long history of diplomacy and has been noted for his ability to get along with even the most difficult people. Not being personally ambitious, he has never cared about being Number One in the Party, but has always been content to play the role of mediator and administrator. As a member of a younger generation, about seventeen years his junior, Chiang Ch'ing has shown great respect for him and has indicated that she is not concerned about being Number One either. "It is not necessary to have titles,"[6] she once said.

Prominent in the Party hierarchy are her protégés Chang Ch'un-ch'iao, who was a Shanghai administrator and propaganda worker, and Yao Wen-yüan, who was a literary critic, before they were lifted from obscurity to the Politburo (in 1969) through Chiang Ch'ing's support. They are both accustomed to working with her, having been her deputies during the Cultural Revolution and having carried out her assignments ever since. Chiang Ch'ing's rise to the top carried them along also. They have been of great help to her since they understand and share her ideology and have been able to help implement Maoist policies.

Yeh Chien-ying, the apparent head of the PLA since Lin Piao's purge, and Li Hsien-nien, the finance minister, are both leading members of the coalition led by Mao that emerged victorious from the Cultural Revolution. During the Cultural Revolution Chiang Ch'ing protected them from the Red Guards and defended them as "good comrades."[7] Since the Cultural Revolution, Yeh has demonstrated his approval of her stand and methods by flooding the army with her model works and educational materials, and by working with people such as Li Teh-sheng, director of the General Political Department of the PLA General Staff, whom she has placed in key positions.

During the recent Tenth Party Congress held in Peking August 24-28, 1973, several of Chiang Ch'ing's closest friends made significant gains with her assistance.[8] Wang Hung-wen, a former Red Guard leader from Shanghai, was elevated to the rank of China's third post in the Politburo; K'ang Sheng, her oldest friend and a member of the Standing Committee of the Central Committee, became a vice-chairman of the Central Committee; and Li Teh-sheng, head of the PLA Political Department, was promoted to the rank of vice-chairman of the Central Committee and also made a member of the Standing Committee of the Politburo.

With her husband, close friends, and colleagues in the Politburo, it would be difficult to contend that Chiang Ch'ing does not wield influence. Mao's health being frail, Chiang Ch'ing and Chou En-lai are the two leading members of the Politburo, and Chou, whatever his real attitude may be, has repeatedly displayed respect for and solidarity with Chiang Ch'ing, as when they appeared together publicly on September 11, 1971, following Lin Piao's fall.

In Government and Official Circles

Chiang Ch'ing is considered by many as powerful and influential in her own right, even though this power may not always be readily visible, partly because of the secretive and unique nature of the Chinese Communist system and partly because of her own wishes at a particular time and circumstance. It is likely that Chiang Ch'ing is content to hold vital power without fanfare or fancy titles. From her position of influence at the pinnacle of the Chinese Communist Party, Chiang Ch'ing is indeed in a position to provide national leadership and affect every phase of life in China for years to come.

Chapter 5

Chiang Ch'ing on the National Scene

Additional evidence of Chiang Ch'ing's importance on the national scene is had from her prominent role in national festivals. Traditionally, Chinese festivals were celebrated by farmers and workers mostly as family affairs conducted in the privacy of the home. After the Communist takeover, some of these traditional methods of entertainment were allowed to continue, but the material has been changed to make it more consistent with their ideology. Knowing that traditions are hard to eliminate, the Maoists have tried to encourage collective action on the part of the people by shaping traditional festivals into "collective celebrations" with Maoist ideological undertones. The New Year celebration, although still important, has been modified to promote Socialist aims; traveling dramatic and musical troupes perform Chiang Ch'ing's revolutionary repertoires today; and mobile cinema teams are showing her works and other instructive films. Chiang Ch'ing's cultural workers have organized a variety of new activities on the local scene to relieve some of the montony of long seasons of toil.

In Communist China, the two most important national holidays are May Day (May 1), and National Day (October 1). May Day is a salute to the international solidarity of the working people of the world, National Day commemorates the proclamation of the Chinese People's Republic. Both May Day and National Day are celebrated throughout China, but the largest celebration of all is staged at Peking every year, with millions of people participating.

These two major holidays are celebrated in a festive atmosphere with massive parades, singing and dancing, fireworks, meetings, and receptions. It is an opportunity for the national leaders to entertain foreign guests, to mingle with the crowds, and to be photographed, thus reaffirming their official status and their importance on the national scene. Foreign guests from all over the world are invited to attend. Regional leaders and representatives from all walks of life travel thousands of miles to attend in the company of the top Chinese leaders. As the events are covered thoroughly by the mass media, both nationally and internationally, in the press and by television, this is the occasion when it is possible for the world to ascertain who is in power if only by taking note of which national leaders are seated on the reviewing stand. Anyone who is missing is either sick, extremely busy working on other duties, or out of power. A change in seating order sometimes signifies a shift in power.

It was reported that Chiang Ch'ing attended the National Day celebration in 1964, but it was in the 1966 National Day celebration that she first took an active part.[1] In 1966, the National Day parade took almost four hours to pass the reviewing stand. Chiang Ch'ing was present on the rostrum with Mao and other leaders and waved to more than one and a half million people in the crowd, over three-fourths of whom had come from other parts of the country. Later in the evening, she and Mao wandered into the cheering crowd during the fireworks display. Since that year, it has become her normal practice to appear in a plain trouser suit, chatting and shaking hands with the people. She also attends many receptions for local groups and foreign guests.

By observing the themes of these celebrations, it is possible for outside observers to draw conclusions about the changes in emphasis of Party policies. In 1967, for example, the first year Chiang Ch'ing appeared on the rostrum at the May Day festivities, numerous revolutionary literary and art floats were features in the parade. Scenes from *Shachiapang,* *The Red Lantern,* and *The White-Haired Girl* were performed, and music from Chiang Ch'ing's model theatrical works was played constantly.[2] One large float bore a legend which read: "Main Points of Forum on Literature and Art in Armed Forces Convened by Comrade Chiang Ch'ing with Comrade Lin Piao's

Authorization." Following the float in eight cars were the performers of the eight model works. On the rostrum viewing these symbols of Chiang Ch'ing's increasing influence were the Prime Minister of the Congo and delegations from Albania, Burma, Indonesia, South Vietnam, New Zealand, Pakistan, Tanzania and Mali.[3]

While the Red Guards were an important influence throughout the country, hundreds of thousands of them marched in the parades; when outside aggression was feared, military strength was suggested with 500,000 troops passing in review. Chiang Ch'ing has been prominent at May Day and National Day festivities regularly down to the present except on one occasion. The National Day parade in 1971 was cancelled without explanation, and it was not until much later that the official explanation was offered that Lin Piao's plane had been shot down in flight to the Soviet Union on the night of September 12-13.

Since her first appearance, Chiang Ch'ing has made important contributions to the celebration of national holidays. As the leading authority in cultural and political affairs and as a ranking Politburo member, she has jurisdiction in planning national celebrations; it is she who often sets their tones and selects their themes.[4] During the 1971 National Day festivities, her revolutionary literary and art workers in both Peking and Shanghai presented the piano music from *The Red Lantern* with Peking Opera singing, the piano concerto *The Yellow River*, and the symphonic arrangement of the Peking Opera *Shachiapang*.[5] In addition, new operas, *Fighting on the Plains*, *The Tuchuan Mountains*, and *Ode to the Dragon River*, and the revolutionary dance drama *Ode to Imeng* were presented.

Chiang Ch'ing has other important symbolic and ceremonial functions to perform as a national leader. On September 8, 1944, while still in Yenan, Mao Tse-tung had delivered a funeral oration at the special memorial ceremony for Chang Szu-teh, a comrade who had distinguished himself in his service to the cause. "All men must die," Mao said, "but death can vary in its significance . . . we have the interests of the people and the sufferings of the great majority at heart, and when we die for the people it

In Government and Official Circles 35

is a worthy death."[6] He went on to say that when anyone in the Communist ranks "who has done useful work dies, we should have a funeral ceremony and memorial meeting in his honor."[7] Thus, by increasing the prestige of the sacrifice made for the cause, Mao hoped to lessen, his followers' fear of death, because, as he pointed out, "If we are unafraid of death, there is nothing on earth that can intimidate us."[8]

As head first of the Central Cultural Revolution Group and later as a Politburo member, and also as Mao's representative, Chiang Ch'ing has attended many such ceremonies over the years. On March 3, 1968, Chiang Ch'ing, Chou En-lai, and others expressed their deep sorrow at the death of Hsu Kuang-ping, member of the Standing Committee of the National People's Congress.[9] On April 13, 1968, Chiang Ch'ing, Chou En-lai, and others attended the funeral ceremony of Ch'eng Ch'ien, vice-chairman of the Standing Committee of the National People's Congress and vice-chairman of the National Defense Council.[10] On January 10, 1972, Chiang Ch'ing attended the memorial ceremony for Ch'en I, foreign affairs minister, vice-premier, and vice-chairman of the Military Affairs Committee of the CCP Central Committee;[11] and on March 29, 1972, she expressed sorrow at the funeral ceremony for Hsieh Fu-chih, Politburo member, public security minister, chairman of the Peking Municipal Revolutionary Committee and vice-premier.[12] Since July 1972, she has also attended the memorial services for other comrades, such as Wang Chi-fan, Ho Hsiang-ning, Teng Tzu-hui, Wang Shu-sheng and Wang Chia-hsiang,[13] who have passed away.

Thus, on the national scene, Chiang Ch'ing has been performing all the functions of a major political leader. In addition to formulating and recommending policy, leading a political and ideological revolution, and helping to give direction to all Party and government activities, Chiang Ch'ing has served essentially as "a symbol of unity, a magnet of loyalty, and a center of ceremony."[14]

Chapter 6

Chiang Ch'ing in International Affairs

Since the Cultural Revolution, there have been major changes in China's foreign policy. In the fall of 1971, China was finally admitted into the United Nations. This event marked the beginning of her growing participation in international organizations and international affairs.

Because Chiang Ch'ing is an influential member in the Party Politburo, which makes all major national and international policies, it is unlikely that any policy could be approved without at least her passive support. Her influence in foreign affairs began to increase in 1967 when the Central Cultural Revolution Group, under her leadership, took over the day-to-day work of the Central Committee. Her frequent appearances at public functions, receiving and meeting with foreign ministers and heads of state, her other activities on the international scene, and her position and status—all suggest that she has a keen interest in foreign affairs and has played a substantial role in formulating and implementing China's foreign policies. She has probably influenced Mao's decisions to some extent by sharing with him her own views and interpretations of occasions she has attended and personalities she has met.

As China's leading voice on cultural and political affairs, Chiang Ch'ing can exert influence on international affairs not only by exercising her actual governing and administrative powers as an important member of the Politburo but also through the ideas she has implanted in her cultural output. Examples are her *Red Lantern* and her more recent revolutionary piano concerto entitled *The Yellow River*. The theme of both concerns the people's war, and by arousing strong anti-

Japanese feeling, the works are credited with having spurred the press's attack on the revival of Japanese influence in Asia.[1] China's firm policy toward the Soviet Union, her pledges of aid to Hanoi throughout the Vietnam war, her statements extolling the atmosphere of world revolution, and the recent improvement of relations with the United States as a counterweight to the Soviet Union all seem to be consistent with the foreign policy views of Chiang Ch'ing and her followers.

Considering the enormous burden of her activities and responsibilities as director of the Maoist Party Secretariat, as leader of the Central Cultural Revolution Group, and as a powerful member of the Politburo, it is remarkable that Chiang Ch'ing has devoted as much time and effort as she has to foreign affairs. Obviously she organizes her time carefully, allotting it as is necessary in accordance with Peking's main foreign policy objectives. Since the Soviet Union is viewed as the major "contradiction" facing China, Peking has attempted to neutralize or undermine Soviet influence everywhere, to distract Soviet attention away from China by various means, and generally to compete with the Soviet leaders for Communist world leadership.

One of the methods used has been to approach the Soviet Union from behind by making considerable efforts to establish friendly relations with Eastern European countries, especially Albania and Romania.

On January 11, 1967, Chiang Ch'ing and other leaders received the Albanian ambassador and artists of the Albanian national song and dance ensemble.[2] Three days later Chiang Ch'ing received members of the Albanian Politburo, the Albanian minister of defense, head of the Political Department of the Albanian People's Army, and the Albanian ambassador to China.[3] A grand banquet was given in their honor,[4] and the Albanian leaders were also invited to performances of *The Red Lantern* and *Shachiapang*. During the Albanian leaders' visit to Peking, hundreds of Red Guards met their comrades from Albania at the Great Hall of the People, singing popular songs of both countries. Since that time relations between China and

Albania have grown closer and friendlier. In June 1967 a Red Guard delegation headed by Yao Wen-yüan was invited to attend the Fifth Congress of the Union of Working Youth of Albania,[5] and in August a rally of more than ten thousand Red Guards was held to welcome Yao Wen-yüan and his delegation on their return.[6] Another huge rally was held in November 1971 to celebrate Albania's thirtieth anniversary.[7] At all these events, Chiang Ch'ing was regularly in attendance.

In February and also in late November 1967[8] Chiang Ch'ing attended several state banquets given by the Albanian ambassador and Albanian leaders in Peking. In October of the same year she escorted them to her model theatrical works and also attended a performance rendered by Albanian dancers of *The Red Detachment of Women*.[9] In addition, Chiang Ch'ing gave state banquets in honor of visiting leaders from Albania and attended Albanian ballet performances on a number of occasions.[10]

A similar pattern was revealed in several meetings with Romanian leaders. In June 1971 President Nicolae Ceausescu led a Romanian delegation to Peking.[11] He was greeted at the guesthouse by Chiang Ch'ing, who escorted him and his party to a performance of *The Red Detachment of Women* on the following evening.[12] Several days later President Ceausescu gave a grand banquet at which he proclaimed, "We note with deep satisfaction that your country has made tremendous progress in all fields."[13] More recently, in March 1973, Chiang Ch'ing greeted and entertained members of the Romanian Cultural Group led by the chairman of the Romanian Council of Culture and Education.[14]

With respect to its Asian neighbors, Peking's foreign policy objectives tend to seek the promotion of better relations with Asian countries for both political and economic advantages, the establishment of friendly "buffer states" around China, and the diminution of Soviet influence, particularly in Southeast Asia.

In support of these objectives, Chiang Ch'ing has encouraged and supported pro-Chinese forces in Japan and personally received a delegation of the Japan-China Friendship Association on

May 4, 1967.[15] In October of that year, she and Mao received all the members of the "Haguruma theater revolutionary literary and art workers of Japan,"[16] and she also held a reception and banquet in honor of a delegation from the Japanese Communist Party in September 1971.[17] In February 1973 Chiang Ch'ing attended a performance by the Japanese Ballet Troupe in Peking, and later, in December, she and Chou En-lai met Japanese friends, Masao Shimizu, his wife, Makiko Matsuyama, and Yoshiaki Tonozaki, who accompanied them on their visit.[18] Leading members of Chinese government departments and literary workers and artists were also present on this occasion.

Chiang Ch'ing and Mao have also been active in establishing better relations with Indonesia. They entertained President Sukarno's wife as early as 1962. On April 30, 1967, she and Mao personally received Chinese diplomats who had been ousted from Indonesia.[19]

Peking has gone to similar lengths to affirm its friendship with North Korea. On June 25, 1970, Chiang Ch'ing attended a rally of about 100,000 to commemorate the twentieth anniversary of Korea's war against the United States.[20] In the same week, she escorted a North Korean delegation to see one of her model operas and attended a banquet held at the Korean Embassy,[21] and on June 28 she went to the airport to greet Politburo members who were returning from a celebration in Korea.[22] On October 25, she attended another rally which commemorated the entry of the Chinese People's Volunteers into the Korean War.[23] When the Pyongyang National Opera Troupe of Korea gave a performance of *The Sea of Blood* in Peking in December 1971, Chiang Ch'ing unsurprisingly was seen attending with Cambodian Prince Sihanouk and his wife.[24] On June 18, 1973, Chiang Ch'ing also attended a performance by North Korea's Mansudae Troupe, and, in turn, invited the troupe to see a Chinese opera.[25]

China has consistently shown support for Prince Sihanouk of Cambodia. In September 1964 Chiang Ch'ing attended the Cambodian Order of Independence celebration in Peking with Prince Sihanouk; in July 1970 the Chinese Communist Party

Politburo members gave a banquet for Prince Sihanouk followed by a sports performance sponsored by the Chinese Foreign Ministry and the Physical Culture and Sports Commission; more recently, in March 1972, a banquet was given to hail Sihanouk's second anniversary in China, and this was followed by another banquet in his honor four months later; and in October 1972 a celebration was held in Peking for his fiftieth birthday. All of these events were attended by Chiang Ch'ing.[26]

Over the years, Chiang Ch'ing has also held meetings with North Vietnamese and National Liberation Front leaders, even up to the present.[27] In November 1971 she escorted them to see performances of her new model opera, *Fighting on the Plains,* and also *The White-Haired Girl.*[28] On May 11 and November 20, 1971, Chiang Ch'ing and other leaders gave banquets to welcome Vietnamese leaders to Peking, and in return attended a banquet given later by the Vietnamese.[29] Approximately 18,000 Peking spectators and foreign diplomats, including Chiang Ch'ing, watched an exhibition by Chinese and Vietnamese table tennis players on November 6, 1970.[30] Chiang Ch'ing also delivered a speech when the sixth anniversary of the founding of the National Liberation Front of South Vietnam was being celebrated in December 1966.[31] On two occasions (March 18, 1968, and November 20, 1971)[32] she attended rallies to welcome Vietnamese leaders and celebrate Vietnamese victories. When Premier Phan Van Dong paid homage to the memory of Ho Chi Minh at the house where Ho had lived in Peking, Chiang Ch'ing and other leaders accompanied him.[33] In February 1973 Chiang Ch'ing attended a banquet in honor of Le Duc Tho (member of the Political Bureau of the Vietnam Workers' Party) and Foreign Minister Nguyen Duy Trinh and was present also at a rally held the next day to hail the signing of the Vietnam agreement. In June 1973 she was also to be seen at a municipal rally held in Peking to welcome the delegation from North Vietnam.[34]

Chiang Ch'ing has been particularly active in demonstrations of Chinese opposition to Soviet revisionism. On February 11,

In Government and Official Circles

1967, she participated in a rally of more than 100,000 in Peking to denounce the "Soviet revisionist ruling clique for breaking into the Chinese Embassy in Moscow on January 25, to assault the Chinese diplomatic personnel."[35] On the same day she addressed a mass rally of Red Guards to denounce the Soviet Union,[36] and on November 7, 1967, she attended a meeting to accuse the Soviet leadership of having betrayed the October Socialist Revolution. The *People's Daily* supported this charge, stating that "the leadership of the Soviet Party and State has now been usurped by revisionists . . ."[37]

In an effort to compete with the Soviet Union in South Asia and offset Soviet influence in India, Peking embarked on a policy of cultivating friendship with Pakistan and neighboring countries. Thus, in August 1968, Chiang Ch'ing escorted the Pakistani foreign minister to a performance of *The Red Detachment of Women*, and the Minister was also honored a few days later by Mao and Chiang Ch'ing at a reception.[38] In addition, she personally met with Empress Farah of Iran in September 1972 and with King Birenda and Queen Aishwarya of Nepal in December 1973.[39]

The Third World, Africa especially, is important to China for both political and economic reasons. China has been providing aid to Africa and other developing countries in order to gain more friends and extend its influence in those areas. Chiang Ch'ing has similarly made personal contact with leaders of many developing countries, including, among others, President Julius K. Nyerere of the United Republic of Tanzania and other Tanzanian officials who visited Peking on July 21, 1968. Mao, Chiang Ch'ing, and other Chinese leaders received them at the reception hall and posed for pictures with them. At a banquet in their honor which was given that evening, President Nyerere delivered a speech praising China, saying, "The last three days have confirmed my conviction once again that we have a lot to learn from China."[40] Chiang Ch'ing met also with President Kaunda of Zambia and President Boumediene of Algeria when they were in China in February 1974.[41] In her capacity as a

Chinese Party and government leader, she personally received an economic delegation from Peru and held a soiree for them as well.[42]

Peking has also been anxious to penetrate the Atlantic community. In August 1968 Mao, Chiang Ch'ing, and other leaders had very cordial talks with members of the Italian Communist Party delegation; in the evening, a banquet was given in their honor.[43] In August 1971 Chiang Ch'ing and members of various groups from literature and the performing arts had friendly meetings with Dutch film director Joris Ivens and French filmmaker Marceline Loridan. She gave a banquet in their honor and escorted them to a performance of her model opera *The Red Detachment of Women*, and to an experimental performance of *Ode to Imeng*, a modern revolutionary dance drama.[44] In September 1971 Chiang Ch'ing, Chou En-lai, and other members of the Central Committee met with French Communist leader Jacques Jerquet. Dinners were given in their honor as well.[45] On September 12, 1973, a ballet was sponsored by Chiang Ch'ing to honor French President Pompidou, and on December 7, 1973, members of the delegation of French Marxist-Leninist Communists of the *Journal l'Humanite Rouge* were feted by Chiang Ch'ing, Chou En-lai, and Wang Hung-wen.[46] On December 31, 1970, Chiang Ch'ing and other Central Committee members were reported to have had very cordial talks with British Communist Party leaders, and in the following year, in October, she met and received British Communist Party leader Reginald Birch.[47]

A major event in China's foreign affairs was its admission to full membership in the United Nations. On December 22, 1971, Chiang Ch'ing and other leaders greeted the Chinese delegation to the United Nations on their return from a successful first session of the General Assembly. With China on the international stage, the groundwork was laid for friendlier relations with the United States.[48]

For decades, Chiang Ch'ing and Mao had been friendly with various Americans who had expressed sympathy for their ideals and cause. On Anna Louise Strong's eightieth birthday, November 24, 1965, Chiang Ch'ing and Mao held a reception for the writer and later attended a banquet in her honor.[49] Miss Strong died on March 29, 1970, and at a memorial service for her on April 2, 1970, Chiang Ch'ing presented a wreath and placed it beside a white ribbon which read: "To progressive writer Miss Anna Louise Strong, a friend of the Chinese people."[50] Similarly, when author Edgar Snow died in Switzerland on February 15, 1972, at the age of sixty-six, Mao, Chiang Ch'ing, Chou En-lai, and other leaders sent messages of condolence to Mrs. Snow.[51] The joint condolence message sent by Chiang Ch'ing and Chou En-lai read: "We were shocked to learn of the untimely passing of our respected friend, Mr. Edgar Snow. . . . Even during his serious illness, he never ceased turning his mind to working for better understanding and friendship between the Chinese and American people. . . ."[52]

However, to protest American bombing of Indochina, a rally was held on May 21, 1970, at Tienanmen Square in Peking. Chiang Ch'ing and Chou En-lai sat in places of honor on the rostrum. Also attending the event were diplomats and friends from Indochina, Asia, Africa, Latin America, Europe, and Oceania.[53]

An American Progressive Students delegation led by Cheryl Hill and Jerry Tung visited Peking Physical Culture Institute in Peking on December 19, 1971. As a gesture of friendship with the American people, Chiang Ch'ing and other leaders and members of the Physical Culture and Sports Commission escorted the American visitors to the sports arena, where they watched table tennis, traditional Chinese boxing, and gymnastic exhibitions. After the exhibitions, the Americans shook hands with the Chinese sportsmen and joined them in singing revolutionary songs in a scene of warm friendship.[54] Some days later, Chiang Ch'ing and other leaders had extensive cordial talks with all the members of the American Progressive Students delegation, at which the leading members of the Chinese table tennis team were also present.[55]

In February 1972 President and Mrs. Richard Nixon made their historic journey to China. In addition to attending meetings and banquets and touring various places of interest, the President and Mrs. Nixon went to a performance of *The Red Detachment of Women* to which they were escorted by Chiang Ch'ing, Chou En-lai and other leaders. Chinese television stations covered the event and American television networks transmitted coverage to the United States via satellite.[56] Chiang Ch'ing was seen seated between the President and Mrs. Nixon in the position of honor. She was also prominent on several other occasions during the Nixon visit. When Chou En-lai returned to Peking from Shanghai on February 29, after accompanying the Nixons on their visit to southern China, Chiang Ch'ing, other leaders, and more than five thousand people greeted him at the airport to express their approval of improved relations with the United States.[57]

Subsequent to the Nixon visit, contacts with Americans in various walks of life began to develop. In May 1972 Chiang Ch'ing attended a banquet held in honor of Mrs. Edgar Snow,[58] and in October of the same year she received the American pianists Frances and Richard Hadden and also the American physicist Li Cheng Tao.[59] In June 1973 Chiang Ch'ing was on hand to greet visiting U.S. athletes;[60] in July she appeared as a surprise observer at an unscheduled exhibition held by visiting U.S. swimmers especially for her, and was also reported to have been seen at the Sino-U.S. ball game two days later wearing a skirt and white shoes and carrying a matching bag.[61] In September Chiang Ch'ing sponsored the concert tour of the Philadelphia Symphony Orchestra in China,[62] and in October of the same year she personally placed a wreath before Edgar Snow's ashes.[63]

Chiang Ch'ing has spent considerable time and effort helping China acquire support from various left-wing international organizations and foreign Communist parties. In the spring of 1967, a seminar sponsored by the Afro-Asian Writers' Bureau was held in Peking to commemorate the twenty-fifth anniversary of Chairman Mao's talks at the Yenan Forum on Literature and Art. On June 5 Chiang Ch'ing and Chou En-lai sat at the rostrum for the closing ceremonies. Kuo Mo-jo, China's most

In Government and Official Circles

highly respected literary figure, delivered a poem that he had dedicated to Chiang Ch'ing:

> Dear Comrade Chiang Ch'ing, you are the fine example for us to follow.
> With courage you lead us toward literary and artistic goals,
> And the heroic image of the workers, peasants, and soldiers now dominates our stage.
> China's yesterday is the today of many Afro-Asian countries.
> And China's today will be their tomorrow.
> We will fly the great red banner of Mao Tse-tung's thought over the Afro-Asian countries
> And the six continents and the four seas.[64]

On the afternoon of June 9, Chiang Ch'ing, together with Chairman Mao and Lin Piao, received eighty writers from thirty-two countries and regions.[65]

On November 24, 1967, Chiang Ch'ing attended a soiree in honor of E. F. Hill, chairman of the Australian Communist Party; her model opera *Taking the Bandits' Stronghold* was presented.[66] A year later Chairman Hill expressed warm praises for Chiang Ch'ing's model revolutionary works in an article published in the Australian publication *Vanguard*. He wrote: "They all stand in striking contrast to what is seen in Australia. . . . Never before has there been such a thorough-going, painstaking, systematic, conscious carrying out of the proletarian line in literature and art . . . [and] Chiang Ch'ing, herself a gifted artist, stood in the forefront of the struggle of the revolutionaries against the revisionists."[67]

V. G. Wilcox, Secretary General of the New Zealand Communist Party, attended a party arranged in his honor on the evening of March 18, 1968, and was accompanied by Chiang Ch'ing and Chou En-lai to see a performance of *Taking the Bandits' Stronghold*.[68]

In December 1969 Chiang Ch'ing sponsored a soiree for "leading comrades of fraternal Marxist-Leninist parties now in Peking." Present on the occasion were officials from Vietnam,

Australia, Burma, Indonesia, France, and Albania, and comrades of the Albanian People's Army Art Troupe. During the evening the guests attended a performance of one of Chiang Ch'ing's model operas.[69]

On November 14, 1971, twenty thousand spectators watched Chiang Ch'ing and Chou En-lai close the Afro-Asian Table Tennis Friendship Invitational Tournament in Peking. Attending the event were players from forty countries and regions. On the rostrum were leaders of table tennis delegations from Korea, Egypt, Japan, Mauritius, Nepal, Tunisia, Vietnam, Laos, Palestine, Nigeria, Chile, Colombia, Mexico, Cambodia, the Union of Burma, and officials of embassies of Asian countries in Peking.[70]

More recently, in August 1973, Chiang Ch'ing attended the opening of the Asia-Afro-Latin American Table Tennis Meeting in Peking and observed some of the matches at the Capital Gymnasium.[71]

Chiang Ch'ing's model theatrical works have had international impact. She has used the Peking Opera, the ballet, and the symphony to communicate Maoist ideas, and through this medium she is probably reaching more people throughout the country and the world than any Chinese leader in the past. Color films have been made of all her model productions and have been shown abroad. Her works in booklet form, photos, records, posters, postcards, scripts and reviews, comic books, and buttons have similarly been exported and marketed widely through a variety of outlets in China and around the world.

At the Autumn Export Commodities Fair in Canton in 1968, Chiang Ch'ing's eight model works were shown. One Congolese visitor observed: "*The Red Lantern* teaches us young revolutionaries that we must not be afraid of sacrifice in order to triumph over the enemy."[72] A visitor from Guinea remarked: "We are convinced that by advancing along the road pointed out by Chairman Mao, the Guinean people can create new literature and art which will meet the needs of Guinea's revolutionary struggle and are imbued with our own national characteristics."[73]

Some leaders in developing countries seem to consider Chiang Ch'ing's model works an effective new approach to accelerate change in their countries by using the mass media to establish a revolutionary culture, promote their cause, create favorable public opinion, and consolidate their gains. A delegate from Swaziland said, after attending a performance of *The White-Haired Girl:* "Similar things are still happening in Swaziland.... It can truly be said that this ballet has given me a weapon."[74]

In addition to influencing revolutionary activists in other countries through her model works, Chiang Ch'ing's meetings with foreign leaders, dignitaries, and diplomats have been widely covered in the local and international press, thus increasing her stature at home and abroad. As Chairman Mao's wife as well as a Politburo member in her own right, Chiang Ch'ing's presence is so significant as to be considered by other leaders a special honor at any occasion. In fact, she is probably more effective than Mao for some purposes because she can talk more informally and warmly to people, represent Mao's intentions in a way that is more complimentary to him, feel the other side out first for Mao, and talk without making irrevocable commitments on the spot. By her participation in international affairs she can also check whether Mao's intentions are being carried out and later report her opinions and suggestions to him. In the meantime she is developing personal contacts in government and official circles while gaining expertise in international affairs. Chiang Ch'ing's worldwide contacts are assets which should enhance her political standing at home.

Preliminary talks with and recognition of Maoist China by an increasing number of nations open the door to more international cultural and trade exchanges, thus paving the way for the introduction of Chiang Ch'ing's cultural works abroad, possibly leading to increasing demand for more cultural exports from China. This may increase Chiang Ch'ing's capacity to reach more people throughout the world.

Part Three

THE CHINESE ARMED FORCES AND CHIANG CH'ING

Chapter 7
Chiang Ch'ing's Relationship with the People's Liberation Army

Chiang Ch'ing's relationship with the Chinese People's Liberation Army (PLA) dates back to the 1930s, when she worked as an assistant political officer in the Red Army Military Commission in Yenan.[1] Because of her history as a Communist and a dedicated underground worker, she was entrusted with high-level intelligence and personnel documents through which she came to know the backgrounds and talents of various members of the PLA. Also, as Mao's wife, she was later afforded the opportunity to meet with promising young officers when they came to see Mao at his office or at home. Among the military officers who became her friends were Chou En-lai, Yeh Chien-ying, Li Teh-sheng, and Li Ta-chang.

Throughout the Second Revolutionary Civil War and the war against Japan, Chiang Ch'ing continued to work in the intelligence department. As she read reports and witnessed the sacrifices by leaders and men which were necessary for success, she developed a tremendous admiration for the people in the PLA. She was also struck by the contrast between the suffering and hopelessness that she had witnessed before her arrival at Yenan and the healthy, orderly life of the dedicated PLA people. She became convinced that the PLA was thus capable of improving life for the average Chinese. Many times she publicly expressed her admiration and affection for the army. "I have always respected members of the Red Army," she told a military group in 1967; "I am very close to the Chinese People's Liberation

Army. I still consider myself part of the military."[2] On another occasion she said, "The People's Liberation Army cadres and soldiers have done a great work and scored a brilliant success."[3]

Because of her feeling for the army and her respect for the soldiers, she often wore a military uniform in public, even before the Cultural Revolution. Once, while she was in Yenan, someone pinned a red star on her cap and she became very upset when it was later removed; she always wanted people to know that she too was a soldier. Twenty years later, still unhappy about the incident, she told an audience, "I never did understand why that star had to be taken off."[4]

Military heroism is a strong central theme in most of her works, and soldiers are consistently portrayed by her in glowing terms, undoubtedly reflecting her own convictions. In her model operas she has openly displayed admiration for the soldier by showing him to be courageous, self-sacrificing, loyal, and intelligent—truly a hero to emulate. In *Taking the Bandits' Stronghold*, the PLA's representative, Yang Tsu-jung, risks his life by infiltrating the bandit stronghold as a spy, and in both her model ballets—*The Red Detachment of Women* and *The White Haired Girl*—the heroines are rescued by the Red Army, as is the village of Shachiapang in the opera of that name.

There is a striking difference between the soldier in her works and those in the works of revisionist writers and artists. Yang Tsu-jung, for example, was a vulgar rogue with a devil-may-care approach to life before Chiang Ch'ing revised his role and converted him into an earnest, altruistic Communist.

Over the years Chiang Ch'ing has traveled extensively from one army post to another, investigating conditions, talking to servicemen, observing the results of her cultural and educational programs, maintaining contact with old friends, and making new ones. She has constantly worked to further a good relationship between the army and the peasants, praising their successes. For example, in reporting on one of the trips she took to a garrison in Canton, she pointed out the fine assistance the army had given to a neighboring commune which was in danger of losing its crop because of the sweltering heat. She related how the soldiers who were off duty volunteered to help transplant seedlings and completed the work on seventeen *mow* (two-and-a-half acres of land), even getting out of bed an hour early to complete the task. "Consequently," she said, "all seedlings were transplanted . . . and the company secured the praise of the leaders of the production teams and the commune members."[5] In *Taking the Bandits' Stronghold*, Chiang Ch'ing inserted a scene emphasizing this type of cooperation, with Yang Tsu-jung listening to suggestions by the peasants and then taking their advice.

Apparently Chiang Ch'ing has warm rapport with army men, to which her long friendships with Chou En-lai, Li Teh-sheng, and Yeh Chien-ying attest. She praises leaders and fighters alike when they behave admirably, and she is observant and appreciative. It was she who publicized the fact that some soldiers roused themselves from a deep sleep when a typhoon hit and rushed outside to stand guard and give any help that was needed during the violent wind and torrential downpour that accompanied the storm, even though the roof was blown off their watchhouse and one man was lifted off the ground and blown several feet away.[6] On the other hand, she reminds them of their duty when it is necessary. In a speech she gave at a rally, she said, "The masses should treat the army correctly and support the army; but the army must also treat the masses correctly; it must love the people."[7]

Response to her appearances and speeches has been exceptionally enthusiastic. A typical reaction was that of Wang Yu-chang, an army man, who after hearing "Comrade Chiang Ch'ing's speech . . . pledged to respond to Comrade Chiang Ch'ing's call."[8] It is a common phenomenon for Chiang Ch'ing to stir her audiences to the point where they answer her directly. At numerous meetings and rallies there have been shouts from the audience of "Learn from Chiang Ch'ing and salute her!" to which she replied, "Learn from you, comrades, and salute to you all!"[9]

Through long years of contact with the army, Chiang Ch'ing has developed many deep and lasting friendships.[10] During the Cultural Revolution she became deeply involved with military politics and gradually gained authority to some extent over ideological, political, cultural, and educational works in the armed forces.

Chapter 8

Chiang Ch'ing as "Adviser" of the Armed Forces

In September 1962, at the Central Committee's Tenth Plenum, the Socialist Education Movement was officially launched. Its aim was to "carry out a cleaning up . . . in the political, economic, ideological and organizational fields . . . and to conduct profound class education and Socialist education among the masses of the people so as to promote proletarian ideology and eradicate bourgeois ideology."[1] Chou En-lai stated in his report that "this movement has far-reaching significance for . . . the destruction of the social foundations of revisionism."[2] After three years of half-hearted implementation by the regular Party apparatus, there had been little success along these lines except in the field of the Peking Opera, where Chiang Ch'ing's accomplishments had been impressive. It was not until Chiang Ch'ing, with Mao's support, turned her attention to other aspects of the cultural revolution that it truly became a mass movement and the Maoists began to make rapid political progress.

After the Central Committee Conference in 1965, Chiang Ch'ing took another trip to Shanghai to work with her friends Chang Ch'un-ch'iao and the drama critic Yao Wen-yüan. On November 10, 1965, the article "On the New Historical Play *Hai Jui Dismissed from Office*" appeared under Yao's name in the Shanghai newspaper *Wen Hui Pao,* thus firing the first shot of the Great Proletarian Cultural Revolution (see chapter 18).

Sympathizers of the two camps divided sharply in response to the article, which was an indirect attack on P'eng Chen through his vice-mayor, Wu Han. The Maoists accused Wu Han of being a revisionist and therefore a political enemy; the other side claimed that Wu Han was merely in error academically.

Even after Mao stressed on December 21 that "the Emperor Chia-ch'ing dismissed Hai Jui from office; in 1959 we dismissed P'eng Teh-huai from office; and P'eng Teh-huai is Hai Jui too,"[3] P'eng Chen's group implied that Mao's call to criticize Wu Han was a scholarly issue. On December 27, *Peking Daily* published Wu Han's self-criticism in which he admitted only to have committed academic errors.

On February 2, 1966, the struggle between the two lines within the Party reached a "critical juncture";[4] a Forum on the Work in Literature and Art in the Armed Forces was convened in Shanghai. Chiang Ch'ing was formally placed in charge by Defense Minister Lin Piao, who told the assemblage that Chiang Ch'ing "has many valuable ideas. You should pay good attention to them and take measures to ensure that they are applied ideologically and organizationally . . . from now on the army's documents concerning literature and art should be sent to her, and you should get in touch with her when you have any useful information; keep her well posted on the situation in literary and art work in the armed forces and seek her views."[5] Chiang Ch'ing was presented as the person who would lay down the guidelines for the ensuing Cultural Revolution in the PLA and as the authority who would judge whether or not they were being carried out.

During the forum, Chiang Ch'ing personally took charge by conducting private and group discussions, delivering "many highly important opinions,"[6] attending films and theatrical performances with army men, explaining the theoretical rationale and necessity of the coming Cultural Revolution, and giving them many new instructions. She also exchanged ideas with many "activists" and members of art and literature units within the armed forces. Chiang Ch'ing stated that the military leaders "must take personal charge and see to it that good . . . heroic models of workers, peasants and soldiers" are created. "Only when we have such models and successful experience in creating them will we be able to convince people, consolidate the positions we hold, and knock the reactionaries' stick out of their hands."[7] She thus spent three weeks of intensive work with the military men, preparing them for their role in the Cultural Revolution. The forum also marked the beginning of important changes within the armed forces as plans developed for greatly expanding political and cultural activities in the men's daily lives. The number of military personnel handling cultural and political activities was therefore increased, and all were subjected to Chiang Ch'ing's supervision to some extent. Many of Chiang Ch'ing's supporters were placed in these new positions, among them her daughter, Hsiao-li, who was assigned to the editorial staff of the army's newspaper, *Liberation Army Daily*, as early as 1966, later advancing to the post of chief editor.

In Chiang Ch'ing's talks with the military leaders, she exposed for the first time the struggle which had been going on between the Maoists and the revisionists during the previous sixteen years. She pointed out that Mao's basic guidelines for creating a proletarian art and literature had not been carried out because of the "domination of a bourgeois and modern Revisionist countercurrent." She declared: "We must resolutely carry on a great Socialist revolution on the cultural front and completely eliminate this sinister line. . . . Our struggle is an arduous, complex, and long-term struggle demanding decades or even centuries of effort. This is a cardinal issue."[8] She explained the two lines and presented a list of documents that the armed forces should read in order to understand better the differences. She pointed out that during the previous three years the Maoists had succeeded in dealing "a powerful blow at conservatives of various descriptions" by launching "a heroic and tenacious offensive against the literature and art of the feudal class, the bourgeoisie, and the modern revisionists" through the presentation of Peking operas on contemporary revolutionary themes. This proved that "even the most stubborn stronghold, Peking Opera, can be taken by storm and revolutionized . . . and that foreign classical art forms such as the ballet and symphonic music can also be remolded to serve our purpose."[9]

The Maoists' ultimate aim was to involve the masses in the creation of cultural works, and Chiang Ch'ing told the forum that the workers, peasants, and soldiers "are now producing many fine . . . articles which splendidly express Mao Tse-tung's Thought in terms of their own practice." She said, "Listen to the opinions of the masses, analyze their opinions, accept the good ones and reject the others. . . . We must encourage revolutionary mass criticism in literature and art." (During the Cultural Revolution that followed, this advice was followed; numerous articles were written by the masses and large character posters were displayed on every available surface.) Finally, Chiang Ch'ing emphasized that cadres and writers had to be reeducated and reorganized. Many workers in the art and literature fields had bourgeois education and the time had come to broaden their experiences and help them understand the real problems of the masses. It was also necessary to encourage them to "study Marxism-Leninism and Chairman Mao's works, in order that they might remain revolutionary all their lives and maintain proletarian integrity in later life."[10]

After this forum, the PLA formed "study groups" to review Chiang Ch'ing's "many highly important opinions," speeches, and documents, and to discuss their implementation. Chiang Ch'ing also directed the PLA to carry out some new far-reaching measures to effect their Cultural Revolution. A new office was set up in charge of writing and producing new works, especially on the subject of the three major military campaigns. This office was to initiate programs to train a "nucleus" of writers and artists; literary and art workers were to take the mass line; an "army" of literary and art critics was to be created; literature and art columns were to be set up in newspapers to analyze and criticize literary works; and the film studios of the General Political Department was to provide stronger leadership over literary and art work.[11] All these changes and reorganizations moved the army further in the Maoist direction and greatly expanded Maoist influence throughout the army.

During this period, Chiang Ch'ing served as an important link between Mao, who was in poor health at that time, and the PLA, planning and coordinating the military aspects of their programs and bringing them to fruition. She was intensely involved in the timing and arrangement of military support for the repudiation and removal of P'eng Chen and other leading members of the Peking Party Committee, the Propaganda Department, the Ministry of Culture, and media workers in literary and cultural circles. The first phase of the political revolution culminated successfully in the CCP Central Committee's public announcement on June 3, 1966, that the Peking Municipal Committee was reorganized. In the shakeup, Li Hsüeh-feng and Wu Te were appointed—Li as first secretary and Wu as second secretary. The new Municipal Committee quickly relieved two revisionists—its president and deputy secretary—of their duties within the Peking University hierarchy. The *Peking Daily*, under new management by Maoists, promptly published an article entitled "Sweep Away All Freaks and Monsters." These events had tremendous impact on the entire country, especially on the regular Party apparatus.

The launching of the Cultural Revolution, in which Chiang Ch'ing was heavily involved, was reportedly well received within segments of the armed forces. According to the New China News Agency (NCNA):

> Commanders and fighters of the PLA ground, naval and air forces have expressed their warmest support for the establishment of the revolutionary Peking Municipal Committee. . . . Celebration meetings and discussions have been held by the commanders and fighters. They put up wall papers and slogans and paraded near barracks to mark the formation of the revolutionary Peking Municipal Committee. . . . The masses of PLA commanders and fighters have angrily condemned the towering crimes committed by the counterrevolutionary revisionist clique of the former Peking Municipal Committee.[12]

During the summer of 1966, Chiang Ch'ing worked closely with Lin Piao, Liu Chih-chien, deputy director of the PLA's General Political Department, Hsieh Chang-hou, and others to help organize the historic series of Red Guard mass rallies. Over thirteen million students, teachers, and youths from all parts of the country came to Peking to see the nation's leaders, especially Chairman Mao. More than 100,000 commanders and fighters were assigned to Chiang Ch'ing, and the PLA men, many of whom were not much older than the young Red Guards themselves, made the visitors feel at home in the capital throughout their stay.

On November 28, 1966, after working with the PLA for almost a year, Chiang Ch'ing was officially named PLA adviser. At the same time it was announced that major literary and drama studios and organizations had been incorporated into the PLA, among them Peking Opera Company No. One, the National Peking Opera Theater, the Central Philharmonic Society, and the ballet troupe and orchestra of the Central Song and Dance Ensemble. These all became constituent parts of the army for political, literary, and art purposes, and were directly responsible to Chiang Ch'ing and under her leadership and command. Delivering the keynote speech at an important rally on that date, one at which important instructions were given for the next stage of the Cultural Revolution, Chiang Ch'ing called for extending the Cultural Revolution into industry and throughout the provinces. According to NCNA:

> Chiang Ch'ing received a thunderous ovation from the entire rally. . . . The important speeches were carefully studied on the following day by the broad masses of professional and spare-time literary and art workers of the PLA. . . . They paid tribute to Comrade Chiang Ch'ing's special contributions.[13]

Chapter 9

Chiang Ch'ing, the People's Liberation Army, and the Red Guards

Beginning in 1966, the People's Liberation Army (PLA) commanders and men had numerous dealings with Chiang Ch'ing which strengthened their relationship with her, gained her many new followers in the armed forces, reinforced their confidence in her leadership, and increased her capacity to influence them. On December 19, for example, she organized a mass rally at the Peking Workers Stadium to thank the PLA for supporting the Red Guards. Braving the icy Gobi Desert winds that often sweep through Peking in December, Chiang Ch'ing waved to the men as her car moved slowly around the inside oval track of the stadium.

At the rally, as first speaker, she rose to tumultuous applause and began skillfully to exploit her unique position as Mao's wife. "Chairman Mao sends you his best regards!" she told them. "You all must want to know how Chairman Mao is. Let me tell you: he is in robust health!"[1] The servicemen again burst into thunderous applause. In her speech she expressed her deep appreciation for the wonderful job the armed forces had done for the Red Guards during their struggle; and she ended her speech by praising the PLA warmly. "You have done an excellent job! You are an invincible force!" The PLA men enthusiastically pledged to carry out her instructions and serve the Red Guards well.

During the Cultural Revolution, all PLA members participated in "study groups," and new groups, such as the Red Vanguards of air force headquarters, were formed to review in depth and discuss Chiang Ch'ing's speeches, her instructions, and other documents, and to actively carry out the Cultural Revolution within the armed forces. Chiang Ch'ing's words and directives were consistently endorsed by Mao and echoed by Chou En-lai, Lin Piao, and others, and the PLA became accustomed to following Chiang Ch'ing's leadership and her authoritative opinions.

In an effort to bring the Red Guards ideologically closer to the PLA, Chiang Ch'ing formulated a series of instructions to help the Red Guards turn their hikes to the capital into "long marches," in emulation of the PLA's Long March to Yenan in 1935. The instructions covered guidelines on how to carry out ideological mobilization work, how to organize leadership, launch mass mutual-aid activities, propagate Maoist Thought, do good deeds for the masses, and learn the revolutionary traditions of the workers and poor and lower-middle-class peasants.[2]

On numerous occasions in her talks Chiang Ch'ing urged the Red Guards to emulate the discipline and heroism of the PLA and to become a strong reserve force for them. "It is our hope that you will modestly learn from the Liberation Army, vigorously destroy self-interest, and foster the collective spirit," she told them on one such occasion.[3] She repeatedly praised the PLA and told the Red Guards to treat the army men with respect. As a result, at Red Guard rallies, representatives from the PLA, according to an NCNA release describing one such rally, "pledged in their speeches to be the powerful backing of the young Red Guards and expressed determination to unite, fight, and win together."[4]

Rallies held on March 28, 1966, February 22, 1967, March 25, 1967, and April 3, 1967, illustrate this point beyond doubt. In her keynote speeches, Chiang Ch'ing urged the young Red Guards to learn some lessons from the PLA men. "We want you to humbly learn from the PLA," she reiterated. "Third Political Commissar Liu Shao-wen of the PLA . . . voiced their determination to act as a powerful backing for the Red Guards . . ."

and "carry to the end the Great Proletarian Cultural Revolution . . ."[5]

As a result of her affection for the armed forces and through her combined use of praise and parental strictness, Chiang Ch'ing has managed to convey to the men her admiration and her high expectations for them: "The masses should adopt a correct attitude toward the PLA . . . the army for its part should also adopt a correct attitude toward the masses."[6] The PLA men in turn have responded warmly and have repeatedly pledged their loyalty to her.[7] The impact of their common experience in the Cultural Revolution consolidated Chiang Ch'ing's political position.[8] In following her lead to success, the army has been well conditioned to follow her leadership and guidance.

Chapter 10

Chiang Ch'ing and the Military Leadership

During the Cultural Revolution, it was necessary for Chiang Ch'ing to exercise her powers in order to implement her policies. The style which she used to persuade military personnel and gain their loyalty is evidenced by her behavior during the entire Cultural Revolution, as for example in a speech she made to an enlarged meeting of the Military Commission. On April 12, 1967, she called the military leaders together, and in accordance with Maoist principles, began by reminding them that they were all comrades and could criticize each other in a friendly way if they wished. "I am just an ordinary Communist," she told them, ". . . if I am wrong, please criticize me." But by pointing out that she had been serving in effect as the general secretary of the Standing Committee of the Politburo since 1965, she let them be aware of her position of power, even though she was receptive to suggestions.

By recounting a parable, she implied that anyone who failed to make new contributions to his country might eventually lose his position. She chided the commanders who did not want to get involved in the Cultural Revolution. The fact was, she told them, they had already become involved and there was no way out but to support the left in the movement. She reassured those who had backed the wrong faction that it was not too late to correct their mistake. She ended with an appeal: "Generals, please do not think it is the field of literature and education only. If we don't concern ourselves . . . they will take over!"[1]

In order to guarantee that the Maoists' reforms would be carried out efficiently, it was necessary for Chiang Ch'ing to place trusted followers in key positions within the PLA; other-

The Chinese Armed Forces

wise "it would not take long, perhaps only several years or a decade, or several decades at most, before a counterrevolutionary restoration on a national scale would inevitably occur, the Marxist-Leninist party would undoubtedly become a revisionist party or a fascist party, and the whole of China would change its color."[2] Serious mistakes had been made by entrenched PLA commanders who had given armed support to several fake leftist units, such as the United Action Red Guards, a "Million Heroes," and other reactionary and conservative groups.

Although Chiang Ch'ing tactfully pointed out that it was hard to distinguish "the right from the wrong" and refrained from pointing an accusing finger at anyone, her intelligence network had informed her that subversion existed within the military. Chou En-lai stated: "We knew nothing about such inside information . . . it was Comrade Chiang Ch'ing who exposed [them]." She realized that it was necessary to remove some of the commanders who did not follow the Maoist line.[3] As Chou pointed out, "Comrade Chiang Ch'ing imposes strict demands on herself as well as on the comrades. She examines every comrade according to the standard of the Thought of Mao Tse-tung and draws a clear line between friend and foe. In the case of comrades, she will earnestly help them, but in the case of renegades and bad elements, she will courageously expose them."[4]

Early in 1966 Chiang Ch'ing accused Lo Jui-ch'ing, the PLA chief of staff, of conspiring with P'eng Chen and Lu Ting-yi to stage a coup d'etat.[5] In the official report of his dismissal it was stated that he had made "the mistake of a bourgeois individual ambitionist in usurping the leadership in the army and opposing the Party."[6] Liu Chih-chien, the deputy director of the Political Department of the army and deputy chief of the Cultural Revolution Group within the PLA, was removed after Chiang Ch'ing denounced him at a Red Guard rally. Twenty-one days later Chiang Ch'ing led a rally to denounce Yang Yung, a deputy chief of staff. He was similarly dismissed.

A new All-PLA Cultural Revolution Committee was organized under the direct leadership of Chiang Ch'ing. Its role was "to strengthen the leadership over the Great Proletarian Cultural Revolution in the whole army."[7] She chose her own committee and carefully made adjustments until it suited her purposes. Hsu Hsiang-chien, whom she placed in the position of director in January, was removed by her in April. Hsu had been a powerful figure in China, a military man for almost four decades and a member of the Politburo since the summer of 1966, but when he failed to meet Chiang Ch'ing's standards, he was removed. Hsiao Hua, director of the PLA Central Political Department, was generally thought by the Cultural Revolution Group to be hostile to Maoist aims. Chiang Ch'ing claimed that the General Political Department should criticize him for shutting "the door to the Cultural Revolution."[8] She worked very hard to remove him from office, leading four different public repudiations of his "closed-doorism."[9] When she succeeded, he was replaced after an interval by Li Teh-sheng. According to *The New York Times*, Li's appointment represented a tactical gain for Chiang Ch'ing since Li had no known affiliations with either the defense minister Lin Piao, or Huang Yung-sheng, the chief of the General Staff. However, he did have links with Chiang Ch'ing. The article reported too that Chiang Ch'ing had extended her influence into the sphere of military affairs.[10]

By the time Chiang Ch'ing had finished overhauling the PLA, three out of seven members of the Military Affairs Committee had been removed, in addition to three out of seven vice-ministers of National Defense, the chief of General Staff and four of his eight deputies, the director as well as two out of the five vice-directors of the General Political Department, three out of eight vice-commanders of the air force, the first political commissar of the navy, the commanders of the armored force, the artillery and the railway corps, and scores of regional military commanders and political commissars.[11]

Even Lin Piao was brought down eventually. It is not clear how this was done, but Chiang Ch'ing and Chou En-lai were the chief beneficiaries of his departure. Although she had worked closely with him during the planning and implementation of the Cultural Revolution, Chiang Ch'ing and Lin Piao undoubtedly did feel differently about a number of things. For instance, it was reported that a book entitled *Quotations from Lin Piao* was being compiled and would be printed by the CCP Military Affairs Committee. This would surely have diluted the impact of Mao's Thought and made Chiang Ch'ing's work more difficult. Lin's insistence that he be publicly designated as Mao's successor was probably another source of friction.

Chapter 11

Military Problems and Chiang Ch'ing

One of Chiang Ch'ing's many assets as a national leader is the very valuable experience she had with the PLA and with military problems during the Cultural Revolution which gave her a competitive advantage over those who had never played a comparable role in the all-out political and military struggle.

Chiang Ch'ing explained that it was the responsibility of her organization to gather facts and investigate them so as to be "able to keep up with the constantly developing revolutionary situation."[1] Because of her access to extensive daily intelligence, she shouldered the grave responsibility of authoritatively identifying and revealing, throughout the revolution, the names of revisionists who posed as members of the left in order to further their own purposes. It was she who led the mass repudiations of these opponents. One example of such a function on her part is associated with the term "February adverse current," referring to efforts made to reverse the gains that had been made by the Maoists and "restore the Liu-Teng rule."[2]

T'an Chen-lin, a vice-premier, allegedly organized a "fake seizure of power . . . at all the offices of the agricultural system," and when the revolutionaries gathered to counterattack, T'an branded their group as a "rightist rally." Because of influence he had gained while working in the new Fourth Army, local PLA units believed him and gave him active support.[3] Chiang Ch'ing accused T'an and his associates of trying to "throw the PLA into disarray and rock the foundations of the newly formed Revolutionary Committees." But what was even more intolerable, according to Chiang Ch'ing, was that "T'an Chen-lin deceived Premier Chou. . . . Consequently, Premier Chou did receive" members of T'an's false revolutionary group. "T'an did so to foster the conservative force and thus acquired more political capital."[4]

In the hope of preventing the PLA from supporting the wrong side in the future, Peking sent out a directive on April 6, 1967, which stated: "Before taking any important action, a report should be made to the Central Cultural Revolution Group and the All-PLA Cultural Revolution Group and their advice sought."[5] Both of these groups were under Chiang Ch'ing's effective direction.

The problem of "adverse currents" continued to arise in various parts of the country, and Chiang Ch'ing for more than two years was preoccupied with ferreting out the "rascals" and mustering support for the favored factions. As late as March 1968, in a speech she made during a reception for a group from Szechuan, Chiang Ch'ing said: "At present the rightist reversal of verdict is the chief danger all over the country. I don't believe that this wind of reversing verdict is not present where you come from. If Peking students try to reverse the verdict on the February adverse current, we will bombard them. We must see the victory of the Great Cultural Revolution."[6]

Another type of military problem, common during a revolution, is the resistance to civil authority by powerful military leaders. A well-known incident of this nature occurred in Wuhan when a revisionist faction calling itself "One Million Heroes," and supported by Ch'en Tsai-tao, the military regional commander, broke into armed conflict with the revolutionary forces. A peace mission headed by Hsieh Fu-chin and Wang Li was sent by the Maoists to reason with Ch'en. In defiance Ch'en allowed his Million Heroes to seize Hsieh and Wang, imprison them, and subject them to considerable abuse. According to Minoru Shibata, a Japanese correspondent, ten warships were sent up the Yangtze River and placed in position opposite the Wuhan waterfront. The following day an airborne division seized key facilities and disarmed the local troops. Hsieh and Wang were released, and when they arrived in Peking, they were greeted at the airport by "the thunderous applause of tens of thousands from the revolutionary masses," including Chiang Ch'ing and Chou En-lai.[7] Ch'en Tsai-tao and his associates were escorted to Peking for denunciation and dismissal. The next day a "Rally of One Million" was held in Peking to emphasize the Wuhan case as an example to others who might be tempted to resist Maoist authority. One of the leaders of the rally was Chiang Ch'ing, who appeared on the Tienanmen balcony to wave to the crowd.[8]

When it became necessary to increase the effectiveness of the "proletarian revolutionaries" by giving them permission to use arms, again it was Chiang Ch'ing who gave them the go-ahead signal. On July 21 she urged them not "to be naïve," as their comrades in Wuhan had been, but to "take up arms to defend yourselves."[9] Lin Piao, echoing Chiang Ch'ing's words, also urged the recalcitrant opposition military leaders to admit their mistakes and give up their old-fashioned ways or they would "have their pigtails grabbed."[10]

Chiang Ch'ing played an important role in "tempering and steeling" the armed forces by expanding their duties and functions and by promoting the Cultural Revolution within the PLA. As early as December 1966 she criticized the public security forces, the procurator-general's office and the Supreme People's Court on the grounds that they were "bureaucratic organs" modeled on those of bourgeois countries and that they had opposed Mao during the preceding several years, while the revisionists were still in power. She proposed that, except for traffic police and firemen, the security forces should be completely taken over by the PLA, and added that Hsieh Fu-chih, minister of Public Security, had agreed to this proposal.[11] Later she called for reform of security and legal organizations in Tientsin. In the following months she proposed the same move in other provinces, urging the assertion of military control. On February 11, 1967, a directive issued to the State Council and the Military Affairs Committee announced that the PLA Peking garrison was taking over the capital's public security bureau and police organizations. Military control was soon established over public security offices in other provinces.

When he introduced Chiang Ch'ing as the person who would give instructions on the establishment of the Hunan Revolutionary Committee, Chou En-lai said: "Comrade Chiang Ch'ing takes a firm stand. She holds the most positive banner. She sees questions most sharply. We must learn from Comrade Chiang Ch'ing."[12] This was the way Chiang Ch'ing was frequently introduced, and in time, the audience naturally accepted her as a national leader in her own right.

Her exceptional leadership qualities were apparent to many who brought their problems to her. One of her talents was an ability to smooth out problems between quarreling factions within the Maoist camp. On September 5, 1967, in speaking extemporaneously to a conference of two warring factions from Anhwei, she said: "I have come rather hurriedly, and I have no idea what is going on here. Old K'ang just dragged me here. Nor have I prepared for the few words which I shall say here." She immediately began to discuss the situation that existed in Anhwei, disclosing an unusual insight into its status. "The small handful headed by Li Pao-hua has been dragged out, and even such bad characters as Liu Hsiu-shan. . . . Hasn't Cheng Ming-yuan also been exposed in broad daylight?" Members of one group cheered for a long time. She said, "Comrades, whatever the case, and in spite of the fact that you had quarrels and fights before, aren't you sitting down together for talks? Isn't this an excellent situation?" Most of the audience again cheered enthusiastically, but one small group continued their discussion among themselves. Chiang Ch'ing turned to them and said: "Why is there no answer from comrades on this side? Do you approve of it?" They then assured her that it was an excellent situation. Before she finished speaking to the assemblage, she had convinced them that they should resolve their differences peacefully. She asked if they wanted an alliance with each other and they shouted, "Yes, yes!"

As Chiang Ch'ing was the authority who could give the young revolutionaries permission to arm themselves, she was also the one whose influence was needed to restrain them when many of their goals had been achieved. In the same speech, she praised the PLA for its role in the Cultural Revolution and described it as "the pillar of the proletarian dictatorship to defend the Great Proletarian Cultural Revolution." She told the representatives: "Everywhere we seized their guns, beat them up, and scolded them. But they did not strike back, nor did they argue. Is there such an army in other parts of the world?"

There were answering shouts of "No!"

She insisted that everyone must refrain from attacking the army under all circumstances, "for they are our boys and we must protect their honor." When the meeting concluded, there was thunderous applause and loud shouts of "Learn from Comrade Chiang Ch'ing, and salute to her."[13]

This speech was published in Chinese newspapers and periodicals and posted everywhere for the people to read. Tapes of her speech were also shipped throughout the country for broadcasting and for study. It was believed that Chiang Ch'ing's words constituted the most effective way to bring about the restraint that was needed in the army, the factories, the schools, the communes and elsewhere. Hsinhua News Agency reported: "Comrade Chiang Ch'ing's speech is the combat call issued by the proletarian command."[14] The General Office of the CCP Central Committee on September 9 issued a circular "calling on the proletarian revolutionaries throughout the country to seriously study Comrade Chiang Ch'ing's speech dated September 5." The circular explained: "Comrade Chiang Ch'ing . . . made a correct analysis of the present situation . . . and set forth specific tasks for the proletarian revolutionaries. All revolutionary committees, military control committees and revolutionary mass organizations should conscientiously organize the masses to listen to the recording of this speech . . . and do well in the work of supporting the army and cherishing the people."[15]

Chapter 12

Chiang Ch'ing and Military Conferences and Receptions

While the key positions in the government and the PLA were being filled in 1967 by people who appeared to be sympathetic to the Maoist goals, Central leaders began in 1968 to consolidate power and rebuild the country. Because it was necessary for the Central leaders to rely on the local military leaders throughout the country, large numbers of military personnel from all outlying provinces were brought to Peking for military conferences. Radio Shanghai reported: "They came from the roof of the world, from snowy forests, from the frontier and coastal defenses of the motherland, and from the forefront of helping the left, helping industry and agriculture, exercising military control, and giving military and political training."[1]

The "Mao's Thought" conventions which were planned, organized, and supervised by the All-PLA Cultural Revolution Group under Chiang Ch'ing's direction were designed to serve several purposes. Their basic motivation was an attempt to preclude rebellions and factionalism by reinforcing the delegates' allegiance to the Maoist camp. It was especially important to bring the military into the Maoist ideological sphere as it had the means for creating serious problems if it wished to do so. For example, on April 9, 1968, "a counterrevolutionary army . . . had been mobilized by Chang Jih-ching, vice-chairman of the Shansi Revolutionary Committee." Chang supposedly led a group of armed commandos who tried to "penetrate Peking and kidnap the Central Committee member in charge of Shansi provincial affairs."[2]

The conventions were designed to unite all factions by building on the one trait they had in common—the acceptance of Maoist Thought. Through the involvement of the delegates in study groups and discussions, Chiang Ch'ing's organization tried to implement the directive that "the PLA should be a great school." In addition to Mao's Thoughts, Chiang Ch'ing's speeches and model operas were studied.[3] The delegates were urged to "take firm hold of ideological-education work . . . fight self-interest, repudiate revisionism . . . and further unify our action and thinking."[4] Special emphasis was placed on combating self-interest by resisting conceit. "It was unanimously held that conceit is a signal for the danger of being divorced from the masses . . . all comrades should keep up with the practice of being humble and prudent."[5] By reexamining themselves and opening different types of study classes, it was thought that the PLA members would be able to "stimulate production, work, and combat-readiness." They were also urged to streamline their organizations and place one-half of their personnel into Mao Tse-tung Thought-propagation teams.[6]

Another function of the conventions was to inform the leaders of the tasks they were expected to perform. The delegates were encouraged to discuss their experiences in order to help their colleagues solve problems that might arise. At a conference held on January 23, 1968, for example, the Chaochou County Revolutionary Committee discussed methods that it had used to correct their "support the army" campaign among the people, and the Harbin Municipal Revolutionary Committee "related its experience in strengthening the leadership in organizing and mobilizing a large number of propaganda teams . . ."[7]

Chiang Ch'ing's All-PLA group, hoping to maximize the results of these conferences, planned their details and timing very carefully. NCNA quoted delegates on February 19, 1968, thus: "[One rally] . . . at a time when the situation in the Great Proletarian Cultural Revolution was becoming ever more excellent, was the greatest concern, inspiration, encouragement, and stimulus to them and to the army men and people throughout the country."[8] On another occasion, many commanders and fighters spoke "highly of the significance of the conference, coming at a time of great victories in the Proletarian Cultural Revolution." One typical statement declared: "It will give a great impetus to the army's mass movement for the 'living study' and application of Chairman Mao's work and will promote the revolutionization of the ideology of the army men."[9]

The programs were carefully engineered by the All-PLA group so that the delegates would be inspired by their trip and would have a memorable experience to sustain their emotional involvement with the Maoists and give them exciting episodes to recount to their associates and friends in the provinces. The atmosphere was usually kept festive. "The buildings were lit up brightly, drums and gongs were sounded, and firecrackers exploded till the early hours . . . after the activists returned from the reception . . . colored fireworks were set off at the headquarters of the navy."[10] Delegates who had been received personally by the Central leaders "sang songs and told their comrades their impression of the happy event, which they described as the most unforgettable moment in their lives."[11] Many delegates "wrote on the flyleaf of their treasured red books" to record meetings with leaders.[12] In a speech delivered after returning home, young Fang Ming, a PLA man of the Canton regiment, stated: "Comrade Chiang Ch'ing's eyes were reddened as a result of insufficient sleep, and yet she worked energetically. We were deeply moved. We young people must emulate the Central leaders revolutionary enthusiasm and must work hard."[13]

There were frequent reports of the delegates remaining in the hall after the reception was over, still "beside themselves with joy" as the result of singing and cheering wildly. "They warmly shook hands with each other and congratulated each other. They sang time and time again . . . the song 'Chairman Mao, We Are Always Loyal to You!' "[14] One delegate recalled: "After the train pulled out of the railway station we continued to cheer and jump about with tear-laden eyes. . . . What a happy and deeply stirring moment for all of us!"[15]

One of the important functions of the conferences was to inspire the delegates to make public pledges of allegiance to

Maoist goals. After some discussion, meeting, speeches, and rallies, many of the representatives pledged themselves and their entire regions to the support of Maoist ideals. A commander of the 574th gunboat of the East China Sea Fleet pledged to "turn the seacoast of the motherland into a great steel wall." "Leading cadres of a certain PLA air force group . . . vowed to 'turn the airspace of the motherland into an unbreakable air stronghold.' "[16] The revolutionary workers from the NCNA Printing Works in Hunan province were so inspired while attending a reception for "revolutionary fighters of the navy and communications corps of the PLA and other comrades" that they pledged to "turn out more [volumes of Mao's works] so that the great Thoughts of Mao Tse-tung could spread throughout the world."[17] The political commissar of a "certain PLA unit stationed along the frontier bordering India . . . vowed to 'build the frontier into a steel wall against imperialism and revisionism.' "[18]

According to NCNA and radio broadcasts, Chiang Ch'ing participated in at least twenty-five such military conventions held between July 7, 1967, and October 14, 1969, greeting 10,000 to 100,000 delegates each time.[19] Chiang Ch'ing personally received delegates from a wide-ranging variety of units, such as the headquarters of the general staff of the PLA, the general logistics department, the navy, the air force, the artillery corps, the armored corps, the railway corps, the Signal Corps, the Anti-Chemical Corps, telecommunications units, the Higher Military Academy, the Political Academy of the Chinese PLA, the metallurgical industry, the Science and Technology Commission for National Defense of various services and branches, and the Seventh Ministry of Machine Building, and the nuclear establishment.

These conferences gave Chiang Ch'ing and her staff an opportunity to meet many local military leaders and to decide on whether or not they were suited for their jobs. They also increased Chiang Ch'ing's prestige among PLA subordinates as they listened to her speeches, studied her printed addresses and model operas, participated in discussions with her, and became accustomed to seeing her strongly entrenched in a position of power, giving instructions and sharing the podium with the top government leaders. They also discovered that she was the final arbiter of what Mao would hear. She told one group: "If you have something to say, just let me know. You can be sure that I'll convey your ideas directly to the Chairman."[20] In her speech of April 12, 1967, she let it be known that if she did not favor conveying certain information to Mao, she would say, "No, the Chairman is very tired."[21]

The meetings also gave Chiang Ch'ing an opportunity to make new friends within the military establishment and to charm more people, as she did, for example, when she delivered her speech at the 100,000-man rally of March 17, 1968. She announced: "I have not always been right. I have made many mistakes and have many shortcomings. . . . Some schools have declared that they want to fry me in oil and struggle too. When I have time I will go and let them fry me in oil. [Laughter]"[22]

Chapter 13

Cultural Workers within the Chinese Armed Forces

Since the Cultural Revolution, Chiang Ch'ing's capacity to influence the ideology and behavior of military men has apparently remained at a high level. By having placed her supporters in key positions, she appears to have gained considerable influence on the PLA leadership. She has also gained access to and influence on the communications media within the armed forces and has thereby facilitated the vertical flow of information and ideas between the soldiers and the Party and PLA leaderships. Her daughter, Hsiao-li, serves as chief editor of the *Liberation Army Daily,* and the editorial opinions in all PLA publications present a glowing image of Chiang Ch'ing. Her name is frequently mentioned in connection with her works, and her praise of the PLA is quoted and publicized, pointing out the importance of her cooperation to their interests.

Since the establishment of Revolutionary Committees in 1967-1968, ideological education, concentrating largely on the study of Maoist Thought, has been given first priority:

> The most urgent task of a Revolutionary Committee . . . is to grasp the work of ideological education of the masses and to ideologically consolidate and strengthen the Revolutionary Committee itself through the running of . . . study classes. This is the most important key to exercising and using power well.[1]

This has facilitated the propagation of Chiang Ch'ing's ideas and the unprecedented expansion of ideological and cultural activities throughout both the armed forces and the civilian population.

All the ideological programs begun during the Cultural Revolution have been continued and expanded. Political and cultural activities now dominate the soldiers' lives. From all over the country there are reports confirming this development: "PLA Unit 6294 has initiated a movement to study and sing model revolutionary theatrical works."[2] "PLA ranking units [in Nanking] . . . held an exchange-experience meeting on the popularization of model revolutionary theatrical works."[3] "Recently the workers, peasants, and soldiers in the province have whipped up an upsurge of study and popularization of these operas."[4]

The cultural activity of the armed forces has kept pace and increased substantially; new activities have been initiated, among them art and literature festivals; propaganda teams and all members of the PLA have been encouraged to write, perform, and participate in these; and PLA propaganda teams have been sent around the country to perform skits and operas for the masses, to organize them into study groups, and to encourage amateurs to study and perform Chiang Ch'ing's model operas and other works. "Many worker-peasant-soldier amateur . . . teams have learned to perform sections and highlights of the revolutionary model works," which the reports describe as "personally cultivated by Comrade Chiang Ch'ing."[5] One group in Kwangsi "made their own costumes, scenery and props as required by the operas."[6] Another source reports that "the soldiers as well as the revolutionary people are learning about and staging these model revolutionary plays."[7] "The three services . . . prepared to do the play *Taking the Bandits Stronghold* accompanied by an orchestra and an enlarged choral group . . . and also present the music of *Shachiapang*."[8] Through these activities, the army has spread Chiang Ch'ing's influence among the masses, and in factories and villages throughout China.

In recognition of the soldiers' efforts and to encourage them, Chiang Ch'ing has attended many of their events. On June 9, 1967, "a theatrical performance was given . . . in the Great Hall of the People by revolutionary art fighters of the units of the Chinese People's Liberation Army's three services stationed in Peking." Attending the performance with Chiang Ch'ing were Chou En-lai and other important military leaders.[9]

In addition to studying and performing Chiang Ch'ing's works, the PLA men were encouraged to create new works based on hers. "Guided by model revolutionary theatrical works, some of the units have already written revolutionary stories, reports, short dramas, and operas. . . . Some of their efforts have been selected and published and are widely welcomed by the broad masses."[10] The new programs "resulted in an unprecedented upsurge of spare-time cultural activities in the armed forces. . . . One company has composed and staged more than one hundred cultural items. . . . Many fighters without much education have taken up the pen to do creative writing, many cadres who never before appeared on the stage have participated in the performances."[11] Through these activities, every member of the PLA has become a cultural worker under Chiang Ch'ing's ideological leadership.

The legend of Men Ho is a nationally publicized example of the "boundlessly loyal" character of a model soldier. Son of a formerly poor peasant of Hopei Province, Men Ho served twenty years in revolutionary activities and was a political instructor of a battalion of the People's Live Action Army. Once, while helping farmers to fire rockets into the sky to disperse clouds and prevent hail from forming, a charge suddenly began to hiss and smoke. Men Ho, "selfless and fearless . . . threw himself on the charge. There was a tremendous explosion. . . . With his own life, Men Ho had protected the lives of twenty-seven comrades."[12] Before his death, Men Ho was active in cultural activities in the army. A pamphlet about his life which is distributed to all PLA personnel recounts that once, while he was helping to educate one of his comrades, he asked him if he had seen any of the model plays. The comrade answered that he had recently seen three of them and had enjoyed them very much. Men Ho asked him, "Do you know under whose leadership they were produced?" The soldier answered, "Comrade Chiang Ch'ing. Everyone knows that."[13]

Because of her activities, her speeches, and the unique character of her works, Chiang Ch'ing's name appears frequently in the news media and within study groups. This has resulted in further consolidating her independent authority and prestige within the armed forces. Members of the PLA have often written articles commenting on her model plays. Hung Wen and Hai Yen wrote an article stating that "under the guidance of Comrade Chiang Ch'ing, the great image of the Chinese PLA has been given the warmest praise and excellent presentation."[14] A July 12, 1969, program "broadcast two articles praising Chiang Ch'ing's achievements in the creation of model revolutionary plays."[15] From time to time the entire libretto of one model play or another is published in newspapers, magazines, or book form. These invariably draw responses from the readers, such as the NCNA article "Veteran Praises Revolutionary Opera *Shachiapang*."[16] Chun Ching announced, "From now on, under the leadership of the Military Commission, the General Political Department and Comrade Chiang Ch'ing, we shall never forget class struggle . . ."[17] This praise, whether sincere or not, inevitably conditions the listeners to admire and respect Chiang Ch'ing. She gains their confidence and they become her loyal supporters, thus legitimizing her authority and leadership in Chinese military affairs.

Chiang Ch'ing has frequently revised her model works. In the revisions she tries to incorporate suggestions received from the ranks and to make her model heroes fit the country's changing needs. *The New York Times* declared that Chiang's revisions portray heroes "as even more brave, resourceful [and] devoted to the masses," with increased emphasis on selflessness, with the people being asked to work harder, to serve the state and the people. "The themes are designed . . . for a time of internal consolidation . . . not a time of struggle for political power, as was the case in 1967 and 1968."[18] Prior to the showing of the newly revised *The Red Lantern*, Radio Wuhan announced, "Revolutionary literature and art workers must take Comrade Chiang Ch'ing as their example, carry through to the end, and create revolution in literature and art."[19]

Chiang Ch'ing's influence has extended still further and her identification with the PLA made even stronger when the television versions of her model operas were filmed and circulated throughout the country. "On the glorious occasion of celebrating the forty-third anniversary of the founding of the great PLA, the documentary films . . . *Taking Tiger Mountain by Strategy* and *The Red Lantern* were released for showing."[20] A rally of 50,000 was held in Nanching "to celebrate the release of the revolutionary model films."[21] In Lhasa, Tibet, "many people . . . have been greatly encouraged and enlightened by the films, pledging to learn from the heroic figures."[22]

Not only are films shown, but special events are also organized by the armed forces to discuss the films. On October 28, 1970, "workers, peasants and soldiers in Canton municipality held a forum after having viewed the color film *Taking the Bandits' Stronghold*,"[23] and the *Tachung Daily* invited some workers, peasants, soldiers and revolutionary art and literary workers to a symposium to discuss their reactions after seeing the television documentary films.[24]

Every year festivals are held to encourage the creative use of the PLA men's leisure time. Radio Wuhan has reported: "In order to popularize the revolutionary plays among the army units, the Wuhan PLA units recently held their third amateur literature and art festival."[25] "The fourth amateur arts festival of the PLA Kunming units opened in Kunming on December 15. . . . They all praised the revolutionary operas nurtured personally by Comrade Chiang Ch'ing."[26] Many new festivals have been organized. "A Workers, Peasants and Soldiers Festival of Singing, Dancing, and Drama is taking place in Kweiyang, Southwest China. It opened on April 30 to mark the twenty-fifth anniversary of Chairman Mao's 'Talks at the Yenan Forum on Literature and Art.' . . . In the past few days 16,000 soldiers of units of the PLA stationed in Kweiyang . . . have put on performances . . . in more than twenty open-air theaters, in the streets, squares, railway stations, parks, factories, people's communes, and army units."[27] "A festival to study and popularize revolutionary model plays . . . was held from October 15 to November 3 in Changsha."[28] "The PLA Canton units have held an amateur literature and art festival . . . in order to mark the tenth anniversary of the Resolution of the 1960 Enlarged Session of the Military Affairs Commission."[29]

As a rule, Chiang Ch'ing appears with regularity at public functions, making personal contacts with PLA personnel and identifying herself with important PLA causes. She has opened PLA literature and art forums, attended rallies to commemorate various military victories, attended performances by PLA fighters, and frequently attends her own model operas with other Central leaders. She personally received tens of thousands of army men during the anniversaries of the founding of the Chinese PLA and the CCP. During PLA conventions and conferences, she attends meetings, forums and receptions, and every year since 1967 she has played a prominent role in Army Day activities. Her picture appears usually on the front pages of the nation's newspapers with military and other top leaders. She was reported with units of the three services of the PLA during the anniversary of the CCP in 1968, and two days later, her All-PLA group sponsored an opera performance to celebrate the occasion. Over 10,000 "revolutionary fighters," including PLA commanders and fighters, were said to have attended.[30] In July 1972 she was prominent at the National Defense Ministry Reception hailing Army Day, and more recently, in September 1973, was in attendance at the PLA soiree sponsored by the General Political Department of the PLA. Songs and dances selected from army-wide theatrical performances of modern revolutionary operas were presented.[31]

Since the beginning of 1967, Chiang Ch'ing's name and photographs have appeared in army editorials, newspapers and publications, showing her as she receives foreign military delegations,[32] as she denounces the Soviet Union for border clashes or other issues of concern to the PLA, or as she welcomes airmen of the PLA who had distinguished themselves.[33]

By attending her model operas, other leaders have indicated their support of Chiang Ch'ing and her interpretation of Mao's Thought. In merely the first six months of 1967, the top leaders of the Chinese Communist Party and armed forces were seen attending Chiang Ch'ing's model theatrical works ten times. This demonstration of solid support has continued to the present time. Documentary films of Mao attending her model operas, ballets, and symphony have also been made and shown throughout the country.[34] Her model plays are often selected for special honors which pointedly associate them with Maoist Thought. "In commemoration of the twenty-eighth anniversary of the publication of Chairman Mao's brilliant work 'Talks at the Yenan Forum on Literature and Art,' the *People's Daily* today devotes three and a half pages to the full text of the new May 1970 stage version of the modern revolutionary Peking opera *The Red Lantern*. Earlier, this new stage version was printed in the journal *Red Flag* in its fifth issue of 1970."[35]

As a powerful member of the Politburo since the Ninth Party Congress, Chiang Ch'ing has an important role in formal controls of the army, which is under the jurisdiction of the Politburo. From 1971 to 1973 (from the fall of Lin Piao to the Tenth Party Congress), she was usually ranked above everyone except Mao and Chou En-lai in the Party hierarchy, and above Yeh Chien-ying, the top military man. Over one-third of the army's personnel are Party members who have stronger discipline, extra duties, and tighter organization than the regular PLA men. Through her control of the Party, Chiang Ch'ing has exercised organizational control over the armed forces.

In her November 9, 1967, speech to political and cultural workers of the PLA, Chiang Ch'ing announced that she had wanted to establish two armies dedicated to the service of the people: one army of creative writers and one army of critics. She explained this move by saying, "In the process of the current Great Proletarian Cultural Revolution movement . . . the problem of troop formation in the cultural circles is basically solved."[36] Through her expert use of these forces and by constantly promoting Maoist Thought and her own interpretation of it, Chiang Ch'ing has virtually established herself as a foremost authority and interpreter of Mao's Thought on every subject, including military affairs.

Part Four

CHIANG CH'ING IN THE IDEOLOGICAL AND CULTURAL SPHERES

Chapter 14

The Maoist Line on Literature and Art

After two years of discussions and deliberations with Chiang Ch'ing, Mao was ready to enunciate their line on literature and art. In his "Talks at the Yenan Forum on Literature and Art,"[1] he observed: "All literature and art are for the masses of the people . . . and in the first place for the workers, peasants, and soldiers; they are created for the workers, peasants and soldiers and are for their use."

Mao had always believed that the pen was as important as the sword in the proletarian revolution. Within this category are included all types of performing arts. Chiang Ch'ing frequently reminded him that, throughout history, military conquests alone have not sustained the power of any leader; it has always been necessary for him to win the hearts and admiration of the people. The Maoist cultural workers or cultural army consisted of writers, performers, propagandists, and mass media writers, and because of Chiang Ch'ing's interest in political culture, never before in Chinese history have they been utilized as fully or has so much attention and effort been paid to literature and the arts. Even Hu Shih's New Culture Movement of the 1920s seems relatively insignificant.

During the Yenan days, Mao and Chiang Ch'ing worked out a program to "ensure that literature and art fit well into the whole revolutionary machine as a component part, that they operate as a powerful weapon for uniting and educating the people and for attacking and destroying the enemy, and that they help people fight the enemy with one heart and one mind."[2]

To the Maoists, the Party principle of primary importance is identification of oneself with the peasants and the masses. Chiang Ch'ing observed that even during the Yenan days, when most writers and artists were fledgling members of the Party, full of zeal, distressed by social ills and angered by foreign invasions, many of them slipped back into their old ways and produced works that benefited special interests. For this reason a basic strategy was outlined in the cultural field stating that it is not just with the enemy a writer must deal; he must also relate to his allies and the masses of the people. When dealing with his enemies, he must expose their duplicity, their cruelty, and point out the inevitability of their defeat; he must support his allies' resistance, praise their achievements, and criticize their mistakes; he must correct the shortcomings and backward ideas of the masses, which hinder them in their struggle.

Literature for the masses must not dwell on their negative side or ridicule them but must serve to fire them with enthusiasm, impel them to unite and struggle, to transform their environment, to make progress and develop their revolutionary zeal. The cultural worker must instruct, yet be mindful that he is the servant of the masses. The Maoists have consistently emphasized the idea that the masses, composed mainly of peasants, workers, and soldiers, are the masters of the country. In creating literature and art, therefore, the creator must understand his audience, speak their language, and then create accordingly. "The cadres of all types, fighters in the army, workers in the factories and peasants in the villages, all want to read books and newspapers as soon as they become literate, and those who are illiterate want to see plays and operas, look at drawings and paintings, sing songs, and hear music; they are the audiences for our works of literature and arts."[3]

In communicating with the masses, the Maoist line insists that the writer not only mingle with the masses but also study the various classes in society, their mutual relations and respective conditions, their physiognomy, and their psychology. Unless he has insight into all conditions, he will not be able to change and remold the masses' thinking and their feelings. As a revolutionary writer, especially one belonging to the Party, he must

In the Ideological and Cultural Spheres

also have a knowledge of Marxism-Leninism, and allow class and national struggle to determine his thoughts and feelings. A new culture must create a product that is simpler, plainer, and therefore acceptable to broad masses of people. As the people are engaged in their struggle, they are eagerly demanding enlightenment, and in order to meet this need, literature and art should be easy to absorb and capable of strengthening their confidence and unity. The need is not for "more flowers on the brocade, but fuel in snowy weather."[4]

On occasion Chiang Ch'ing has pointed out to Mao that his standards in the cultural sphere have not been satisfactorily met by the country's cultural workers. In subsequent chapters of this study, the multiple ways by which their efforts after the Yenan period were hampered by "revisionists in authority" will be examined in greater detail.

Chapter 15

Early Ideological and Cultural Struggles

In the 1940s Mao's chief targets were Japanese imperialism and the bourgeois and capitalist interests represented by Chiang Kai-shek. Even the left-wing literature initiated by Wang Ming at that time seemed inadequate to Chiang Ch'ing and Mao. It had "the clothes of working people but the faces of petty bourgeois intellectuals."[1] The Yenan Forum launched a large scale attack against the "counterrevolutionary" culture and at the same time set forth the Maoist outlook and theory on literature.

Even in Yenan, Chiang Ch'ing had made efforts to implement the new policy in the arts and had written and staged a P'ing opera, *Pinghsing Pass*. But at that time there was overwhelming opposition to her program from people who were satisfied with the old types of stories. After the Communist triumph and move to Peking, Chiang Ch'ing "wanted to establish two armies for the worker-peasant-soldier on the basis of the proletarian revolutionary line: one army of creative writers, and one army of critics."[2] But she continued to meet strong resistance from cultural workers who did not share her views.

In her work she applied two important principles which she and Mao had worked out during their discussions: the problem of class stand and the problem of attitude. She believed firmly in taking sides with the proletariat and the masses against people in authority taking the capitalist road. On the question of attitude, she believed that a work of art should expose the enemy's duplicity and point out the inevitability of his defeat while praising and educating the masses, being patient with their shortcomings, and helping to correct them, but never ridiculing them.

In the Ideological and Cultural Spheres

In producing and creating new material for the performing arts or in revising the old, Chiang Ch'ing never deviated from these basic principles and soon established a professional reputation as an outspoken, tenacious fighter for her ideals. She argued the importance of new material that would help in the mobilization of the peasants and workers, raise the morale of the soldiers, and educate the illiterate. She insisted that Mao's Thoughts should be dramatized, communicating them through songs, plays, and films, and that the old works, which were irrelevant and had nothing to do with reality or glorified the past and ignored the opportunities to build a better future, should be banished.

When Chiang Ch'ing decided to reform the Peking Opera, she launched her first attack against her most formidable opponent, "Mr. Peking Opera" himself, the leading star, Mei Lan-fang.[3] She wrote articles criticizing his views, and after meeting with strong resistance, finally persuaded him and many others to pledge their support to Party leadership, to improve the ideological and artistic level of the drama, and to influence audiences in Socialist patriotic ways. Her object was to stage more plays of rich educational and technical value, and not to stage any more plays that were ugly, indecent, or harmful to the physical and mental health of the people. Continuing her campaign in 1949 in direct opposition to Liu Shao-chi, she insisted on banning such plays as *Picking Up a Jade Bracelet* and *The Emperor and the Waitress*, plays for which Liu Shao-chi had already given the green light.

In 1950 she caused a national controversy by condemning the already accepted Hong Kong-made film, *Inside Story of the Ch'ing Court*. The film, depicting the conflict between the weak young Emperor Kuang-hsu and Dowager Empress Tz'u-hsi, was shown all over China as a patriotic film, but in Chiang Ch'ing's opinion it was a film of national betrayal. In one scene a member of the eight-power allied expedition announces: "Since the Sino-Japanese War of 1894, China has suffered financial losses, her armed forces are poorly equipped and weak . . . and she is far inferior to the enemy in strength. China must not engage in hostilities with any foreign country."[4] Scenes like this throughout the film reflected attitudes and responses contrary to Chiang Ch'ing's belief that "before the wild beasts of imperialism, revolutionary people must not show the slightest timidity."[5] Later, the film portrays the revolutionary action of the Boxers against imperialism as a sort of barbarous turmoil. Throughout, it "glorifies the Emperor Kuang-hsu, praising him as a 'good emperor,' helping us, the people." On his departure the film shows "the people kneeling along the roadside to see him off, . . . giving credence to the picture of the submissive, bovine masses who are grateful for any crumbs of attention from a lofty personage."[6] At another time the emperor's concubine assures him that the foreign aggressors are really his friends, and she adds, "I am sure that the foreign powers will help Your Majesty restore the throne and regenerate the imperial regime."[7]

Repeatedly Chiang Ch'ing demanded that the film be repudiated, but Lu Ting-i, Hu Ch'iao-mu, Chou Yang, Yuan Mu-chi, and other members of the Department of Propaganda, backed by Liu Shao-ch'i, "desperately resisted." Finally Mao spoke out, declaring: *"The Inside Story of the Ch'ing Court* is a film of national betrayal and should be criticized and repudiated. Somebody called it patriotic; I consider it national betrayal—national betrayal through and through."[8] As a result of Mao's statement, *People's Daily* and *Peking Weekly* stated that "the opposition had to give way, but perfunctorily appointed a historian of reactionary views to write a short fake criticism which was really aimed at shielding the film."[9] Even this was considered too harsh by the opposition, and publication of the criticism was withheld for seven months.

In 1951 Chiang Ch'ing's efforts again resulted in nationwide debate in cultural, educational, and ideological circles when she criticized *The Life of Wu Hsun*. The film involved the experiences of a famous Shantung beggar who lived during the reign of Emperor Kuang-hsu. Wu Hsun was originally pictured as a humble man who begged from the rich in order to build a school; this was later proved to be false. He was actually a confidence man whose devices were so lucrative that he became a rich landlord and loaned money at usurious rates. Chiang Ch'ing felt that the story as depicted in the film "praised the landlord class, advocated slavishness and capitalism, and maliciously slandered the peasants' revolutionary struggles."[10] Chiang Ch'ing pointed out that begging, even for noble reasons, was undignified behavior and that, although Wu Hsun lived in a period of struggle against foreign aggressors and feudalism, he devoted full energy to supporting the status quo, emulating the rich and fawning over them in order to get what he wanted.

"Ought we to praise such disgusting conduct?" Mao asked in an article he wrote later for the *People's Daily*. "Can we tolerate such conduct being publicly praised, especially when the failure of the revolutionary peasant struggle is used to heighten the contrast? In the view of many writers, history develops by the exertion of every effort to preserve the old from extinction, not by class struggle to overthrow the reactionary feudal leaders who had to be overthrown, but by submission to these rules, in the manner of Wu Hsun."[11]

When he heard Mao's criticism, Chou Yang, the leader of the opposition and the "grand old man" of literary and art circles, alarmed about possible loss of prestige, exclaimed: "Why make such a to-do about a little bourgeois reformism?" And he proceeded to explain that there were more important things to worry about: "Many writers are not getting enough praise from the Party leaders, and it has upset them and made them depressed."[12]

The controversy finally reached such a pitch that Chiang Ch'ing organized a special investigating team, which she led personally under the name Li Chin. They visited the village in Shantung where the real Wu Hsun had lived, and investigated the man's actual history. The records revealed that Wu Hsun had been a completely unprincipled rogue who lived by his wits, made a fortune through trickery, and during his later years founded a school in the hopes of improving his image. When the investigating team returned to Peking and presented their seventy-thousand-word report, Chou Yang, Kuo Mo-jo, and Hsia Yen had to admit publicly that they had been wrong.

Immediately Chiang Ch'ing wanted to use the material obtained from the investigation as a basis for a realistic opera entitled *Sung Ching-shih*, but Chou Yang quickly blocked her efforts.

Still Chiang Ch'ing persisted, reviewing hundreds of films and plays and attacking those which she believed failed to meet "standards of significance to all the masses of the people, dealing with their lives, thoughts, and age-long strivings, with the insight of revolutionary artistic vision."[13] According to the Peking *Ching-kang-shan*: "Comrade Chiang Ch'ing worked tirelessly, leaving her footprints everywhere." She tried to ban such films as *With Troops under the Walls of the City*, *Lin's Shop*, *Nightless City*, *Press Ganging*, *Early Spring in February*, and *Pei-Kuo Chiang-nan*, partly because most of the characters that were portrayed sympathetically in them were of the big landlord or rich bourgeoisie class.[14] She also attacked films in which major emphasis was placed on selfishness, as in *Sisters of the Stage*, a story about a girl who was concerned only with furthering her own career at the expense of her associates; or films in which revolutionaries were portrayed as generally disheartened and hopeless, as in *Red Sun;* or those in which proletarian leaders were shown as buffoons, as was Senior Li, who made a fool of himself by performing the queue-swinging movement of salesgirls, teenagers' leg exercises, and "broadcast drills" in front of the workers of his workshop.

Chiang Ch'ing felt that with the development of mass communication in China, the content of any material presented had to be correct. Thinking especially of the peasants who perhaps saw only one movie or play a year, Chiang Ch'ing knew that the emotional impact of that piece would be enormous and it was of vital importance to present material which would strengthen the country's moral fiber and influence the viewers' thinking positively, rather than confuse and depress them.

Chiang Ch'ing was especially anxious to involve young people in political activity and social criticism, and she took time from her busy schedule to encourage them and lend support. In 1954, when two young men submitted a criticism of *Study of the Dream of the Red Chamber* to the *People's Daily* and were turned away because they were "nobodies," she personally visited the publication's office to argue on their behalf. Finally, Mao himself submitted the criticism to the Political Bureau of the Central Committee of the Chinese Communist Party with a letter in which he deplored the stranglehold on the literary organs by "old ladies with bound feet." He observed: "We have the strange situation in which Yu Ping-po's bourgeois idealism is tolerated but lively critical essays by 'nobodies' are obstructed. This deserves our attention."

In spite of Chiang Ch'ing's tenacity over the years, art and culture in China remained essentially "a pool of stagnant water." The Ministry of Culture, which had been formed for the express purpose of creating a new social culture, produced nothing new. Liu Shao-ch'i, when presented with suggestions for improvements which would bring the arts more closely in line with Party policies and would present stimulating, encouraging experiences for the masses, chided, "We must not do anything rash."

Finally, after twenty-two years, with her patience at an end, Chiang Ch'ing decided to push aside all opposition. Singlehandedly, she "opened fire on that bastion of feudal and capitalistic culture . . . the Peking Opera."[15]

Chapter 16

Reform Movement in Peking Opera, Ballet and Symphony

The period following the Great Leap Forward was an especially trying time for Mao and Chiang Ch'ing. Mao's prestige was at its lowest ebb; his directives were ignored by Liu Shao-ch'i, Teng Hsiao-p'ing, P'eng Chen, and others, and he believed that the country was gradually sliding back toward private ownership and capitalism. Thinly disguised attacks on Mao like the "anti-Mao" column entitled "Evening Chats at Yenshan," carried by *Peking Daily* and *Frontline*, were beginning to appear in the mass media. Chiang Ch'ing protested against the play *Hai Jui Dismissed from Office*, which was a blatant denunciation of Mao's policies and his dismissal of P'eng Te-huai. Mao's and Chiang Ch'ing's problems were compounded by the fact that the mass media were controlled by the opposition.

Early in 1961 Chiang Ch'ing was invited to watch a performance by some young actors and actresses who had written a new opera with a contemporary theme. She found it fresh and exciting. After the performance she met with the cast and told them that she was delighted with their revolutionary enthusiasm. She pointed out to the troupe that they had proved the old art form was perfectly capable of being used for presenting operas with modern revolutionary themes.[1] Realizing that the young artists were anxious to express themselves in new works but were being stifled by P'eng Chen and his associates, she decided to try again to reform the Chinese theater and resolved this time not to let anything stop her. She zeroed in on the largest

In the Ideological and Cultural Spheres

and most established company, the Peking Opera Company No. One, as her first target.

Throughout China, of the estimated 3,000 theatrical companies in existence, more than 2,800 were performing Chinese opera of some kind. They had the trained personnel and facilities available for the presentation of new material. Since Peking Opera was such a prestigious art form and was so popular among the Chinese people, Chiang Ch'ing felt that if she could revolutionize the Peking Opera, the other Chinese theatrical forms would quickly follow its lead. Furthermore, the Peking Opera form was particularly suitable for presenting the heroic images of workers, peasants, and soldiers with its use of selected singing voices for clearly defined characterization and music to heighten the emotional effect of dramatic moments.

She began to prepare for her project. By the winter of 1962 she had completed an extensive review of more than 1,000 Peking operas which were then being staged in various cities.[2]

In April 1963 Chou En-lai sided with Chiang Ch'ing publicly when he spoke to a conference of literary and art workers. He urged writers and artists to use contemporary themes and the Socialist Revolution as the subjects of their works. To reinforce the effect of his words, Chiang Ch'ing quickly organized the publication of articles attacking the "theory that ghosts are harmless."[3] These appeared in the Shanghai newspaper *Wen Hui Pao*. Chou Yang commented, "I still don't see what's wrong with traditional and historical plays."[4]

In September 1963 Chiang Ch'ing selected the story *Sparks Amid the Reeds* and, bypassing all the officials who had blocked her efforts in the past, notably Lin Mo-han, Chi Yen-ming, Chang Keng, and P'eng Chen, went straight to the young performers, called a meeting, and gave them the script to adapt. The story centered around the Communist New Fourth Army and their fight against the puppet army which had been under Japanese control (1937-1945) in the interior of China.[5]

At first P'eng Chen, the mayor of Peking, who was in control of Peking Opera Company No. One's purse strings, refused to let Chiang Ch'ing use any of the actors and actresses for her project and also withheld theater space for rehearsals. But in the face of her persistence, he suddenly reversed his tactics and approved the experiment, scheduling *Sparks* for performance after only ten days of rehearsal. When Chiang Ch'ing watched the dress rehearsal, she realized that the performance was going to be a disaster. She quickly sent for the Shanghai People's Opera Troupe to watch the play and then began extensive revision of the script.

She objected to the production on several counts. Her first objection was one of principle. The leading role of Sister Ah-ching had been given to a man. "Female impersonation is a product of feudal society," Chiang Ch'ing pointed out to the actors. "It would be a strange phenomenon for female impersonation to appear on a Socialist stage."[6] As an actress with thorough training and lifetime experience in drama, Chiang Ch'ing knew how she wanted the play to be performed. She felt that the story should "concentrate on the portrayal of revolutionary characters, from whom the audience could draw inspiration and courage,"[7] and that it should emphasize the role of armed revolution to smash armed counterrevolution. It should, therefore, she said, end on a high note, with a dramatic assault on the enemy. P'eng Chen and his group, on the other hand, insisted that it end with the wedding feast of the enemy commander. Chiang Ch'ing wanted to make the dominant musical image that of the Communist political instructor, but the opposition insisted that, for balance (according to the old rule of Peking Opera construction), the enemy officer should be emphasized. As a result, the enemy officer's arias were often broadcast on the radio, and even the children began to hum them.[8] Chiang Ch'ing insisted also that the music should express clearly the difference between the revolutionary and the counterrevolutionary elements, but the opposition pointed out, that, by tradition, Peking Opera music is neutral; therefore, revolutionary heroes and their enemies must be treated alike.

In the meantime Chiang Ch'ing was trying to gather support for her cause, but P'eng Chen and his friends were in control of China's major news media and they were successful in blocking

In the Ideological and Cultural Spheres 99

all her efforts to air her side of the controversy by marking all her statements and directives "classified" and filing them away as state secrets. P'eng Chen was still withholding funds and refusing to give the company rehearsal space or a stronger cast. And so, finally, Chiang Ch'ing gathered her cast and scriptwriters together and took them out into the country to live with the army in the hope that they would develop more realism in the script and in the performances. When he heard they were leaving, P'eng Chen took some of the young singers aside and reportedly said, "You'd better not go. The country wind will harm your voices."[9]

Chiang Ch'ing continued nevertheless with revisions and changes to make the opera more effective. She considered every detail and its importance to the overall effect. When the opera was finally premiered, the Peking Municipal Party Committee met afterward to discuss it. P'eng Chen remarked, "It's tasteless, like pure boiled water." Later, when Chiang Ch'ing heard of his comment she asked, "What's wrong with pure boiled water? No one can live without it, and you have to have it to make tea or wine."[10] Another member complained that there was overmuch concern with what was only dialogue and singing, to which Chiang Ch'ing's reply was, "Without dialogue and singing, what would an opera consist of?"[11] Teng Hsiao-p'ing, the secretary-general, countered, "I'll raise both hands and vote yes as long as I don't have to watch any of them."[12] Likewise, T'ao Chu muttered, "I don't want to look at them. I'd rather even play mah-jong with Teng Hsiao-p'ing."[13]

In July 1964 Chairman Mao finally saw the opera and proclaimed it a success. He asked that the title be changed to *Shachiapang*, and after a few more changes, the opera took its final form. It has since become enormously successful. The final version tells the story of Sister Ah-ching, a Communist Party underground liaison officer in the village of Shachiapang, south of the Yangtze River, who, during the war of resistance against Japan, sheltered eighteen wounded soldiers and their leader, the company political instructor of the New Fourth Army. The opera emphasizes the "relations between the people and the army, and the relations between the hardships of the revolutionary struggle and revolutionary optimism,"[14] two vital facets of Communist life which Chiang Ch'ing was anxious to stress.

While working on *Shachiapang*, Chiang Ch'ing also brought the Honan opera *Chao Yang Ditch* to the Chinese Stage Songs Research Institute in Peking, requesting that it be adapted for Peking Opera. Chou Yang and Chang Keng opposed the adaptation, but in a compromise allowed the material to be changed into a combination of Honan and Szechuan style, resulting in a mongrelized product which Chiang Ch'ing repudiated and stopped. Lin Mo-han argued that adapting Honan Opera to Peking Opera was too big a stride, to which Chiang Ch'ing replied, "You did not take too big a stride; you simply stepped sideways."[15] When Chou Yang, Lin Mo-han, and Chang Keng complained about the problems Chiang Ch'ing was creating for them, Teng Hsiao-p'ing declared, "I have no objection to her reforming the drama, if people will just stop arguing about it."[16]

On November 8, 1963, Chiang Ch'ing took the second play she had selected, *The Red Lantern*, to the China Peking Opera Institute for adaptation. This is the story of the struggle waged by Li Yu-ho, a railway worker and underground Party member, and his family against the Japanese invasion in northeast China. Again she met resistance all along the way. One of her stars pleaded illness and the other was sent on tour abroad. Chiang Ch'ing had called for "fine, powerful singing by the hero in the execution scene at the opera's climax, in order to show his noble ideals and emotions, as well as his powerful revolutionary feelings," but the opposition "wanted to stress 'human nature' and 'family sentiment'" to create an atmosphere of tragedy, which Chiang Ch'ing felt would "distort the theme of revolution and the portrayal of revolutionary heroes."[17]

Ah Chia, the director, sought to delete a scene which Chiang Ch'ing insisted should remain in the opera to bring out the heroism of Li Yu-ho. Over persistent objections, Chiang Ch'ing stressed that Li Yu-ho should be given the most important part in the play in order to inspire the youth of the country. "You have all acted in the traditional Peking Opera," she reminded them, and urged them to consider the classical role of Chou Yu, an energetic symbol of heroism. "You will remember that not only the plot, but costumes, music, and style of singing were so planned as to serve this one character and build his image. When we play the roles of workers, peasants, and soldiers today, why can't we do the same for them?"[18]

As usual, she was concerned with having every detail correct. "She was attentive to the reading of every phrase and provided instructions on performances as well as props and lighting."[19] Old Lady Li's costume, for example, was ill suited to the character she played, and Chiang Ch'ing pointed out to the actress: "Old Lady Li is a poor woman with torn clothes. She works all day. Her clothes don't get torn first around the stomach but on the arms and legs. You've mended your clothes in the wrong places. I don't blame you, though, because you've never lived the life of a poor woman."[20]

As soon as they realized that Chiang Ch'ing's operas were gaining popular support, Chou Yang and Chang Keng hurried to prepare a "modern Socialist drama." They assigned the Experimental Drama League to write a play about the inner workings of a government bureau, but it failed to achieve popularity.

The following year Chiang Ch'ing suggested to the Peking Ballet Company and the Shanghai Ballet Troupe that they jointly present two ballets with contemporary revolutionary themes, *The Red Detachment of Women* and *The White-Haired Girl.* On this occasion it was Liu Shao-ch'i himself who openly objected, declaring, "We can't present stilted imitations of everyday life."[21]

The Red Detachment of Women is about Wu Ching-hua, a poor slave girl who suffered great wrongs and finally joined a detachment of the Workers and Peasants Red Army during the Revolution. While working out her plans for this ballet, Chiang Ch'ing took her performers and assistants on a trip to Hainan Island, where the action of the ballet takes place, in order to ensure the realism of the settings and general background. Again she met strong resistance from Lin Mo-han. During rehearsals he decided to remove a number of leading players and send them to Hong Kong to perform *Swan Lake*. Following Chou En-lai's protests and Party members' boycott of the company, Lin Mo-han backed down.

When Chou Yang saw the final rehearsals, he said: "I don't understand the story. We must not let foreigners see it."[22] However, Chairman Mao liked it and said that the portrayal of the Revolution was excellent. Lin Mo-han indignantly announced to the news media that it was an artistic disaster. "It can only be described as a baby with bottomless pants, sucking its thumb . . . an ugly daughter-in-law who ought to be kept out of sight."[23]

In 1963 Chiang Ch'ing also saw a performance of a Shanghai Huai Chu (folk) opera and promptly began to adapt it into the Peking Opera *On the Docks*. In this instance, besides presenting characters who were model Communists worthy of emulation, she tried to present a story that would give the masses pride in menial labor and would express her strong feeling for giving moral support to workers in other countries of the world. The original version had been composed with the cooperation of the Shanghai dock workers, according to Chiang Ch'ing's guidelines. When they heard that Chiang Ch'ing was going to use the Peking Opera to show their heroism, they were elated. "Before liberation we wanted to see operas," one of them said, "but how could we go to the operas when we didn't even earn enough to eat?" Another said, "In the old society we were looked down on and called 'stinking hired hands' and 'dirty coolies.' We had no right to watch from the audience, let alone go to the stage." But Chiang Ch'ing's opposition promptly began to make changes in the script. When the dock workers saw the modified version, they were furious. One said, "Every one of our families has a history of bitter suffering. . . . Before liberation we worked on the docks simply to keep alive. The Communist Party liberated us and we have boundless proletarian feelings for the Party and Chairman Mao. . . . When it comes to the revolutionary cause of the Party, we veteran workers are prompt, ready and decisive. Your opera makes us stupid and sluggish. This is

In the Ideological and Cultural Spheres

an insult! We will never approve such an opera!" The opera was then readapted under Chiang Ch'ing's instructions to incorporate the ideas of the men on the wharf.[24]

Later when she was adapting *Taking Tiger Mountain by Strategy,* Chiang Ch'ing again personally wrote and directed several scenes to "show the living process by which the people's soldiers . . . go out to mobilize and organize the masses."[25] When she suggested that a symphonic version of *Shachiapang* be written, she followed every detail of the development, attending rehearsals and listening to tapes. She told the composers, "This is a significant experiment . . . the idea of nationalizing things and adapting foreign things for use in our country." She made a number of suggestions, such as, "Begin with Peking Opera music; it is richer than Hopei pang tzu. . . . The high seventh-degree singing should not be left out here, as that would weaken the climax. . . . We need true voice instead of falsetto in this place."[26] During the rehearsal of *Raid on the White Tiger Regiment,* she refused to approve the results until one particular scene portrayed the hero properly, emphasizing his "heroic quality and class origin and how he grew up as an internationalist fighter of the proletariat under the cultivation of the Party and Mao Tse-tung's Thought."[27]

Chiang Ch'ing had her staunch supporters throughout this period who appreciated what she was trying to accomplish. She won the affection of many of the creators and performers with whom she worked. Yu Hui-yung, the composer of the music for *Taking the Bandits' Stronghold* and *On the Docks,* stated: "Every word and sentence, every tune and beat, is permeated with pains Comrade Chiang Ch'ing took in remolding this art."[28] T'an Yuan-shou, a performer with Peking Opera Company No. One, said, "Our respected and beloved Comrade Chiang Ch'ing has given us courage and strength. She has warmly encouraged us to do what had not been done by our predecessors and to cut open a new path through briers and brambles."[29] Wang Meng-yun, another performer said, "I have constantly received education from Comrade Chiang Ch'ing."[30] Tu Chin-fang, the famous Peking Opera actress, told everyone,

"I was so excited that I could not sleep. . . . Comrade Chiang Ch'ing has given us invaluable guidance, ranging from the structure of the play, the feelings of the characters, music, and singing, to artistic designs."[31]

By June 1964 Chiang Ch'ing had generated so much feeling about revolutionizing Peking Opera that a Festival of Peking Opera on Modern Themes was organized in Peking. Five thousand people attended, including opera company representatives from the provinces and all the major cities, as well as the Chinese cultural hierarchy. Speaking for the old guard, Lu Ting-yi assured the delegates that "we appreciate new historical plays written from a historical materialist point of view and of educational significance, particularly those on historical subjects since the Opium War." At the same time his followers reiterated, "We are not opposed to traditional plays which are good."[32] To many it seemed that P'eng Chen "voiced enthusiastic support of revolutionary plays during the day, but at night retired to his heaven full of emperors, ghosts and beautiful ladies."[33]

The Festival was planned to last from June 5 to July 31, with thirty-seven operas to be presented. *Raid on the White Tiger Regiment,* a story about the Chinese Liberation Army's fight in Korea during the Korean War, was one of Chiang Ch'ing's operas chosen for presentation. During the Festival the leading man, Sung Yu-ch'ing, became ill. Chiang Ch'ing visited him in the hospital and told him, "Little Sung, Chairman Mao expects you to be a Red and an expert crusader for revolutionary literature and art."[34]

In July Chiang Ch'ing delivered a major speech at the forum of theatrical artists and workers who were participating in the Festival. She "discussed the great significance of the revolutionization of Peking Opera and expounded its guiding principles."[35] She reiterated that the stage should be occupied by "workers, peasants, and soldiers, who are the real creators of history and the true masters of our country. We should create literature and art which protect our Socialist economic base." She also took time to praise and encourage young writers who were basing their works on these concepts. "The opera *Little Heroic*

In the Ideological and Cultural Spheres

Sisters on the Grassland, performed by the Peking Opera Troupe of the Inner Mongolian Theatre, is very good. The playwrights wrote the script for this opera with their revolutionary feelings inspired by the outstanding deeds of the two little heroines. The middle section of the opera is very moving."[36]

After the Festival, Chiang Ch'ing's doctor sent her to Shanghai, ostensibly to rest and divorce herself from intense concern with opera reform, but, nevertheless, while there, she continued to devote a large portion of her time to revising the scripts and music of her operas and reviewing new material. The magnitude of her accomplishments is staggering. Most impresarios are pleased if they can complete one major production successfully within a three- or four-year period; Chiang Ch'ing had completed eight in such a short period, and controlled every aspect of each: selecting the story, researching it for authenticity, revising it, preparing the script and revising that, casting the roles and recasting them until the players were right for the parts and the roles were properly balanced, supervising the composition of the music and revising it until it was effective, directing the works, planning and overseeing the choreography, outlining the types of costumes she wanted and making changes when the color or design were not suited for the mood of the play, planning the scenery and lighting, and making endless revisions.

Through her tireless efforts a new form of Socialist theatrical art has emerged, a combination of the old and the new as well as East and West, and it has created new heroic characters in the workers, peasants, and soldiers of China. But it was not until after the launching of the Great Proletarian Cultural Revolution that she succeeded in removing her opposition and was able to make her works available to everyone.

Chapter 17

Chiang Ch'ing and the Mass Media of Communication

Early in 1965, determined to remove the revisionists who were blocking the spread of the new literature and art based on Maoist Thought, Chiang Ch'ing launched a concerted campaign to oust and replace the personnel then in control of the mass media. She prepared a series of articles which ultimately launched the Great Proletarian Cultural Revolution and led to the downfall of P'eng Chen, the mayor of Peking, who was accused of discarding the Maoist theory of "class and class struggle" against revisionism. P'eng Chen's ouster was followed by that of Chou Yang, deputy director of the Department of Propaganda of the CCP Central Committee who "had wormed his way into the Communist Party" and was "the ringleader of the black line against the Party, socialism, and Mao Tse-tung's teaching in literary and art circles";[1] Hsia Yen, the vice-minister of culture, who was guilty of "extreme hostility toward the Thought of Mao Tse-tung and rabid opposition to its propagation";[2] and Lin Mo-han, deputy director of the Department of Propaganda, "the No. 1 accomplice of Chou Yang, arch-chieftain of the counterrevolutionary revisionist clique in literary and art circles."[3] All the men who had directly or indirectly blocked Chiang Ch'ing's efforts to reform Peking Opera were removed from their posts, including hundreds of newspaper editors, presidents and vice-presidents of universities and colleges, and thousands of "authorities," "literary giants," and "officials" within the cultural and ideological spheres.[4] The CCP Central Committee made the provision that these "literary and art workers should go to rural villages and industrial factories in an organized and

In the Ideological and Cultural Spheres

planned manner, so as to mingle with workers and peasants and reform their own world outlook."[5]

Chiang Ch'ing spearheaded the attack against revisionists throughout the mass media, delivering keynote speeches at hundreds of rallies from February 1966 on.[6] Through her political leadership and reorganization of the mass media, she was able to disseminate her works quickly and easily to the masses. Soon Chiang Ch'ing's model works were in evidence everywhere. Her music and songs were heard constantly on the radio, television, and loudspeakers; posters showed scenes from her operas and ballets; there were even stamps and "comic books" depicting the characters and scenes. Klaus Mehnert, after a month of traveling throughout China in 1971, observed:

> I had read that the 1,300 Peking operas that were still listed in a 1963 catalogue had been replaced by only eight new works. But until I witnessed it at first hand, I had had no idea what such a monopoly meant.[7]
>
> . . . .
>
> [The eight model plays] are the only ones performed on the Chinese stage today, and . . . were all—as every theatergoer knows—produced under the direction of Mao's wife, Chiang Ch'ing.[8]
>
> . . . .
>
> In China, the new theater stamps its indelible mark on all of China's cultural life; at every turn, the visitor meets with it in some new guise. Most of the postage stamps now in use (I saw fourteen different designs), as well as nearly every picture postcard I saw, and every kind of calendar, show scenes from these operas and ballets. They are on the covers of magazines. They are framed and hung in hotels, in railroad cars, in buses, in shops, in private homes. They are the standard gift for all occasions, either as prints or in embroidered wall hangings, sculptured in wood and even sometimes in jade. They are hung as giant posters along the streets. At the Industrial Fair in Shanghai I was shown a steel saw that turned out not machine parts but neat little silhouettes of the heroine from one of the operas.[9]

The new Socialist culture is propagated by specialists as well as by amateurs, through formal and informal channels of communication. Formal channels include state-controlled newspapers, radio, television, theater, publications, billboards, and the educational system, as well as organizational hierarchies. Revolutionary committees, the Party, the army, the government, and mass organizations all have their own "armies" of specialized propagandists to disseminate Chiang Ch'ing's works by organizing study groups to discuss newspaper reviews, films, and books based on her guidelines; gathering people to see cultural parades, demonstrations, and rallies; transcribing radio broadcasts of her activities into handwritten wall posters; conducting meetings; and organizing amateur shows and skits dramatizing her themes. They also stimulate amateur activities in the arts and literature along Maoist lines. Their efforts reach into the farthest corners of the nation. Tens of thousands of mobile cinema service units are also operating throughout China, taking films and lantern slides of her works into the villages.[10] The *Liaoning Daily* stated: "The showing of the televised documentary films *Taking Tiger Mountain by Strategy* and *Red Lantern* is a major event in the political life of the people in the province.[11]

In such places as the Sinkiang Autonomous Region and Inner Mongolia, mobile culture troupes "have proved a good example of how to carry out Chairman Mao Tse-tung's principle that art should serve the workers, peasants, and soldiers and . . . advance socialism."[12] There is evidence that cultural troupes exist all over China and that they cover all the provinces, giving performances under all kinds of conditions—even between shifts in factories, in the fields, teahouses, and at meeting places."[13] It was reported that in four months, one ensemble alone, the Central Nationalities Music Ensemble in the Langya Mountains, "visited sixteen production brigades of eight communes in six districts and, besides helping with the farm work, gave musical and operatic performances to audiences totaling over 210,000 people." While they were working, eating, and living with commune members, they coached the amateurs in the area. Even circus performers were devising ways to project the new heroes of the model operas. "If Peking Opera can project the heroic image of our times, why can't we, with our somersaulting, balancing tricks and magic?" they asked.[14]

Klaus Mehnert recounts, "Wherever I attended an amateur performance (even in the nursery schools!), the scenes either were taken from the prescribed new works, or were paraphrases that adhered closely in type and subject matter, including the abruptly frozen tableau at the end [exactly like the end of the model operas]."[15]

Amateur cultural activities have been increasing everywhere with the encouragement and coaching of the cultural workers under Chiang Ch'ing's leadership. A Shanghai shipyard worker, Chu Yu-sung, was illiterate until 1958, but since then he has been trying to write poetry. "I am a workman in the heat-treating shop," he said. "Those bourgeois 'poets' treated us workers with disdain, and never wrote any poems to praise us workers in the heat-treating shop. So I am determined to write them myself."[16] Lu Yen-hua of Chingpu County said, "While taking an active part in physical labor, I told nearly a hundred revolutionary stories. In recent years . . . I have written many revolutionary stories which spread Mao Tse-tung's Thoughts and eulogize the poor and lower-middle peasants."[17]

To stimulate these activities, clubs and many other institutions have been newly organized to encourage writers, performers, and artists; help advance new literary journals; and get access to radio broadcast time, cultural festivals, and art exhibits. One exhibition of revolutionary art which opened October 1, 1967, in Peking contained 1,600 works, from huge oil paintings to delicate papercuts, life-size clay sculpture, and badges. They were displayed in twelve halls of the Museum of Chinese Art. During five months, starting in the spring of 1969, six festivals were devoted to drama alone.[18]

The content and Maoist orientation of the mass media and the unprecedented upsurge in cultural and ideological activities throughout the country (a Great Great Leap Forward), all reflect Chiang Ch'ing's influence and represent some of the concrete achievements of the Great Proletarian Cultural Revolution, discussed in the following section.

Part Five

CHIANG CH'ING'S ROLE IN THE GREAT PROLETARIAN CULTURAL REVOLUTION

Chapter 18

Planning and Launching of the Great Proletarian Cultural Revolution

During a work conference of the Central Committee held in September and October 1965, Mao Tse-tung called for the criticism of Wu Han, the noted historian and vice-mayor of Peking, who had written the play *Hai Jui Dismissed from Office*.[1] The play was a thinly veiled attack on Mao for his dismissal of P'eng Te-huai, the former defense minister. In the play, Hai Jui—and by implication P'eng Te-huai—is presented as "a perfect and noble character," and the emperor, symbolizing Mao, as a tyrannical despot. The Central Committee's response to Mao's request was to set up a Group of Five in Charge of the Cultural Revolution headed by P'eng Chen, the man who had opposed all of Chiang Ch'ing's efforts to reform literature and the arts. Chiang Ch'ing realized the situation had become so serious that the time had come to defend their political stand or give up everything she and Mao had worked for over the years.

At an enlarged meeting of the CCP Military Affairs Committee in April 1967, Chiang Ch'ing recounted the fact that she had spent several months writing a critical analysis of the play. "I had some materials which I hadn't shown the Chairman because I didn't want to overburden him. . . . I went ahead in preparing the article. But I kept it a secret for seven to eight months and corrected it numerous times. . . . We knew that once they found out about it, they would try to prevent it from being published."[2] However, by working with her close friends in Shanghai, Chang Ch'un-ch'iao and Yao Wen-yüan, Chiang Ch'ing succeeded in having the article published under Yao's name on November 10, 1965, in the Shanghai newspaper *Wen Hui Pao*.[3]

Chiang Ch'ing pointed out in the article that, "as is known to all," China fell victim in 1959 to a series of natural calamities which lasted for three years and resulted in economic setbacks. Because of this, the "modern" revisionists clamored for "individual farming," demolition of the communes, and the restoration of "rule of the landlords and rich peasants . . . who were responsible for numerous grievances of the working people in the old society."[4]

The play tells of the experience of a Chinese official during the Ming Dynasty who supposedly resisted the emperor's demands in order to protect the poor peasants from seizure of their land. In his *Stories of Hai Jui,* Wu Han states: "The seizure of land is the cause of all grievances . . . return of the land is a means to help poor peasants."[5] The return of land was also the cause for the dismissal of Hai Jui in the play, the implication being that P'eng Te-huai's dismissal came about also as the result of his objections to the collectivization of land during the Great Leap Forward.

The true story of Hai Jui is quite different from the play. The article states, "We are not historians," indirectly reminding the readers that Wu Han was a distinguished historian and professor specializing in the Ming dynasty. As his distortions of Hai Jui's life were deliberate, there was an implication that he must have had a purpose.

Actually, Hai Jui was concerned with increasing and collecting taxes for the Ming emperor, and by removing land ownership from the hands of government officials who were tax-exempt and placing it into the hands of rich peasants and landlords, he was able to enrich the emperor's coffers. "In no case did he consult the poor peasants and try to solve" their land problems. In fact, "He again and again admonished the peasants to submit to feudal rule." He even advocated the use of the army to "pacify" peasants who protested abuse. He stated that "the people south of the lower reaches of the Yangtze are knavish and rascally in character" and asserted that it "is better to wrong the common people than the retired officials in order to preserve prestige. . . . Preservation of prestige is called for because the retired officials are of patrician birth while the common people are of lowly birth."[6]

When the article was reprinted by *People's Daily* on November 30, 1965, the editor added a preface noting that views on the play were varied because the main issues had not been systematically debated; thus it transferred Chiang Ch'ing's criticism from a political into an academic context. On December 30 *People's Daily* also published Wu Han's twenty-three page self-criticism. He admitted that newspapers and magazines had published many articles criticizing his play and reported, "I have read only a few of them." After several pages discussing the tax setup during the Ming Dynasty, he admitted that Hai Jui's character was true to the form as described by Chiang Ch'ing in her article, and in conclusion stated: "Finally, I must say that this self-criticism of mine . . . lacks depth . . ."[7] The Maoists agreed with Wu Han that his self-criticism lacked depth, and Chiang Ch'ing began to prepare a further repudiation of Wu Han and his two associates within the "Three-Family Village."

On February 2, 1966, Chiang Ch'ing spoke to a Forum on Literature and Art in the Armed Forces.[8] After three weeks of meetings, discussions, and lectures with military leaders, a summary of the Forum was published enumerating Chiang Ch'ing's ten guidelines for reorganizing the cultural units within the armed forces and setting up new methods and institutions for their implementation.

While this forum was in session, P'eng Chen's Group of Five in Charge of the Cultural Revolution met with the hope of counteracting the effects of Chiang Ch'ing's work. Under the guise of supporting Mao's requests, they announced: "The policy of 'opening wide' propounded by Comrade Mao Tse-tung . . . calls for full expression of all kinds of opinion (including anti-Marxist things)"[9]—which was actually the opposite of what the Maoists were trying to achieve.

On April 18, 1966, with the assistance of her daughter, who

was on the editorial staff of *Liberation Army Daily*, the article "Hold High the Great Red Banner of Mao Tse-tung's Thought and Actively Participate in the Great Proletarian Cultural Revolution" was published.[10] The article clearly set forth the guidelines for the forthcoming Great Proletarian Cultural Revolution, and these guidelines were used to inspire the masses and implement the movement until the sixteen-point decision of the Central Committee was passed by the Eleventh Plenary Session of the Eighth Central Committee of the CCP on August 8, 1966. The April 18 article instructed the masses to create new and original Socialist and proletarian works and foster good models; emancipate the mind; overcome superstition; practice democratic centralism; follow the mass line; encourage revolutionary, militant, mass criticism of literature and art; use Mao Tse-tung's Thought to reeducate cadres in charge of literature and art; and reorganize the ranks of writers and artists.[11]

On May 10, 1966, Chiang Ch'ing again turned her guns on Wu Han, this time with an article under Yao Wen-yüan's name, entitled "On 'Three-Family Village,'" which was published in Shanghai's *Liberation Daily* and *Wen Hui Pao*. The fusillade was aimed also at two other members of the Three-Family Village, Teng T'o, editor of the *People's Daily*, and Liao Mo-sha, propaganda director of the CCP Peking Committee. They, together with Wu Han, had written a series of approximately 150 articles under the collective pen name of Wu Nan Shing. The three men not only followed Liu Shao-ch'i's revisionist line but also attacked Mao through parables, insinuation, and satire. Chiang Ch'ing regarded the three as an anti-Party clique supported by P'eng Chen, the mayor of Peking. They had been carrying out a deliberate, systematic, and well-organized attack on Mao, using the three publications under their control—*Chien-hsien, Pei-ching Jih-pao,* and *Pei-ching Wan-pao*.

Of all the articles, Teng T'o's series entitled "Evening Talks at Yenshan" were considered the most vicious. By featuring "Great Empty Talks," he ridiculed Mao's Thoughts, pointing out that they rambled on endlessly and no one understood what they meant. "Coincidentally," the author said, "there is in my

The Great Proletarian Cultural Revolution

neighborhood a child who has recently often imitated the ring of a great poet and composed quite a number of Great Empty Talks. Not long ago he wrote:

> 'The sky is our father,
> The earth is our mother,
> The sun is our nurse,
> The East Wind is our benefactor,
> The West Wind is our enemy.'

"In this poem," the author continued, "although there are such eye-catching words as sky and earth, father and mother, East Wind and West Wind, benefactor and enemy, yet their abusive use has made hackneyed tunes of them." The author's advice, therefore, was to read more and talk less. "When you want to talk, go take a rest and don't waste people's time."[12] Besides slandering Mao's dictum, "East Wind is prevailing over West Wind," (symbolizing that the revolutionary forces of Asia, Africa, and Latin America will overcome the imperialist forces represented by West Wind), the article represented a cutting satire against the Communist leadership and implied that they had made many empty promises.

Under Chiang Ch'ing's direction, six writers wrote a lengthy rebuttal: "Teng T'o's 'Evening Talks at Yenshan' Are Shady Articles Against Party and Socialism." It appeared in the Peking *People's Daily* on May 9, 1966, and criticized Teng T'o for maliciously attacking the Party, accusing by insinuation that although the Party leadership pretended to be wise, it actually despised the masses. It also pointed out that Teng T'o's article accused the Party of going back on its word and of being "unworthy of trust," opposing the general line of building socialism and the Great Leap Forward, and attacking the dictatorship of the proletariat.[13]

To launch the Great Proletarian Cultural Revolution, Chiang Ch'ing carefully prepared another article entitled "The Reactionary Nature of Evening Talks at Yenshan and Notes from Three-Family Village," which was published under Yao Wen-yüan's name in the *People's Daily*, May 11, 1966. The article accused the "Three-Family Village" authors of writing fake criticisms of "black weeds." It pointed out that a person who has acted negatively all his life finds it impossible to "act a positive role convincingly, and so leaves a great many holes." In addition to accusing the "Three-Family Village" authors of making an attempt to "turn big issues into small ones and slip through," it said they had grossly slandered the Central Committee of the Party and Chairman Mao.

Encouraged by these articles, youth groups and Red Guard units began to form on campuses to air their grievances and demonstrate against the revisionists, whom they considered to be "a privileged class within the Communist Party itself, an almost tyrannical bureaucracy that had managed to gain control of the machinery of government."[14]

Over the years Chiang Ch'ing had invited young scholars and theoreticians to Wanshow Shan on the western outskirts of Peking for political and ideological discussions. Among the students and young intellectuals who met there were Kuan Feng, Chi Pen-yu, Yao Wen-yüan, and Mme. Nieh Yuan-tzu, a philosophy professor at the University of Peking.[15] On May 25, a "big character" poster attacking Lu P'ing, written by Mme. Nieh, appeared on the University of Peking campus. Demonstrations followed, and later an announcement was made that a new Cultural Revolution Group had been organized to replace P'eng Chen's Group of Five. P'eng Chen's name was conspicuous by its absence; the first deputy chief and leader of the new group was Chiang Ch'ing. In the same month the editor of the *People's Daily* was replaced, and the newspaper, along with the *Liberation Army Daily*, became an important instrument in effecting the Cultural Revolution under Chiang Ch'ing's leadership. Among those also removed from office at that time were Lu P'ing, president of Peking University, and Li Ta, president of Wuhan University. Both were replaced by men with Maoist sympathies.

Youth groups were forming throughout the country within the middle schools and colleges, and demonstrations were held regularly. Liu Shao-ch'i's associates organized and sent out "work teams" to the campuses, ostensibly to "promote" the Cultural Revolution but actually to "keep an eye on the movement."

In June Chiang Ch'ing engineered the publication of several important editorials, spelling out further what she wanted the youth groups to do. In the first, published on June 1, 1966, in the *People's Daily*, she urged her followers to "Sweep Away All Freaks and Monsters," stressing the necessity for ridding the country of those revisionists and reactionaries entrenched in ideological and cultural positions, including bourgeois "specialists," "scholars," "authorities," and "venerable masters."[16]

On June 7, 1966, in an effort to unite her forces firmly on the basis of Maoist Thought, Chiang Ch'ing published an article in the *Liberation Army Daily* entitled "Mao's Thought Is the Telescope and Microscope of our Revolutionary Cause."[17] It stressed that the most powerful ideological weapon—the only one—was Maoist Thought, for it served as China's ideological-political telescope and microscope for observing and analyzing all things; it was the only weapon to be used for storming the enemy's positions and achieving victory.

The article "We Are Critics of the Old World" appeared in the *People's Daily* on June 8, 1966. It was designed to encourage the youth movement, stimulating members toward new and stronger efforts in the future, and noted that the rapid and vigorous development of China's Great Proletarian Cultural Revolution was shaking the world.[18] China's great masses, eight hundred million strong, had started to criticize the old world, old things, and old ways of thinking on an unprecedented scale. The paper pointed out that criticism was absolutely necessary for consolidating the dictatorship of the proletariat and for building socialism and communism. A thorough job had to be done for, according to Mao, "This is also like sweeping the floor; as a rule, where the broom does not reach, the dust does not vanish by itself."

On June 13 the Party Central Committee, in a joint directive with the State Council, ordered a sweeping reorganization of higher education and a six-month suspension in the admission of new students. In fact, all universities, colleges, high schools, and elementary schools were closed for the next two years in order to let the students learn through participation in the Great Proletarian Cultural Revolution. Liu Shao-ch'i's work teams, taking this opportunity, became more active in the universities and in other organizations, all of which resulted in increasing clashes with Chiang Ch'ing's revolutionists. During July, Liu's "work teams" brought mounting criticism on themselves by their evasive and disruptive behavior. The Central Committee finally ordered their removal during the second half of July, but Liu-Shao-ch'i and his followers, ignoring Mao's directive, sent them into schools, factories, and communes. It was reported that even the Red Guards began to have disagreements among their own ranks.

The strategy of Chiang Ch'ing's Red Guards was to carry out the revolution by "reasoning things out," holding rallies, organizing attack teams and struggle meetings, issuing Red Guard newspapers, and erecting large-character posters. Their stated objectives were to defeat the handful of power-holders in the Party organ who clung to the reactionary line, to apply Maoist Thought, to defend the Party Central Committee and Chairman Mao, and to attack every negative thing in the old world.

In July, Chou Yang, deputy director of the Department of Propaganda, and others were denounced at a meeting held by the department. Soon mass meetings condemning him were held all over the country, and he was branded as "the big red umbrella covering all monsters." On August 5 Mao personally wrote a large-character poster entitled "Bombard the Headquarters," urging all-out war against "top Party persons in authority taking the capitalist road."

On August 8, 1966, during the Eleventh Plenary Session of the Eighth Central Committee of the CCP, the Sixteen-Point Decision was adopted, outlining Maoist guidelines for the Great Proletarian Cultural Revolution.[19] The sixteen main points were, in brief:

The Great Proletarian Cultural Revolution

1. The proletariat must meet, head on, every challenge of the bourgeoisie.
2. The revolutionaries must dare to move forward in the struggle in spite of resistance.
3. They must place priority on daring above everything else and boldly arouse the masses.
4. They must let the masses educate themselves in the movement "and any method of doing things on their behalf must not be used."
5. They must firmly apply the class line of the Party and distinguish their friends from their enemies.
6. They should utilize the correct method of handling contradictions among people; that is, there should be full debate which should be conducted by reasoning, not by coercion or force.
7. They must guard against those who brand the revolutionary masses as counterrevolutionaries, as "a number of persons . . . are taking advantage of certain shortcomings and mistakes in the mass movement to . . . engage in agitation."
8. There are four categories of cadres: good, comparatively good, those who have made serious mistakes but have not become anti-Party, and a small number of anti-Party, anti-Socialist rightists. The last category should be exposed, but they should be given an opportunity to reform.
9. The excellent new Cultural Revolutionary Committees and Congresses should hold elections and encourage members to criticize their leaders.
10. The educational system must be reformed.
11. Criticism of reactionary views in philosophy, history, political economy, and education should be organized, but criticism of anyone by name in the press should be decided on only after discusssion with the Party Committee.
12. A policy of unity-criticism-unity should be applied to scientists, technicians, and ordinary members of working staffs as long as they are not opposed to the Party and socialism.
13. The Cultural Revolution should add momentum to the

Socialist Education Movement and clean things up in the fields of politics, ideology, organization, and economy.
14. Through the Cultural Revolution, "greater, faster, better, and more economical results" should be achieved in all fields of work.
15. The Cultural Revolution and the Socialist Education Movement should be carried out in the armed forces.
16. All acts and actions of the Cultural Revolution should be guided by Mao Tse-tung's Thought.

With the Sixteen Points adopted by the Central Committee, the Great Proletarian Cultural Revolution was formally launched under the guiding influence of Chiang Ch'ing.

Chapter 19

Red Guards and Mass Rallies

Throughout the summer of 1966 and until the end of the year, Chiang Ch'ing conducted and participated in all kinds of Red Guard meetings and mass rallies. At these rallies she encouraged the students and revolutionary teachers, and gave them authoritative instructions. Sometimes she opened the meetings, then held small group discussions and reviewed the wall posters they had made; on other occasions she listened to their discussion and disputes without taking part in them herself.[1]

On July 25, when she met with students at Peking University, she greeted them in her typical manner: "We shall come at the call of the revolutionary students, teachers, and staff members whenever we are needed . . . We are service personnel of the revolutionaries."[2] Throughout August huge Red Guard rallies began in Peking, and by the time the last one was held, she and Mao had greeted a total of over thirteen million young people. Chiang Ch'ing personally assumed responsibility for them and placed the Red Guards under the protection of the PLA, which fed them, provided housing, and kept them safe while they were in the capital.

In mid-August Chiang Ch'ing presided over the first Red Guard rally at the Peking Workers Stadium. The August 31 rally also opened under her chairmanship, and she played an important role in organizing and conducting the eight huge rallies that were held between August 18 and November 26 of that year, each of which was attended by one to three million Red Guards. During that period she also "received them in groups, talked with them, and had pictures taken together with them."[3]

In addition to arranging these huge rallies, Chiang Ch'ing

organized and participated in many smaller rallies, meetings, and discussions, and to entertain Red Guards arriving from all over the country, she sponsored performances of her model operas that were attended by all other national leaders as well.[4] On October 31 she appeared at a rally commemorating Lu Hsun, and in spite of professed frail health, she was reported to be present at all other important occasions during that period, as vivacious and full of energy as ever.[5]

The Russian sinologist A. Zhelokhovtsev described a meeting he attended. After several students had given short talks, he noted: "Chiang Ch'ing came up to them, and exclaiming, 'Very good!' gave them a glass of water . . . The students roared with admiration—how simple, how charming that public figure was!" Zhelokhovtsev added, "Chiang Ch'ing's slim-waisted figure, dressed in a closely fitted green army uniform, was constantly in motion." From time to time she asked the speakers questions, playing games with the audience which kept bursting into applause.

> After the speeches made by Chen Po-ta, K'ang Sheng, and Li Hsueh-feng, whose speeches I am completely unable to remember, since they so skillfully said nothing of interest, the floor was given to Chiang Ch'ing. . . . "You are the revolutionary new generation," Chiang Ch'ing said. "You are leading our revolution forward. We, the older generation, are leaving, and as we go, we give you our revolutionary traditions. Chairman Mao is leaving China to you. You will govern China. The school of the Cultural Revolution is a great school!" The effect was immediate. From the moment that the leaders departed, the meeting continued without let-up. Speakers replaced one another, everyone trying to outdo the other by his enthusiasm. . . .[6]

At a farewell party for a group of Red Guards, Chiang Ch'ing outlined her instructions for their basic approach: "First, you must act in a matter-of-fact way and verify facts, so that your position will not be vulnerable. Second, you must work hard and be meticulous in your work. Win the majority, and turn your minority into a majority."[7] She advised the students to be flexible in observing and judging the enemy, warning that the opposition was still strong and that many people in the majority had been fooled.

Anna Louise Strong happened to visit a "service center" for the Red Guards one afternoon in September 1966. "It had been set up . . . to handle the hundreds of thousands of Red Guards who were flocking to visit Peking from all over the country."[8] From time to time she noticed that small groups of Red Guards would rise and leave the building. She was told that they were on their way to catch trains and return home to the provinces, carrying instructions and ready to begin the revolutionary work.

On November 28, 1966, 20,000 literary and art workers held a rally to pay special tribute to Chiang Ch'ing's contributions in "resolutely persisting in the literary and art line of Chairman Mao, in personally taking part in the struggle against the pernicious counterrevolutionary revisionist line, and in the practical struggle to create a new proletarian literature and art."[9] Chou En-lai said in a speech: "The success achieved in the revolutionization of literature and art is the result of a firm struggle against the black revisionist line . . . throughout the period from the 1930s to the 1960s, Comrade Chiang Ch'ing personally participated in the . . . struggle . . ."[10]

At each gathering Chiang Ch'ing gave elaborate and specific instructions for the particular group she was addressing. Observers all seemed to agree that her word was authoritative. According to the Japanese reporter Minoru Shibata, an eyewitness at the Peking rallies of 1966,[11] almost immediately after Chiang Ch'ing's November 28 speech in which she attacked the "old Peking Municipal Party Committee," the Central Propaganda Department and the Ministry of Culture, P'eng Chen was dragged out to the Red Guards' rally and compelled to wear a big name-tag around his neck; following P'eng Chen's public humiliation, many other leaders "taking the revisionist line," including Lu Ting-yi, Lo Jui-ch'ing and Yang Shang-k'un, were similarly denounced.[12]

On December 18, 1966, Chiang Ch'ing called on the Red Guards in her audience to "rise up and take over bureaucratic organs which had been modeled on those of bourgeois countries."[13] The revolutionary left responded to her call enthusiastically and set the stage for the important break in Shanghai, the "January [1967] Revolution," which in turn touched off a power-seizure movement on a national scale. As the movement expanded to include revolutionary rebel organizations in industrial and mining establishments, the power struggle toppled many Party and government figures at local levels everywhere. Chiang Ch'ing's call to "rise up against the political oppression and economic exploitation by Liu Shao-ch'i" motivated large numbers of contract workers, temporary workers, and apprentice workers all over the country to agitate. On December 28, she greeted 100,000 Red Guards who called themselves the "Long March Detachments"[14] and had walked all the way to Peking.

The youth movement had been organized to exert public pressure against entrenched Party revisionists, but it had also been planned to encourage young people to participate in making history and actually to bring about far-reaching changes through their own efforts. It was a positive way of channeling their idealism and molding them into an active force of veteran revolutionaries who would look back on their experiences and sacrifices, and would be motivated to continue working toward Maoist goals.

As the movement gathered momentum, Chiang Ch'ing set the stage for greater revolutionary activities in 1967. On New Year's Day the *People's Daily* published a long editorial entitled "Carry the Great Proletarian Cultural Revolution Through to the End," outlining the main political tasks that confronted the revolutionary masses in 1967. The article explained:

> The Great Cultural Revolution should be carried out on a large scale in the factories and rural areas; revolutionary students, teachers and intellectuals should go to the factories and rural areas to integrate themselves with the worker-peasant masses; fully develop extensive democracy under the dictatorship of the proletariat to prevent the restoration of capitalism; continue to carry out mass criticism and repudiation of the bourgeois reactionary line.[15]

Chapter 20

Chiang Ch'ing and the Development of the Great Proletarian Cultural Revolution

On April 12, 1967, Chiang Ch'ing delivered a speech in which she declared: "You see, without these youths, it would have been impossible to expose the traitorous clique . . . who occupied leading positions in this front. What a great contribution these youths made!"[1] According to Chiang Ch'ing's instructions, Red Guards and "revolutionary rebels" had been returning to their homes and making efforts to take over political power in their local and provincial governments, in the factories, and in the communes. Their method was to put up large-character posters that accused leaders they wished to remove, then call a public meeting and insist by persuasion or force that the accused leaders attend, and publicly criticize and remove them from office. Then new Revolutionary Committees were set up to carry on government pursuant to the Maoist line.

In many cases the revisionist leaders quickly organized fake Red Guard units to fight against the true Red Guards.[2] In other cases, true Red Guard groups who were in disagreement with each other quarreled over who was to be purged and who was to represent them in the new Revolutionary Committees. The revisionists also organized groups who concentrated on performing acts of sabotage and flagrant atrocities in order to discredit the true Red Guards. There were cases in which local revisionist leaders felt seriously threatened and used small personal armies or paramilitary units to attack and open fire on the Red Guards.³ Because of these problems, incidents of disorder and bloodshed began to occur throughout the country.

During this period Chiang Ch'ing was deluged with important tasks. It was she who was the ultimate judge of who were the true Red Guards, and she had to defend and protect the people who she knew belonged to the Maoist camp. It was also her responsibility to convey Mao's intentions to the other leaders and to her followers. She was the one who drew up the directives and orders, and it was she who interpreted them for the Red Guards when they were in doubt. Her word was law. When she named a target for attack, the Red Guards immediately dragged him out of his house for public criticism and put up wall posters of denunciation.⁴ She also implemented orders and purges, kept in close contact with her lieutenants, and saw to it that they followed through on their instructions. She met with them to answer questions and told them how to handle their problems. She arbitrated disputes, explained her views,⁵ tried to unite quarreling factions, and gave her followers encouragement and support. She provided them with secret information to facilitate their work, sponsored rallies and meetings, and in general tried to smooth out the operations of the Cultural Revolution.

The first major disruption that was obviously a case of sabotage occurred prior to the January Revolution in Shanghai. At the instigation of the "top leaders taking the capitalist road," many students created problems in the streets, blocking traffic and transportation with government trucks which they were using as propaganda vehicles. In factories, workers staged strikes for higher wages and disrupted rail service by rushing in vast numbers to Peking to present their case to Maoist leaders, namely Chiang Ch'ing.⁶ According to the wall posters of the Peking Red Guards, Ch'en Pai-hsin, first secretary of the Shanghai Committee of the CCP, and Ts'ao Ti-ch'iu, mayor of Shanghai, used 30,000,000 People's currency ($12,000,000) to bribe workers to strike and to fight the young Red Guards. These Shanghai workers also organized their own fake Red Guards,

The Great Proletarian Cultural Revolution

and on December 27 they forced many factories to close, causing enormous damage to the economy. By means of "economism" they had "made both national economy and people's livelihood suffer setbacks." The state had to use emergency measures to freeze government funds. This chaotic situation continued in Shanghai until the middle of January 1967.[7]

Distinguishing the sincere Red Guards from the insincere proved to be the most difficult task of all because all youths involved in the struggle worked under the banner of Mao. Chiang Ch'ing warned the Red Guards to be wary of "two-faced" people who had infiltrated their ranks. She particularly pointed to Lu Cheng-ts'ao, who had been a close associate of P'eng Chen's and instead of repenting had come out again to "hoodwink" the revolutionists. He had said to the Red Guards: "'We will support you,' but . . . [as the result of] instigation . . . in a number of important communication junctions, the railway services have been interrupted."[8]

She told the Red Guards not to be afraid of straightforward people who made mistakes and then admitted them or of those who spoke their minds. "For instance, Comrade Ch'en I once spoke some wrong words . . . wrote a poem and exaggerated in his talks sometimes . . . but he is not a fence rider. . . . He and I sometimes argue seriously until our faces turn red."[9]

Chiang Ch'ing worried about the possibility that people would be unfairly wronged, especially those who were her friends and those who had always been loyal to Mao at critical times. When the United Action Committee, the opposition's Red Guards, "turned their spearheads" against the two loyal Maoists who had originally exposed Teng Hsiao-p'ing, she cautioned the Red Guards to exercise restraint.[10]

Difficulties developed within the military hierarchy when commanders tried to instigate trouble against each other. Liu Chih-chien, for example, incited people to oppose Yeh Chien-ying and thus created misunderstandings and dissension among the military leaders. Chiang Ch'ing let it be known that she was well informed about which generals and marshals were causing friction, but she argued for patience. "We cannot treat them all the way we do Liu Shao-ch'i," she said, "or there would be only a few left in our state."[11]

During the early part of 1967, the true Red Guards were indeed Chiang Ch'ing's "powerful little generals" supporting her directives and sweeping large numbers of revisionists out of office. Even Liu Shao-ch'i tried to associate himself with them in public. When Chiang Ch'ing spoke to a meeting of the representatives of the revolutionary masses of the Central Documentary Film Studio and the August One Studio, she told her audience that Mao disliked being photographed, especially when people crowded around him to have pictures taken with him.[12] She cited as an example the time when Mao was receiving the Red Guards, and Liu Shao-ch'i, Teng Hsiao-p'ing, and T'ao Chu maneuvered themselves close to him and clustered around him, smiling into the camera.[13] She also urged them to make films for the youth and the masses, but not depressing "revisionist films" such as one she had seen in which everyone in a village except one lonesome old man had died.

During 1967 the opposition not only continued to make revisionist films but their followers even raided studios and carted equipment away. Chiang Ch'ing warned that such acts were very serious, constituting sabotage of production and military equipment.

One of the film people who worked for Liu Shao-ch'i was Ch'en Po, who had made a film about the army's land reclamation projects. In one scene, while standing in a field of opium poppies, the army men sang a song of eulogy to Chairman Mao. Chiang Ch'ing asked Ch'en Po to change the background, but he refused, claiming that opium flowers were seen everywhere in Sinkiang.[14] When she tried to reach Ch'en and insist that he change the scene, she was told: "He is in Tien Shui, getting fat." In response, Chiang Ch'ing remarked, "People like Ch'en Po should be dragged back and subjected to struggle."

In early 1967 factional fighting among the Red Guards grew more serious. Chiang Ch'ing, knowing who was responsible for the disturbances, frequently warned her youthful followers not to be "duped." She pointed out that "the most terrible thing is that the masses fight among themselves." Chiding the quarreling factions, she explained: "You become angry the moment you talk to each other. You are not that angry when you struggle against the persons in authority taking the capitalist road, but you are furious when you argue among yourselves. Surely there must be someone pulling your strings behind the scene."[15] She reminded her youthful followers that when violence started, the instigators "sit comfortably on the mountaintop to watch the tigers fight."[16] Realizing that many of the Red Guards also had personal battles to win, she urged them not only to seize power from the capitalist roaders but also to seize power from their own egoism. "Only when you achieve the latter can we win a complete victory in seizing power from the capitalist roaders in authority," she told them.[17]

The most famous Red Guard group under the control of the revisionists was the United Action Committee, which was composed of children of high cadres. They tried to launch a so-called false power takeover and false unification of the Revolutionary forces. For a short time some of them were imprisoned, then released. Chiang Ch'ing also objected to the fact that they formed a graded hierarchy within their organization, with differing armbands to indicate superior ranks.[18]

Clashes and sabotage continued in the provinces throughout the country in 1967. In Chengtu, anti-Mao elements took over a textile mill as the workers deserted their posts;[19] clashes between Maoists and anti-Maoists were reported also in Shansi Province;[20] Nanchang, in Kiangsi Province, was occupied by anti-Maoists who controlled all vital organizations in that city for several days in January;[21] workers in Fukien Province were incited to strike in an attempt to turn the political struggle into an economic struggle; a similar uprising in Foochow, the capital, resulted in the abolition of revolutionary organizations;[22] pro-Mao Red Guards were attacked by local authorities in Kweichow Province, causing clashes between the PLA and anti-Mao groups and resulting in the imprisonment of many local leaders;[23] after prolonged clashes, the Red Guard rebels finally seized power in

Shantung Province;[24] more serious fighting broke out in Heilungkiang by the end of January and in the beginning of February;[25] and, according to United Press International, on January 29, 1967, forces loyal to Mao were sent to quell large-scale disturbances by an insurgent "field army" in Sinkiang Province.

In February 1967 Red Guard Congresses were held in Peking to organize the Red Guards more efficiently and to ensure their authenticity when they went into the provinces to take over their local governments.[26] Chiang Ch'ing was intensely involved in the setup of the new provincial revolutionary organs, taking special pains to ensure the placement of Maoist supporters in key positions. In order to alleviate the difficulties that were occurring between the Red Guards and the various countermovements, Three-in-One Revolutionary Committees, consisting of one-third pro-Mao representatives from the old leadership, one-third from the new revolutionary mass organizations, and one-third from the military who supported the new line, were set up to head the leadership organizations.

During this period Chiang Ch'ing made many trips throughout the country to mediate problems and help establish local Maoists in power. For example, on January 3, 1967, she went to Canton, where tens of thousands of Red Guards greeted her at the airport, and mounted "a decisive attack on the followers of T'ao Chu . . . to establish . . . control over the city."[27] After this attack on T'ao, Chiang Ch'ing arranged for the publication of two articles by Yao Wen-yüan, who denounced T'ao's two books, *Ideals, Integrity and Spiritual Life* and *Thinking, Feeling and Literary Talent,* comparing them with Liu Shao-ch'i's work *Self-Cultivation.*[28]

After several disturbances in the provinces, notably the February 23 Tsinghai incident in which some Red Guards were killed and others wounded by actions of Deputy Commander Chao Yung-fu of the Tsinghai Military District,[29] Chiang Ch'ing and her colleagues in the Party leadership issued a directive on April 6 specifying that, before taking any important action against mass organizations, advice should be sought from the

Central Revolution Group and the All-PLA Cultural Revolution Group.[30]

To reduce friction, Chiang Ch'ing also decided to stop the "exchange of revolutionary experiences by the students" at a time when students were still coming to Peking and going to other areas in order to establish revolutionary ties. On April 20 she sent out a circular through her Cultural Revolution Group in conjunction with the Central Committee, ordering all Red Guards who were already in outlying areas to return to their own areas and remain there.[31] Because of continued disturbances, Chiang Ch'ing's Cultural Revolution Group, in a joint circular with the Party Central Committee, the State Council, and the Military Affairs Committee, on June 6, 1967, forbade armed struggle, illegal arrest, looting, and sabotage.[32] This was an obvious attempt to segregate the anti-Maoist forces from the true Red Guards and prevent them from harassing the masses.

Throughout the country people were in fact being harassed, arrested, and tried in private courts which disguised themselves as revolutionary organs. Party and army documents and seals had been seized and public properties damaged and destroyed. The circular ordered the garrisons and local troops in various places to take appropriate action against violators; they were authorized to arrest, detain, and punish according to law all those who violated the provisions in the circular order.

Through her intelligence network Chiang Ch'ing learned that the Red Guards' judgments were not always correct. They carried on a great deal of investigative work and exposed groups of "renegades" who had been protected by "Party leaders in authority taking the capitalist road," but mistakes were made. To avoid further injustices, Chiang Ch'ing's Cultural Revolution Group again issued a circular in conjunction with the Central Committee on June 28, 1967, specifying what to do with arrested renegades.[33] It warned the Red Guards not to declare anyone a renegade on the basis of insufficient and unverified materials, and forbade mass organizations to carry on factional struggles on the pretext of catching renegades. The directive clearly indicated that "special agents" had worked their way into some mass organizations and that thorough investigation and search within the organizations were thus necessary.

By September 1967, due to the excessive growth of factionalism among Maoists themselves, Chiang Ch'ing had come to the conclusion that people should stop criticizing each other; the time had come for self-criticsm and unity.[34] All the groups should strive to find common ground for reaching agreement on major matters while ignoring minor differences. There should not be recourse to suppression; instead, an ideological and political program should be initiated to educate those who had made mistakes. As for the "bad" people, she believed that the government and the left should stop making arrests and rather should mobilize the revolutionary masses to deal with the problems by themselves.[35]

Obviously, Chiang Ch'ing and Mao considered it desirable to reduce the numbers attacked, to unite with those who had made mistakes, and to start a reeducation program, including self-criticism, to solve contradictions among themselves. As repudiation and struggle were still carried on, emphasis was placed on discussion and persuasion while armed struggle was deemphasized. It was time to absorb lessons, to learn from past experience and mistakes.[36]

On October 14, 1967, Chiang Ch'ing took another step to direct the youth movement onto another level. Together with other leadership organizations, her Cultural Revolution Group issued a circular ordering all universities and secondary schools to start classes immediately.[37] A Proletarian Educational Revolution was also ordered as a means of eliminating the "bourgeois system of education and of fostering the proletarian system of education." By December 1967 most of the youth had either returned to school to propel the Educational Revolution forward on campus or had gone out to rural and mountainous areas to learn from the peasants. Educational reform along Maoist lines was gradually implemented, and the alliance of all revolutionary organizations was forged.[38]

According to available evidence, and considering the magnitude of the Cultural Revolution, Chiang Ch'ing had probably been collecting intelligence and preparing for the movement long before its launching. It has been observed that many cadres were purged merely at her suggestion; because of her intelligence network and her authority she apparently had the final say as to whether or not a comrade had been loyal to Mao.[39] She appears to have been the ultimate authority, and her responsibility was staggering, considering the number of cadres that were investigated, disgraced, or protected by her during the Cultural Revolution. Those who survived the purges or were protected by her and treated as her friends will presumably feel obligated to be loyal to her in the future. This again tends to strengthen her capacity to influence the Party as well as the government. The less independent a base of power a cadre had, the more likely he would be to appreciate her protection. She has been characterized as a veritable powerhouse, with eyes and ears everywhere.[40] Chou En-lai said, in a meeting in September 1967: "The Central Revolution Group is the staff headquarters of the Great Proletarian Cultural Revolution . . . it is the equal to the former Secretariat of the Central Committee, but the responsibilities it shoulders are even greater than those of the latter . . ."[41] Chiang Ch'ing, of course, was at the helm of the Central Cultural Revolution Group, and since its inception, had been empowered to issue directives in its name.

Among the numerous leaders and cadres whom Chiang Ch'ing protected from disgrace was Hsieh Fu-chih, the security chief, who was repeatedly attacked by factions of the Red Guards.[42]

Chiang Ch'ing's power was obviously pervasive, for it reached down to the local scene. Many in Canton were purged after her speech of January 31, 1968, in which she suggested that "blackline persons like Chang Tung-chuan, Li Shao-chun and Ah Chia must be struggled against until they topple . . ."[43] At the same meeting she provided protection for an old friend, Tsui Wei, by saying, "Tsui Wei wants me to guarantee him. I know that part of his life in Yenan . . ."[44] To defend another friend of hers she said, "Yuan Shih-hai has made mistakes, but he has worked hard in producing model revolutionary plays. In the great Cultural Revolution his attitude toward mass criticism against him was very good, and he never grumbles . . ."[45] Concerning whom to purge and not purge, she gave this advice: "Don't waste time on persons who are historically questionable. The important thing is to see how they are behaving now . . ."[46]

According to an American source, when Chiang Ch'ing publicly denounced propaganda chief T'ao Chu, his career came to an end. The same source also reported: "It has been observed that at the frenzied pinnacle of China's Cultural Revolution, a simple word from Chiang Ch'ing was enough to make strong men tremble . . ."[47] Of T'an Chen-lin she once said, "I formerly protected him."[48] Later on however, she condemned him. Thus she let it be known that she could change her mind if the man changed his attitude. This was a formidable weapon to influence whomever she wished to persuade.

During the Cultural Revolution Chiang Ch'ing played a crucial role in bringing down top Party leaders and government officials. Adopting the same approach she used in her reform of the literature and arts, she "weeded out the old and let the new emerge." Before she had finished purging the Party and government, the ranks of the revisionists had been decimated.[49] Of the six men on the Standing Committee of the Party Politburo, only Mao, Chou En-lai, and Lin Piao remained in power by 1969. Of the thirteen-member Party Politburo, seven members and four alternates were purged;[50] forty-eight members of the active Party's Central Committee were purged; forty alternates were eliminated, and twenty-nine rebuked. Five of the six regional Party bosses were purged and the sixth was demoted, and when Chiang Ch'ing denounced Yang Hsiu-feng, the chief justice of the Supreme People's Court, he committed suicide. Nine out of fifteen deputy premiers and seventeen out of forty ministers of the State Council were ultimately removed.[51]

When Chiang Ch'ing called for the reform of security and legal organizations in Tientsin in February 1968 and in Chekiang and Szechuan in March, urging the introduction of military control, it was accomplished without delay, and the process of reorganization was quickly repeated in other provinces throughout the country. According to the *People's Daily* of May 17, 1968:

> Under the leadership of the proletarian headquarters, hundreds of millions of revolutionary people in China have waged sustained and vigorous attacks on the enemies of the proletariat; have destroyed the bourgeois headquarters . . . hidden within our Party; ferreted out the handful of capitalistic-roaders in the Party and a number of counterrevolutionary revisionists, renegades, enemy secret agents, and counterrevolutionary double-dealers; and smashed their criminal intrigues, which vainly attempted to undermine China's dictatorship of the proletariat and restore capitalism. This is a great political victory.[52]

THE MAOIST CASE AGAINST LIU SHAO-CH'I

Politically and symbolically, the most important man to be removed from office during the Cultural Revolution was Liu Shao-ch'i, chairman of the Chinese People's Republic. Red Guard sources suggest that the "struggle between the lines" of Liuists and Maoists stemmed from Yenan times. They differed in every field, including culture, foreign affairs, and economics.

In foreign affairs, Liu favored closer cooperation with the Soviet Union, yielding on a number of issues, including border and ideological disagreements, in exchange for some material and technical aid. In his book *How to be a Good Communist*, which was published in 1962, he advocated peaceful coexistence with the Soviet Union. *Red Flag* and *People's Daily* attacked this as an anti-Mao book and accused Liu of being "China's Khrushchev."[53] The Maoists, on the other hand, advocated self-reliance in foreign affairs.

In economics, Liu was noted particularly for advocating a slow transition from capitalism to socialism, with material incentives to stimulate the economy and with centralized monopoly of industry.[54] He endorsed the policy of "san-tzu i-pao," i.e., the restoration of individual economy, the extension of plots for private use and of free markets, the increase of small enterprises with sole responsibility for their own profits or losses, and the fixing of output quotas based on the households.

The Maoists, on the other hand, emphasized long-term national stability through balanced growth, decentralization, ideological education to develop nonmaterial incentives, and the promotion of agricultural development, local industry, and handicrafts. They also gave due consideration to the cultural aspects of economic development; for example, instead of utilizing large tractor stations, they believed the peasants should have the machines at their disposal in order to help "free their minds from superstitious attitudes and dogmatism about agricultural mechanization."[55] The Maoists accordingly stressed education and economic development, with emphasis on mass participation.

In culture, Liu formulated a program of "peaceful evolution" for artists and writers in the mid-1950s in an attempt to build his own "cultural army" and propaganda force. Under this program, young talented artists and writers were given professional training and every possible assistance. Contrary to the Maoists teachings, they did not have to go "deep among the masses to learn life." Liu advocated, in short, more freedom for writers in choosing their material.

In his private contest with Mao and Chiang Ch'ing, Liu made use of Mao's own dictum: "In order to overthrow a political power, it is first necessary to mold public opinion and carry out ideological war. This is true for the revolutionary class and it is also true for the counterrevolutionary class."[56]

Liu Shao-ch'i was responsible for advancing the "three-famous" principle: famous writers, famous directors, and famous actors; and also the "three-high" policy: high salaries, high pay for the written word, and high cash awards.[57] Liu called for abolishing the class struggle on the literary and art front, and his aim was generally to foster peaceful evolution and turn his new literary and art circles into a center for shaping public opinion.

On one occasion Liu said: "It is all right for writers and

artists to stay with the masses for only a short period of time."[58] When the cultural conflict intensified in the mid-1960s, he maintained: "If writers and artists have difficulties going to the countryside, they may go there in motor cars so that they can eat and sleep in the cars."[59] This policy was interpreted by the Maoists as trying to turn writers into "bourgeois gentlemen" considered to be above the masses.

Liu Shao-ch'i also directed the Chinese Writers Association to provide travel expenses for writers to encourage creative works. Following plans laid out by Chou Yang, the association established reception centers at the Summer Palace in Peking's suburb, in the Peitai River resort area, and in other scenic spots.[60] In the performing arts, Liu ordered Chou Yang to "lop off" the cultural work teams and substitute his own theatrical troupes. He convened his own forum on literature and art in 1964 advising his cultural workers to be daring and not to fear making mistakes. It was in this context that literature attacking Mao began to appear in China.

After Liu had dissolved many cultural work teams, his own East China People's Art Theater and Shanghai People's Art Theater began to present revivals. T'ien Han, the veteran playwright, dug out all his old plays and enjoyed a comeback. Plays like *Money Is the Thing, The World of Money, A Comic Marriage,* and *Borrowing a Wife* were performed. Liu branded the revolutionary plays performed by the cultural work teams as nothing but "bundles of straw," "vulgar," and "low-grade stuff." Hsia Yen's movie *The Prairie Fire,* produced in 1962, nevertheless exalted Liu as a "hero of great courage and the big savior of the people."[61] In that film Liu was described as the only friend of the workers, and Mao was not even mentioned.

Liu appeared for the last time in a public role at a Red Guard rally in Peking on November 25, 1966. He represented all revisionists, and when he was officially removed from "all posts both inside and outside the Party," his dismissal symbolized the downfall of all the "top Party persons in authority taking the capitalist road," and the monumental victory of the "proletarian revolutionaries" led by Chiang Ch'ing.

Chapter 21

Chiang Ch'ing and China's Youth

Considering the restricted life that the youth of China led before the Cultural Revolution, and the exciting experiences they underwent while traveling and effecting the epoch-making political and ideological revolution under Chiang Ch'ing's leadership, the Cultural Revolution will long be remembered in the minds of many youths as the high point in their lives.

Chiang Ch'ing was looked upon by the youth as a kind and sympathetic person, to whom, of all the top leaders, they felt closest. She personally guided them, provided for them, and supported them. Even when their fortunes were at the lowest ebb, she defended and championed their cause.[1] More than any other national leader of her generation, Chiang Ch'ing appears to have attained a high level of popularity with them.

The 300 to 400 million young people under eighteen constitute a powerful political force in China, a force with which Chiang Ch'ing has quietly begun to consolidate her support. Under her direction, mass youth organizations such as the Communist Youth League, Young Pioneers, All-China Students Federation, and All-China Youth Federation are being restructured and reconstituted.[2] NCNA reports that "preparatory conferences have been held in hundreds of cities and countries . . . calling for young people who have studied Maoist Thought, taken active part in . . . great revolutionary campaigns, and integrated closely with the masses."[3]

Leading the youth of China is undoubtedly a heavy responsibility for Chiang Ch'ing. She has been deeply concerned about channeling their energies into constructive endeavors. Apparently, efforts to do so since the Cultural Revolution have been successful. According to the *People's Daily*, youth from Peking have given a good account of themselves in every field of endeavor in their new surroundings—within the schools, and working shoulder-to-shoulder with local peasants and herdsmen to transform nature and expand production on China's new frontiers.[4] They have also implemented Maoist educational reforms, combining formal education with productive labor. Chiang Ch'ing surely had the youth in mind when she created her model works, hoping to wield a proper influence over them and to prepare them for their role as "revolutionary successors." In addition, she has encouraged and identified herself with youth by attending sports events, theater, and the arts on numerous occasions, such as, recently, the National Sports Tournaments and Sports Awards Ceremonies.[5]

For Chiang Ch'ing as well as for the youth, the Cultural Revolution was an incomparable experience that has deeply affected their lives and mental outlook. Having this common bond and shared experience, a great potential youth force has been created which is eager to again "make new contributions" and "win new victories" under Chiang Ch'ing's political leadership.

Part Six

CHIANG CH'ING'S WORKS AND CONTRIBUTIONS

Chapter 22

Maoist Thought and Chiang Ch'ing's Contributions

In her speech "On the Revolution of Peking Opera," Chiang Ch'ing raised the basic question underlying her entire philosophy: "There are well over 600 million workers, peasants and soldiers in our country, whereas there is only a handful of landlords, rich peasants, counterrevolutionaries, bad elements, rightists and bourgeois elements. Shall we serve this handful, or the 600 million?"[1]

With this principle in mind—that of serving the 600 million— Chiang Ch'ing tried to foster a strong new Socialist cultural medium for the entire country in which the masses would play effective and inspiring roles, surmounting their problems and building a better, cooperative (i.e., Communist) society. The instructions and guidelines which Chiang Ch'ing has developed over the years have been accepted as the authoritative interpretation of Maoist Thought. Some of her most important guidelines for works in the performing arts in a Socialist society, for example, are these:

1. the important roles should depict positive characters drawn from the masses, who show their strength and heroism during cataclysmic disasters and surmount everyday problems with dignity;
2. the story must present life as it has actually existed since the beginning of the people's revolutionary efforts in China;
3. it should suggest the advantages of public ownership as opposed to private ownership (increased productivity through cooperation and mechanization);

4. old operas may be retained if they are not inconsistent with Socialist principles;
5. creation of new theatrical material should involve a three-way combination of the masses, the professional theatrical artists, and the leadership—the masses provided the themes from their experiences, the playwrights learn from the masses and put their stories into dramatic form, and the leadership provides the facilities and support to make the productions possible, returning them to the masses for their enjoyment and inspiration;
6. foreign works should be examined and adapted to enrich China's experience and broaden her knowledge;
7. a new Chinese music and style should be created to serve present needs in line with the instructions given by Chiang Ch'ing to the young creators: "Be bold and follow your own road";
8. the useless parts of the old should be weeded out and the new should be allowed to emerge.[2]

Of all her guidelines, the one urging the creation of positive characters on the stage is the most important to Chiang Ch'ing. A proletarian hero must have courage, diligence, equanimity, loyalty to the cause, optimism, and determination. His speech and behavior must reflect all his fine qualities. The stage hero must be strong and full of health. He braves dangers, volunteers quickly for tasks which require responsibility, is a living example of courage, hard work, and confidence. He performs heroic acts when necessary, his heroism being part of his political and ideological awareness. He is the ideal man to emulate, the person everyone aspires to be and hopes that he is, essentially.

Negative thoughts, like negative characters, are no longer prominent on the stage. Except for anger, the range of negative emotions—worry, fear, apprehension, doubt, frustration, despair, and the like—are rarely manifested by a hero. The purpose of the theater, according to Chiang Ch'ing, is to offer and assert new positive images in the minds of the people. These images should nourish the people's hope, strength, moral inspiration, and high moral values; they should help them cope more successfully with overwhelming obstacles, and replace negative and useless mental burdens with constructive attitudes.

The great majority of Chinese have always been illiterate. After the overthrow of the Ch'ing Dynasty and the establishment of a public education system, illiteracy was still a major domestic problem. Years of war, turbulence, economic dislocation, and natural calamity, as well as the complexity of the Chinese written language, made progress in literacy discouragingly slow. Notwithstanding the strides made by the Communists in this area, illiteracy is still far from being wiped out.

Chiang Ch'ing has been in the vanguard of this fight, compensating for the widespread illiteracy by making the performing arts an audio-visual educational medium. The theaters, in effect, have been converted into vast classrooms, communicating Maoist Thought to the masses through carefully orchestrated innovative entertainment. In this medium the development of new ideas is encouraged along Maoist lines, and old styles, including makeup, costumes, sets, and lighting, are discarded. The traditional makeup calling for red-painted faces to signify uprightness has been replaced by the natural sun-tanned face and intense expression, with painted eyebrows slightly slanted upward. The orthodox white-painted face characterizing dishonesty and deceit and other painted faces symbolizing other characteristics are modified. The characters in the reformed operas and ballets are now simplified, with almost all characters classified as either good or bad. The more complicated characters or the so-called middle characters are all eliminated from the current scene.

In staging, a combination of shadow boxing, old-style opera, and Western ballet has been created, with new, stylized stage gestures replacing old stances and footwork. In the old form, anger use to be demonstrated by an actor blowing his whiskers; in the reformed opera it is expressed by heavy scowling. A number of other kinds of symbolic stage business has also disappeared (such as having a stagehand throw a flag over the face of an actor to indicate his decapitation), while others have been retained (such as the action of stepping over a threshold or waving a red-tasseled whip to symbolize riding a steer). However, the old musical instruments, mainly the xiaoluo (small gong), the daluo (big gong), the bangu (time-beater) and the anobo (small cymbals), are still in use. Ever since Western instruments, especially the piano, were introduced by Chiang Ch'ing, Chinese music has become more palatable. Her innovative combination of contemporary themes and modern techniques with traditional features has given her revolutionary works a broader appeal than that of the old art forms.

In former years audiences barely listened to what was being said on stage. Their attention was focused primarily on the stars, who usually would not appear until the final act. During the four-hour-long program spectators would spend their time cracking melon seeds, sipping tea, gossiping, or discussing business, while peddlers hawked their wares and waiters tossed hot towels back and forth. Today however, such a teahouse atmosphere is unthinkable. Likewise, the practice of having male actors play female roles (with a female occasionally playing a male), as in the old opera, has been abandoned. Today male and female roles are played by members of their respective sexes singing in their natural voices rather than in the falsetto voices typical of traditional opera.

Chiang Ch'ing's conception of the new opera is, in short, a combination of catharsis, "ideological education," and entertainment. It is an approach that stresses the type of hero everyone would like to be. The model everyone is to emulate will be extensively analyzed in the succeeding chapters.

Chapter 23

Chiang Ch'ing's "Revolutionary" Works: A Digest

TAKING TIGER MOUNTAIN BY STRATEGY

In *Taking Tiger Mountain by Strategy*, Chiang Ch'ing proceeds to describe the crucial civil war of 1946 between the People's Liberation Army and the Kuomintang soldiers. Its theme is dramatized by the Maoist saying "Even if the enemy is strong and the people are weak, if the masses are aroused, armed and organized in their struggle, the people will win." It was also written to show the difference in moral fiber between the Communist army and the Kuomintang troops.[1]

The story: After the Japanese surrender in 1945, Chiang Kai-shek concentrates his entire military power in fighting the civil war. A band of defeated Kuomintang troops become common bandits in a mountain hideout. Led by their chief, Vulture, they terrorize the village of Chiapi. Li Yung-chi, a railway worker, is kidnapped by Vulture; his wife and child are murdered. The People's Liberation Army arrives, organizing resistance and liberating the valley. Li, together with Chang, a hunter of Chiapi village, and the latter's daughter, joins the PLA. Yang Tsu-jung, the platoon leader of the People's Liberation Army, disguised as a bandit, makes his way into the enemy's fort. He outwits Vulture and establishes communication with his own unit. A fierce battle ensues in which the bandits are defeated, and Chiapi is freed. The villagers and their liberators then celebrate the triumph and are determined to continue the Revolution.

In this opera Yang Tsu-jung, the model hero, is designed to

inspire the people according to the Maoist slogan "Awaken the masses, fire them with enthusiasm, and impel them to unite and struggle to transform their environment." Yang Tsu-jung is a man of courage, tough and confident. It is easy for the audience to identify with him; he is straightforward, uncomplicated, yet always clever enough to outsmart an adversary. In fact, he is not too different from the traditional heroes in most of the old-fashioned action novels in China. In the early version, hero Yang was portrayed as a daredevil, dashing and rough, with a banditlike air, humming obscene ditties on his way up the mountain to the bandits' stronghold. After Chiang Ch'ing's criticism and analysis, the portrayal of Yang as a hero was transformed to fit the proletarian hero image.

Chiang Ch'ing supervised every phase of the creation closely, diminishing the negative roles by cutting scenes about superstition and murder committed by villains. She added scenes to emphasize the good relationship between the army and the people, making Yang a hero with political consciousness instead of a reckless adventurer divorced from the masses. In Chiang Ch'ing's version, the villains assume less significant positions, which makes the hero stand out in contrast. By outwitting and defeating his enemies so decisively, his hero image serves a definite purpose: "Yang has been deeply engraved on the heart of the broad masses of workers, peasants, and soldiers as the incarnation of proletarian loyalty, bravery, and wisdom."[2]

In the old opera style, one scene shows Yang entering in disguise on his way to the bandit stronghold, executing dances depicting the journey, leaping across a stream, mounting a ridge, dashing down a steep slope, galloping across a distance and then looking around, singing:

> "Let the red flag fly all over the world,
> Be there seas of fire and a forest of knives,
> I'll charge ahead.
> The Party gives me wisdom and courage,
> Risk and hardships are as naught;
> To wipe out the bandits I must dress as a bandit,
> And penetrate their stronghold like a dagger."

In a later scene, while Yang is trying to win the bandits' confidence, the bandits decide to put him to a test. Shooting is heard and the bandits expect Yang to react. But Yang, knowing it is a trick, instead of running out to join his comrades, says to the bandits: "The Communists are here. Come with me and fight." After Yang has outsmarted the bandits and gained their confidence, the real test comes when a captured bandit returns and recognizes him. During a tense scene, Yang gambles with his life in a last daring act. He says to Vulture: "Chief, for your sake I've offended this dog, so he's attacking me. If you believe that I'm a Communist Army man, finish me off at once. Choose him or choose me. You decide as you please." He removes his sash and tosses it onto the ground, and Vulture is fooled.

In another scene, during Vulture's birthday party, Yang urges all the bandits to get drunk while he sends signals to the Communists to attack. While the bandits are heard playing rowdy drinking games in an adjoining cave room, Yang climbs onto a tree stump and looks around, singing: "The bandits are drunk and befuddled. I hope the comrades will come quickly and smash this den of stubborn enemies." When finally the Communists do come, a Western-style gun battle ensues, with the hero chasing the villainous chief. Besides killing several other bandits, Yang ultimately overpowers Vulture, and the Communists capture all the remaining bandits in a colorful and dramatic ending.

Through Yang's dialogue and action the creators have presented a typical proletarian hero with the required qualifications. Hired once as a farmhand, he knew misery in the past, but he has boundless loyalty to Mao. He consistently displayed not only sincere class feeling for the masses, but also courage and wisdom. He becomes in essence an image that symbolizes a galvanizing spiritual force.

ON THE DOCKS

A different theme is presented by Chiang Ch'ing in *On the*

Docks, the first Peking Opera to eulogize the Chinese working class.[3] The opera is entirely about the workers, with Shanghai workers actually participating in its creation. It is clearly designed to build up the hero image of the working man and inject pride and self-respect into a coolie class that had traditionally been despised.

One of Chiang Ch'ing's friends, K'o Ching-shih, began writing *On the Docks* in 1963. K'o Ching-shih was the head of the East China Bureau of the Central Committee. He called on writers and artists of Shanghai to create a Huai Chu Opera. When Chiang Ch'ing saw the tryout, she immediately decided to have it revised and adapted to Peking Opera.

The story: In the summer of 1963, as rice is being loaded by longshoremen on a Shanghai dock to be shipped to support the people's struggle for independence in developing countries, a foreign freighter seeks permission to leave port ahead of schedule because of an impending storm. Fang Hai-chen, a woman Party secretary, is charged with organizing a group to speed up the loading.

In the meantime Han Hsiao-chiang, a young longshoreman who looks down on his work, is being influenced by Chien Shou-wei, an undiscovered class enemy. When Han drops a sack of wheat that is being removed to the warehouse to avoid the storm, Chien sweeps the spilled wheat into a dustpan containing glass fiber and dumps it into the sack. He then motions to Han to pick up the sack of rice to carry into the warehouse. Chien intends through the mixup to have the spoiled sack shipped overseas, thus damaging China's goodwill abroad.

When Fang Hai-chen learns what has happened, she and Kao Chi-yang, the team leader, mobilize the longshoremen and spend the whole night trying to find the spoiled sack of wheat. At the same time she confronts Chien Shou-wei with the event, and hearing his contradictory statements, she becomes increasingly suspicious. Later, in making comparisons between the docks of old and new China, she and the retired longshoreman, Ma Hung-liang, help Han realize that his disdain for dock work has caused him unwittingly to aid the enemy. Aware of his

Her Works and Contributions

mistake, Han then exposes Chien, and the plot is brought to light. By daybreak the contaminated sack has been found, and the shipment goes abroad undamaged.

The prologue to the opera sets the tone. The workers express their determination to maintain their new respectability, which they have gained as a result of their liberation from backward bourgeois ideology, reflecting the Maoist Thought: "The influence of the bourgeoisie who come from the old society will remain in China for a long time to come, and so will their class ideology; hence the necessity for the struggle in the ideological field."

The first scene opens on the docks in Shanghai, amid the usual bustling activity, and the opening song is sung by Kao Chih-yang, the team leader and a Party member, signifying the power of the dock-workers and their friendship for all parts of the world. All the dock-workers in the opera, except Chien and the wavering young Han, are heroes, but Fang Hai-chen, the heroine, surpasses all the others. Selflessness and devotion are constantly expressed through dialogue and action. In the first scene, Ting Ke-chien, a longshoreman and a Party member, reports to Kao Chi-yang, the team leader, that they have accelerated the loading so that now the dock workers are even complaining that there is not enough work to do. "They say we should add another two thousand sacks of rice and they'll get them abroad without even breathing hard . . . good comrades are not afraid of work."

Later in the story, Fang, the heroine, reiterates the opera's theme, saying: "Comrades, this wheat is going abroad to aid our brothers in Asia, Africa, and Latin America. Every sack will play a part in the struggle for freedom. The more difficult the situation and the busier we are, the more we must remember Chairman Mao's instruction: 'Be resolute, fear no sacrifice, and you will surmount every difficulty to win victory.'"

Chien Shou-wei, the former warehouse-keeper who is now working as a longshoreman, represents the revisionist element, missing the "good old days" and longing for an easy life. When he talks about his son, he says to young Han: "How fine it would have been if you could have got into Sea Transport Academy together. One day you would have been first mates, and then—captains' uniforms, visored caps, black leather shoes, shiny gold insignia and epaulets . . ." With a sigh he adds, "That son of mine. A failure. A mere longshoreman. He's made me lose face. . . . Everybody looked down on a longshoreman before liberation. 'Stinking coolies,' they were called. Very menial workers." The character of Chien, on the other hand, is drawn as a composite enemy of the working people, not only trying to corrupt a confused young dock-worker but also seeking to damage New China's international image.

Fang Hsi-chen, the heroine, has many of the characteristics typical of the standard proletarian hero. All through the opera she shows complete devotion to Party principles. When reprimanding the young dock-worker who dropped the sack of wheat, she caustically observes: "The sack you carried came loose because something has come loose in your thinking." When young Han throws down his work pass, Fang restrains her anger but declares that "clearly someone has put you in a boat going nowhere and you're doing the rowing." Out of duty she is determined to help this young man find pride in his work. Her song expresses this objective, stating:

> The evil wind may kick up choppy waves,
> But I'll buck the wind and beat the waves,
> I'll bring this sailing ship back to port.

Later she advises the young man, "Don't look down on the labor of the dock-worker, young Han. Every bale and sack here is linked with world liberation. . . . What you have thrown away is not your work pass but the cause."

SHACHIAPANG

Shachiapang is probably one of Chiang Ch'ing's favorite works, and the first that she has made into a symphony. It was adapted from another play, *Spark Amid the Reeds*.[4]

The story: In the tranquil lakeside village of Shachiapang, eighteen wounded New Fourth Army men are hiding from the Japanese. Led by Sister Ah-ching, an underground Communist Party worker who runs a local teahouse, villagers help the men cross the enemy lines. During a Japanese raid, Kuo Chien-kuang, the political instructor of the company, takes his wounded men to hide in the lake marshes.

The Japanese raids are followed by the arrival of the Kuomintang puppet troops commanded by Hu Chuan-kuei and his chief of staff, Tiao Teh-yi. Sister Ah-ching had once saved Hu's life by hiding him from the Japanese. Now Hu has become a Japanese collaborator. Without knowing who Ah-ching really is, Hu remains of course grateful to her. Playing a double role, she pits Hu and Tiao against each other and skillfully overcomes dangers and difficulties.

Under orders from the Japanese Imperial Army, Hu and Tiao torture the villagers to find out where the wounded Communist soldiers are hiding. Sister Ah-ching, however, outwits the villains, and with Aunt Sha's help, she not only sends help to the wounded but also obtains information about the enemy's headquarters. In the end, the New Fourth Army returns to Shachiapang to capture the puppets and free the village.

The theme of this opera deals essentially with guerrilla warfare, based on the Maoist belief that a people's war cannot be fought without the support of the people. Sister Ah-ching, the heroine, dominates the stage; the well-drawn villain, the puppet commander Hu, serves actually to bring out her admirable qualities through sharp contrast with his inferior maneuvering and decadence. To gain Hu's confidence, Sister Ah-ching says, "The commander is a big tree, and I want to enjoy its shade." By her efficient actions, the audience is led to trust her ability to outsmart her opponents and overcome obstacles. In this sense she resembles the hero Yang Tsu-jung in *Taking Tiger Mountain by Strategy.*

Every Communist soldier is a hero in *Shachiapang*, with Kuo Chien-kuang, the company political instructor, standing out even more than the others. Virtues which Communists are expected to emulate are constantly stressed in the opera. During the evacuation scene, while Ling, a soldier, is sorting bandages and medicine, and Wang, another soldier, is folding sacks, the dialogue is quite revealing:

> LING: Young Wang! Come and let me change your dressing.
> WANG: Change the dressing? No, I won't. It's too hard to get medicine; we should keep it for serious cases.

Aunt Sha, a peasant woman, is a composite character representing all peasants who have suffered brutality and injustices under rich landlords. Her song relates the days when the abuse of child labor was common, and reminding the people of those demoralizing times, she noted:

> "In the dark days we were too poor to raise our children. Of my four boys, two died of hunger and cold. I had to get a usurious loan from the Tiaos in a year of famine. To pay the debt, my third son had to work for them as a farmhand. Tiao had a murderous heart. He made my son toil day and night. Brutally beaten, the boy died of mortal wounds."

Friendship and goodwill between the army and the peasants are frequently demonstrated through short scenes. For instance, Ling, noticing that Aunt Sha is washing the army men's clothes, says, "Aunt Sha, washing clothes again! Let me do that!" In reply, Aunt Sha explains, "The instructor's been helping with our harvest all night. Why shouldn't I wash a few clothes for him?"

Kuo, the instructor, regularly displays the courage and optimism of the model Communist. When he takes the wounded to the marshes, Aunt Sha worries about them. "Aunt Sha," he says, "we have the tradition of the Red Army men who crossed snow-covered mountains and swamps. No difficulty can stop us."

The puppet commander, Hu, is different from other villains. Instead of being vicious and brutal, he is portrayed as a jovial type, corrupt and muddle-headed. But aided by Tiao, his foxy chief of staff, he remains nevertheless a dangerous opponent. Using the traditional opera style, Hu introduces himself in an entrance song:

> "Any man with a few guns can be a chief;
> I get along by keeping in with three sides;
> Chiang Kai-shek, the Japanese, and secret societies."

Throughout the opera Hu illustrates all the decadent habits of the old days—playing mah-jong, drinking, and demanding "voluntary gifts" from the people. Tiao has the worst possible background in a proletarian society, as is shown in his introduction: "This is Tiao Teh-yi, son of the late honorable Mr. Tiao, the wealthiest man in town."

In all modern Peking Operas, peasants and soldiers always tend to show courage and spirit, even in the face of death. When a peasant called Fuken is dragged in for questioning, Hu says: "Speak up! Where have the wounded New Fourth Army men gone?" Fuken points at Hu and shouts: "Traitors! Down with Japanese Imperialism! Down with traitors and stooges!"

"Orderly!" Hu commands, "have him shot for the other riff-raff to see!" And Fuken is dragged off and shot.

In the end, Sister Ah-ching and Kuo lead the commando platoon and militia in a raid on the villains' backyard, with the fighting men doing somersaults and vaulting walls, bringing the opera to a rousing conclusion.

RAID ON THE WHITE TIGER REGIMENT

Raid on the White Tiger Regiment is an opera that represents in essence a dramatization of Maoist Thought.[5] Each scene is based on one of Mao's slogans expressed in his speeches. The idea of the play is based on Mao's observation during the Korean War: "The people who have triumphed in their own revolution should help those still struggling for liberation. This is our international duty."

The story: The Chinese People's Volunteers are helping the

North Koreans fight the Americans and their "puppets" in Korea. Yang Wei-tsai, the platoon leader, builds up a close relationship with the villagers, and together they fight the war of resistance. Following Mao's tactics of encircling the enemy, Yang leads his Dagger Squad behind enemy lines in an attempt to surprise the enemy headquarters. With the help of the villagers, he succeeds, and captures the enemy commander just as the main force of the Chinese People's Volunteers arrive.

This opera was written in an effort to inspire the Chinese people to make new contributions toward international brotherhood. The curtain rises to the beating of drums and stirring music. Chinese and Korean soldiers enter, waving flags, and together march into battle.

Following this rousing opening is a friendship scene based on another Maoist dictum: "The army must become one with the people so that they see it as their own army. Such an army will be invincible." When the Chinese forces arrive in the little Korean village, the Koreans, led by a peasant woman, Aunt Tsui, express their happiness with singing and dancing. When the Chinese People's Volunteers are leaving the village, Aunt Tsui sings to them:

> "As I see you leaving, my sons,
> There is no end to what I want to say in thanks."

Yang sings in reply:

> "We drink from the same river,
> And fight shoulder to shoulder.
> This beautiful land belongs to the people."

The next scene is the dramatization of Mao's concept: "All reactionaries are paper tigers. In appearance, the reactionaries are terrifying, but in reality they are not so powerful. From a long-term point of view, it is not the reactionaries but the people who are really powerful."

Representing the reactionaries are the "puppet soldiers" who, under the command of an American adviser, try to force the local people to repair a damaged road. When the people refuse, the American adviser reprimands the Korean puppet commander, who immediately orders his men to burn down the villagers' houses. Soon the village is in flames and some villagers are herded into the village square by the puppet soldiers, but they still refuse to repair the road. One of them, Aunt Tsui, is questioned, but she gives the puppet commander such a tongue-lashing, calling him and the American adviser "bandits," that the puppet commander finally fires at her. Mortally wounded, she arouses the villagers further by singing: "We will break through the darkness to meet the dawn, we will persist in the struggle and brave the storm."

A fierce struggle between the puppet soldiers and the villagers then ensues, and as a symbol of defiance the civilians lift up the body of Aunt Tsui.

The Dagger Squad, disguised as enemy soldiers and led by Yang, finally gets behind the enemy lines by outwitting enemy guards. With the help of a peasant woman the squad reaches the headquarters of the White Tiger Regiment and proceeds to destroy the enemy. The opera ends victoriously with stirring music and a narration of Mao's words: "The people of the countries in the Socialist camp should unite! . . . All peace-loving countries should unite! . . ."

THE RED LANTERN

The Red Lantern is one of the earliest operas composed by Chiang Ch'ing. Eight years were spent polishing and revising the script under her close supervision.[6] It was created to publicize the courage and sacrifice of the proletariat during their struggle against Japanese aggression, about which Mao remarked: "Thousands upon thousands of martyrs have heroically laid down their lives for the people; let us hold their banner high and march ahead along the path crimson with their blood!"

The story: Li Yu-ho, a railway switchman and a Communist

underground worker, receives a secret code which he must deliver to the guerrillas in the Cypress Mountains. He lives with his foster mother and daughter in a Japanese-occupied town under the control of Hatoyama, the Japanese chief of police. Betrayed by Wang, a fellow underground worker, and refusing to tell the enemy where he has hidden the secret code, he is beaten and tortured. The Japanese then bring his family to him to pry the information out of them, but to no avail. At his wits' end, Hatoyama executes Li and his mother but lets the daughter go. Li's daughter, Tieh-mei, then proceeds to carry out the mission. Helped by neighbors, she succeeds in delivering the secret code to the guerrillas. The "red lantern," a family treasure, develops into their symbol of strength.

During the play, when the young heroine discovers what her father is doing, he explains, "You know everything now, Tieh-mei. The code is more important than our lives. We must keep it a secret even if it costs our heads." From that point on the girl inherits her father's staunch belief in the struggle, which she affirms as she sings to herself:

> "I am seventeen, no longer a child,
> I should share my father's worries.
> If he's carrying a thousand-pound load,
> I should carry eight hundred."

Tieh-mei is a model teen-ager who, once having made a resolution, carries it out through actions designed to stimulate the admiration of her peers in the audience. When she and her family are being questioned and threatened with being shot, her dedication is expressed as she sings to her father:

> "You have given me your integrity
> To help me stand firm as a rock!
> You have given me your wisdom
> To help me see through the enemy's wiles;
> You have given me your courage
> To help me fight."

When the Japanese demand that she deliver the secret code in five minutes or they will shoot the entire family, her convictions are being severely tested, but she replies, "I . . . don't . . . know." Thus she becomes a perfect model heroine, courageous, selfless and dedicated to her ideals. When the Japanese order the family to be shot, the orchestra builds to a stirring crescendo, and the three of them, heads high, march up a slope, defying death.

Audiences find the scene emotional and inspiring. It serves to remind them of the many sacrifices that were made for the cause during the wars of liberation.

Li Yu-po, the father, is a hero with whom the masses can easily identify. He was born and reared as an ordinary worker, and his character expresses the finest qualities of the Chinese proletariat conforming with the Maoist ideal: "filled with courage and strength [he] . . . fought the foe and never gave ground." One review said: "Li Yu-po's struggle against Hatoyama represents the Chinese people's struggle against Japanese imperialism, the proletariat's struggle against the bourgeoisie and the struggle of millions of revolutionary people against a handful of reactionaries."[7]

Underlying the opera are the differences between two basic philosophies, one represented by the hero, urging that "so long as I live, I'll devote my life to revolution"; the other, expressed by the villain: "Enjoy the wine and songs while we can. Better alive than dead."

THE RED DETACHMENT OF WOMEN AND THE WHITE-HAIRED GIRL

Each of these ballets deals with the liberation of a fiery, rebellious, and angry peasant slave girl who finally achieves success in the struggles against the exploiting class.

The story of The Red Detachment of Women: During the Second Revolutionary Civil War (1927-37), Hainan Island, off the southern coast of China, is in a state of turmoil.[8] In the countryside the poor peasants join the Red Army. The women are also organized, using farming tools as weapons to defend themselves against landlords and tyrants; they emerge as the legendary Women's Detachment.

The struggle in the story focuses on the political awakening of the slave girl Wu Ching-hua, beginning with her flight from a tyrant-employer's "prison" and her capture and merciless beating, after which she is left for dead. Rescued by Hung Chan-ching, the Communist Party representative of the Women's Company of the Red Army, she is brought to the Red Army base where she joins the Women's Company. During an attack on her former tyrannical employer, her hatred is so intense that she fires without orders, almost upsetting the battle plans. Through political education and guidance, however, she learns discipline and develops into a model soldier. After her benefactor, Hung Chang-ching, is murdered, she kills their enemy, the tyrant, and pledges to carry on the revolution.

This was China's first modern ballet on a contemporary revolutionary theme. Formerly, the ballet was used only to entertain the elite class in China; its subjects, therefore, were love, escapades about kings and nobles, and stories about fairies. The new ballets, similar to the new Peking Operas, were designed to encourage the workers, farmers and soldiers.

This ballet stresses the point again that the People's Army is led by the Party and that the Party and the army must rely on the people to build a rural foundation for Communism. Hung Chang-ching represents the army and Wu Ching-hua the oppressed working class. The ballet gives a fiery presentation of action, with fighting carefully choreographed to suit the mood and theme. Both hero and heroine are easily understood by the masses and identified with. Wu Ching-hua has a deep hatred for the landlord, and her uncontrolled passion for revenge is finally sublimated by the Party's discipline, which helps her mature into a woman conscious of her greater responsibility. She becomes an explosive force in the ballet, while Hung remains the typical model hero—mature, firm, strong, devoted, and fearless. "Revolution is not simply a matter of personal revenge," he says to Wu Ching-hu during a drill scene. "It's aim is the emancipation of all mankind." Regretfully recalling her mistake in opening fire without permission, she says, "Why do I think only of vengeance for myself?"

After Hung is captured by the tyrant, he is brought to enemy headquarters and is ordered to sign a recantation. He grabs the sheet of paper, rips it up, and throws it on the floor. Later, when he is burned to death, he stands in the flames, raises his right fist and shouts defiance. The ballet was designed in part to give recognition to the many courageous and heroic acts that occurred during the civil war.

The story of The White-Haired Girl: In a village located in North China, the father of Hsi-erh, a young girl, unable to pay his debts, is beaten to death, and Hsi-erh is taken by force to work in the home of the landlord, Huang Shih-jen.[9] Defiant, she is beaten, but she fights back and finally flees to the mountains. After she has endured much suffering, her hair turns white. When the Eighth Route Army frees the village, her boyfriend, who had joined the army, finds the nearly wild girl in a cave. Reunited with her people, she joins the force, kills her oppressor, and goes forth to carry on the Revolution.

The story is based on an actual case in a cave town north of Yenan. In 1936 a crazed woman appeared one day on the edge of a bluff and would not let anyone near her. She was reported to be living in a cave like a wild animal. As stories about a "white goddess" spread, two writers of the Lu Hsun Academy of Literature and Art in Yenan based *The White-Haired Girl* on this event, and it won a Stalin Prize in 1951. When the play was presented to the peasants in 1947, according to eyewitness Jack Belden, "the bitter reality was not lost on the women in the audience, many of whom had had similar experiences . . . old and young, peasant and intellectual, wiped tears . . . one old lady wept loudly through nearly the whole play."[10]

Like Wu Ching-hua in *Red Detachment of Women*, Hsi-erh in the ballet is filled with bitterness, and after her hair has turned white, she harbors an increasing passion for revenge. The original version of the story only served to show that "the old society changes human beings into ghosts." After many revisions the ballet finally appeals sharply to the Maoist theme "Where there is oppression, there is resistance and struggle."

In both ballets the heroine dominates the stage, displaying great physical prowess, fighting like a tigress, and annihilating enemies with as much skill and bravery as any proletarian hero in the modern Peking Operas. Because the role is physically demanding, more than one ballerina is said to be required to play the heroine in one performance.

"Because of the content of life embraced by *The White-Haired Girl*," reports *China Reconstructs*, "some ballet forms, such as free-sweeping movements, high leaps, and other difficult movements, are given full play. It also introduces postures, hand gestures, and acrobatic techniques from national folk dances and Chinese operas, thus making up for the shortcomings of foreign ballet in expressing the life, thoughts, and feelings of the Chinese character."[11]

Both ballets include singing and dialogue, thus departing from the old rule to suit the Chinese working people, who always preferred folk dances and singing. These additions also help the audience understand the plot and tend to increase the emotional impact. In converting the stories into ballets, Chiang Ch'ing changed the emphasis of the plots from negative to positive. In Chiang Ch'ing's versions, the exploited peasants are transformed from pathetic characters to assertive, straightforward, and courageous people who revolt and fight back, entirely different from the humiliated poor of the old days who swallowed insults and only "complained against heaven." In the older version of *The White-Haired Girl*, the raped heroine worked submissively; after she escaped she even dreamed that the landlord would marry her because she was pregnant. In Chiang Ch'ing's ballet, however, she is devoid of self pity. When she is insulted by the landlord, she immediately seizes a candleholder and attacks him, vowing: "I will become a storm! I will become thunder that shakes the nine heavens!" In the adaptations, Chiang Ch'ing is thus able to present characters who encourage people to speak up and fight against their oppressors.

Chapter 24

Popular Response and Impact

Popular response to Chiang Ch'ing's works as reflected in the mass media has been overwhelmingly enthusiastic.[1] The workers at the Locomotive and Rolling Stock Plant in Peking said in an interview: "When we railway workers saw *The Red Lantern*, we felt it was very close to us, that it had great lessons for us, and was a tremendous inspiration. We workers like to see revolutionary modern drama.[2] Workers at the Shanghai No. 2 Machine Tools Plant said that the workers liked most the operas depicting heroes from their own ranks."[3] The peasants also welcomed stories about their lives. The *People's Daily* carried a number of articles by peasants from various rural areas, praising especially *The White-Haired Girl* as "truly serving peasants and showing the unyielding resistance of the oppressed peasants."[4]

Chao Chen-ti, a woman textile worker from Shanghai, expressed her preference for the new Peking Operas that had replaced the old love stories. "Who wants to see those plays that depict foreign and ancient figures, that concern the loves and romances of young couples who call each other lover and sweetheart all day long . . . ?"[5] Wu Shu-yang, a young longshoreman in Shanghai, said, "How happy we were to see safety helmets, carrying poles, and shoulder shields appear on the stage! . . . Excellent! We cheer and applaud!" Huang Pei-yuan, a member of the Tungtan militia, exclaimed, "I support *Shachiapang* a thousand times, I acclaim it ten thousand times. We not only want one *Shachiapang* but thousands and thousands of *Shachiapangs!*"[6]

The main reason the masses enjoy the new operas and ballets stems from the fact that the stories are about people like themselves and the experiences they have undergone in the past. They can understand those readily, and are deeply moved by them. The stories reflect the thoughts, hopes, and feelings of the masses of laboring people. They see themselves portrayed as heroes and heroines, and praised. By identifying with the positive characters they enjoy a feeling of pride as they vicariously forge ahead and rely on their own efforts to win a better life and build a country they can be proud of.

When the Shanghai School of Dance presented the two revolutionary ballets in Shansi Province, the audience reaction was enthusiastic. Chen Yung-kuei reported: "They symbolize the common experience of all poor peasants in the old society . . . We formerly poor and lower-middle peasants love such ballets which teach us never to forget classes and class struggle."[7] Teng Wan-tien, another formerly poor peasant, said, "I like *The White-Haired Girl* for portraying the fighting spirit of Wang Pai-lau and Hsi-erh and for expressing what is in the hearts of formerly poor and lower-middle peasants." He was particularly affected by the ballet because the present-day struggle has a close relationship with the struggle of the poor against the landlords dozens of years ago.[8]

Yin Wei-chen, of the Huangukang Production Brigade, said, after he had seen several model Peking Operas, "What we saw was our own struggles; what was said was what we wanted to say. . . . I would like to see them a thousand times"[9] Wang Tsu-chieh and Yang Yu-hsi, two soldiers stationed in Peking, commented, "If the people armed with Mao Tse-tung's Thought can smash the old world, they can also build a new one. Let the emperors, kings, and all the monsters who once monopolized the stage go to the devil! Workers, peasants, and soldiers have risen in rebellion!"[10]

From 1965 on to the present time, praise of Chiang Ch'ing's leadership and her works has appeared frequently in newspapers, periodicals, and radio broadcasts. These favorable comments by people in all walks of life have been conditioning the populace to share the same high opinion of her and respect her legitimate authority. They have helped to generate widespread mass support for her leadership and popular confidence in her ability to best interpret the "Thought of Chairman Mao." During

Klaus Mehnert's tour of fourteen Chinese provinces in 1971, he noted that music from the operas and ballets, as well as reviews, quotations, and discussions of them were constantly being heard on television and radio.

> Throughout the entire trip, whenever I asked the name of the music coming from the loudspeaker or the car radio, I was invariably told it was one of the operas. It never failed. . . . Strangely enough, no one seems to become bored with this unvaried diet. On the train I was the only person who ever turned off the radio; everywhere else, the loudspeakers were going full blast. On trips by car, I had to ask the driver to turn the radio down so that I could hear my companions; as soon as one opera was finished, the driver would turn his dial until he had found a station that was playing the next one.[11]

The works of Chiang Ch'ing have already become so popular in the rural areas that traveling troupes are reportedly playing to packed houses, a fact suggesting that theater for the first time is apparently becoming an integral part of the peasants' lives. After attending *The Red Detachment of Women*, Mehnert observed,

> The theme songs, especially those sung by the guerrillas, are obviously very popular; during the performances I heard several people around me singing along with the chorus. Later, as we left the theater and went out in the street, people were still humming.[12]

In addition to giving viewers a sense of pride and self-respect, the model works tend to promote a sense of appreciation among the different segments of society. After watching a soldier hero scaling a cliff, leaping barbed wire entanglements, crossing gorges, engaging in hand-to-hand combat in enemy headquarters, and risking his life to improve their lot, it is difficult for workers and peasants not to respect the profession of soldiering. On the other hand, the heroic deeds of peasants and workers are also on display, making soldiers likewise feel more respect for them. As Wan Shih, a veteran of the Sino-Japanese War, said:

"The operas reminded me of the way the people acted as our eyes and ears, and as our support forces. They shielded us, led us on our way, carried our food and ammunition, supplied us with information about the enemy, and tended our wounds. That's the reason we were able to fight so successfully behind the enemy lines."[13] Fang Pei-fu, a writer, observed, "Writings depicting such heroes have a brand new content, as well as a distinctive form and style. Fresh and unadorned, incisive, vigorous, and permeated with ideals, they give readers confidence and strength, encouraging them to continue on the revolutionary path."[14]

Given the mass dissemination of Chiang Ch'ing's works and their special nature, it is fairly reasonable to infer that they do and will affect the people's thinking, living habits, and behavior to some extent. Because her works have set up new and authoritative standards for behavior, replacing traditions and the dictums set down by parents, the young people, women, and the masses will probably be more assertive, more outspoken and more "active" than they have been traditionally. Women will tend to be less subservient to men; inspired by the heroines in the model operas, especially the able and intelligent women in *Shachiapang* and *On the Docks*, they will rise and fall on the basis of their own abilities and contributions to the cause.

As a person's thinking changes, his behavior also changes. Yu Yen-hua, a timid peasant woman who lived in Kwangtung, is an excellent example of a person so impressed by the model works that her behavior drastically changed. One day she dropped in at a village teahouse where a professional storyteller had been hired to entertain the customers, relating a story about T'ang Po-hu, a landlord-class intellectual who did no useful work but chased after women. Although he had eight wives at home, he still tried to force a young maidservant to become his concubine. Overcoming her shyness, Yu Yen-hua then offered her services and told the story of *The Red Lantern*. She succeeded in winning over most of the customers. From that time on, storytelling in that teahouse took a strong turn toward the side of socialism.[15]

Her Works and Contributions

The works of Chiang Ch'ing in effect teach the Chinese people about their revolutionary history. As the people witness the sacrifices made on their behalf, they tend to develop a deeper appreciation of "proletarian revolutionaries," and feel closer to the Party and army. The model works also politicize the people by demonstrating and explaining to them the new political concepts, such as People's War, Communist Party, socialism, communism, nationalism, class struggle, revisionism, etc., illustrating acceptable new attitudes, new standards of behavior, new styles of work and leadership, and new relations among groups. The understanding and acceptance of Mao's and Chiang Ch'ing's Socialist attitudes and behavioral standards by the masses have the potential to accelerate social change and unify the country along Maoist lines.

Many people have expressed their gratitude for her works. Two laborers in Shansi Province, Hsi Shun-ta and Shen Chi-lan, exclaimed: "We had long hoped for the day when those parasites who eat human flesh and drink human blood would be chased off the stage. . . . Today, under the direction of Comrade Chiang Ch'ing, great victories have been won. . . ."[16] The models also display Chiang Ch'ing's knowledge of the actual conditions under which the masses live and struggle, and through her knowledge, understanding and interest in them, the masses should feel closer to her as a person and trust her in other areas. Klaus Mehnert summed up his observations by saying:

> When we consider the unbelievably wide impact of the new theater—the thousands of stage productions and movies; the hundreds of thousands of amateur performances in schools, in factories, and in villages; when we consider that the "eight exemplary works" are now the only ones in existence, and that the next generation will know no other heritage—when we consider all this, it would seem that never before in history has a single woman had so incalculable an influence on the . . . lives of hundreds of millions of people.[17]

Part Seven

SUMMARY AND CONCLUSION

Summary and Conclusion

In conclusion, Chiang Ch'ing has played a vital role in the Chinese Communist movement since joining the Party in 1931. The evidence indicates that Chiang Ch'ing has made major contributions to her Party's cause over a protracted period of time. In addition to serving as Chairman Mao Tse-tung's confidante, representative, and aide since 1939, she appears to have exerted significant influence on his thinking and policies.

The nature of Chiang Ch'ing's contributions to the process of decision-making can be clearly delineated. She and her supporters have collected information and intelligence of policy relevance. From the Maoist vantage point, and with their interests, priorities, and goals in mind, she has then formulated her own analyses and assessments of the problems and situations that have required solutions. She has suggested alternative solutions to Chairman Mao, and sometimes to other members of the top leadership, indicating her own preferences and recommendations. Of course, on major questions she has sought the authorization of and has abided by the decision of Chairman Mao. After a decision has been made, she has often been actively involved in its implementation as well as in the reappraisal of the decision in light of feedback information on the responses to, and impact of, the policy. In this fashion, Chiang Ch'ing has contributed to the formulation and implementation of major political, economic, social, educational, cultural, military, and foreign policies adopted in China. Over the past few decades, these have included the Hundred Flowers Movement, the Great Leap Forward, the Sino-Soviet split, the Socialist Education Movement, and the Great Proletarian Cultural Revolution.

Particularly since 1942, Chiang Ch'ing has spearheaded the

revolutionization of China's culture, especially in the performing arts. Her eight revolutionary works have been seen and evidently enjoyed by hundreds of millions of Chinese and, as a direct result of unprecedented mass dissemination of her works, the Thought of Mao Tse-tung appears to be more influential now than ever before. Chiang Ch'ing has not only exercised a decisive influence on the substance, content, and themes of art and literature, but also on the personnel of leading literary and cultural institutions themselves. She has made important contributions to revamping the educational system so as to conform with Maoist precepts, and has had a major impact on the mass media. Under her direction and inspiration, new Revolutionary Committees, literary and art units, and the armed forces have sent cultural troupes and propaganda teams to the factories, communes, schools, etc., primarily to encourage them to study and perform Chiang Ch'ing's model works but also to create new works based on hers. Novel literary, art, and cultural activities are being sponsored by cultural workers largely to disseminate Maoist culture, thus extending Chiang Ch'ing's overall influence.

Starting at the lowest echelons, Chiang Ch'ing began her Party work in the intelligence and propaganda organs and gained invaluable expertise in the inner workings and structure of the Party apparatus. As a result of the conviction shared by her and Mao—that the apparatus was leading China down the path to Soviet-style revisionism and was restoring capitalism—they decided in the mid-1960s to rectify the Party apparatus through the medium of the mass action, particularly as reflected in the Cultural Revolution. Following a drastic purge of the Party leadership, Chiang Ch'ing helped to establish new Revolutionary Committees throughout the country and to plan for the Ninth Party Congress. The novel features of the recent Constitutions reflect the great progress made toward achieving Maoist goals. Between the Ninth and Tenth Party Congresses, and also more recently, Chiang Ch'ing has been, among other things, actively restructuring the Party, revamping the other political institutions of China, building grass-roots support, and

Summary and Conclusion

helping to determine and implement China's national and international policies.

That Chiang Ch'ing does indeed play a prominent role in a wide variety of governmental affairs can also be seen by evaluating her contributions in other areas. She has, for example, been active in planning and promoting festivals and celebrations at both national and local levels, including the National Day celebrations (beginning in 1964), and the May Day celebrations (beginning in 1967). In international affairs, she has served as a principal contact with representatives and leaders from many parts of the world. Particularly since her election to the Politburo, she has had a role in formulating and shaping Chinese foreign policy.

During the Cultural Revolution, Chiang Ch'ing also became deeply involved in military politics. She was responsible for the removal of generals and commanders; overhauling the political and cultural departments of the armed forces; creating new "armies" of writers, artists, and critics; gathering and analyzing the facts on the "constantly developing revolutionary situation"; and in general issuing orders and directives under the name of the Central Cultural Revolution Group and the All-PLA Cultural Revolution Group. She had to cope with the multiple problems caused, in part, by resistance to civil authority on the part of powerful military leaders and military revisionists. Under her direction, military training conferences and conventions have been organized and conducted. Ideological education, including intensive study of her revolutionary works, has been given top priority. Political and cultural activities have been expanded within the armed forces to such an unprecedented extent that a model soldier, for example, is now expected to explain the history of the ideological and cultural struggle under Chiang Ch'ing's leadership and discuss Chiang Ch'ing's "important opinions," her works, and her contributions to the cause.

During the Great Proletarian Cultural Revolution, Chiang Ch'ing was in the vanguard, providing overall political leadership and coordinating the youth, the military, the press, and other organizational groups, plus other aspects of the movement as first deputy leader of the Central Cultural Revolution Group. It was under her supervision that most of the documents which launched and guided the mass movement were drafted and published. She delivered the major addresses at critical junctures of the Revolution, and traveled to different parts of the country to mobilize the masses. She gave them authoritative instructions and was able to settle disputes on the spot. She became youth's spokesman, Mao's spokesman, and the spokesman for the Central Cultural Revolution Group, the All-PLA Cultural Revolution Group, and the Maoist "proletarian headquarters."

Chiang Ch'ing's political influence was undoubtedly derived at first from Chairman Mao, but with her active, persistent revolutionary service since 1931, she has gradually become a political force in her own right. She appears to have acquired her own constituency in the military establishment, the Party hierarchy, the government bureaucracy, and the mass media, and in educational, literary and art circles, as well as among the youth, women, and "revolutionary masses" of China. She is admittedly a senior figure in an identifiable and important Maoist group which includes Politburo members Wang Hung-wen, K'ang Sheng, Li Teh-sheng, Chang Ch'un-ch'iao, Yao Wen-yüan, and Wang Tung-hsing. As a Politburo member since 1969, she has certainly shared in the exercise of authority over all the crucial areas of the Chinese political system.

Chiang Ch'ing's authority and influence stem from several sources. Her special status as the wife of Chairman Mao, her remarkable record of performance and achievements, and her relative youthfulness set her apart as a leading symbol of the Maoist "revolutionary successors." (She is about twenty years younger than most of the other members of the top Party leadership.) The widespread favorable comments in the press about her leadership, her indentification with popular needs and aspirations, her sustained commitment to the Maoist cause, and her leading and critical role in the Cultural Revolution, together with her many other contributions, appear to have won her

Summary and Conclusion

mass support and public confidence. Her broad, well-balanced, and solidly established base of support certainly suggests that she is an independent and important political force that must be taken into account. In short, Chiang Ch'ing has indeed acquired real authority in all its varied aspects discussed in the Introduction: the authority of ideas, formal and effective authority, the authority of confidence, the authority of prestige, and the authority of special assets.

Inevitably, the question arises as to what Chiang Ch'ing's future in the post-Mao Tse-tung era will be. It appears that there are six major possibilities, assuming there should be no unpredictable drastic change in the regime's environment, such as a serious domestic crisis or a major foreign war. The possibilities are: (1) a fall from power; (2) a figurehead role in the top leadership; (3) a genuinely important role as a member of a "collective leadership"; (4) a final-arbiter role, resolving disputes between contenders for power; (5) personal control over a nominally "collective leadership"; and (6) undisguised and supreme personal power. The evidence suggests that the most probable course of future development for Chiang Ch'ing lies within the range of the third, fourth, and fifth possibilities. The longer Mao lives and remains in power, the greater the opportunities for Chiang Ch'ing to increase her long-term overall strength, with Mao's blessing.

Reference Notes

INTRODUCTION

1. For background purposes, see John King Fairbank, *The United States and China;* Harold C. Hinton, *Communist China in World Politics;* Franklin W. Houn, *A Short History of Chinese Communism;* Chalmers A. Johnson, *Peasant Nationalism and Communist Power;* Franz H. Michael and George E. Taylor, *The Far East in the Modern World;* Nathaniel Peffer, *The Far East;* Benjamin I. Schwartz, *Chinese Communism and the Rise of Mao;* Richard H. Solomon, *Mao's Revolution and the Chinese Political Culture;* Richard C. Thornton, *The Comintern and the Chinese Communists, 1928-1931.*

CHAPTER 1

1. Chapters 1 and 2 are based in part on interviews with some of Chiang Ch'ing's old acquaintances, and with Chinese officers and staff members who dealt with her, and on intelligence sources. It is difficult to determine the precise birthdate of Chiang Ch'ing; the date used is an estimate. Chiang Ch'ing's original name is believed to be Luan Shumeng. She has also used other names—Li Yun-ho, Li Ch'ing-yun, Lan P'ing, and Li Chin.
2. Henrik Ibsen's *A Doll's House* was translated and published in *New Youth* in June 1918 (See C. T. Hsia, *A History of Modern Chinese Fiction, 1917-57.* New Haven: Yale University Press, 1961, p. 607).
3. Chen Chi-hua, *History of Chinese Films* (Peking, 1967).

Reference Notes

4. Mao Tse-tung, *On Literature and Art* (Peking, 1967).
5. *Kuangchou Hungchi*, December 29, 1967.
6. *China Reconstructs*, August 1967.
7. *Chu Yin Tungfanghung*, April 1968.
8. *Chingkangshan*, May 25, 1967.
9. *Kuangchou Hungchi*, December 29, 1967.

CHAPTER 2

1. *Popular Motion Pictures* (Peking, 1961).
2. See details and documentation in chapter 15.
3. *People's Daily*, May 20, 1951.
4. *Liberation Daily* (Shanghai), December 29, 1967.
5. Ibid.
6. *Keming Tsao Fan Pao*, May 15, 1966; *Selected Readings From the Works of Mao Tse-tung* (Peking, 1971), pp. 389 ff.
7. *Liberation Daily*, loc. cit
8. Ibid.
9. Mao, *Selected Readings*, p. 432, and intelligence sources.
10. Mao, *Selected Readings*, p. 476.
11. *Honan Daily*, August 2, 1958; *Hopeh Daily*, August 25, 1958; Anna Louise Strong, *The Rise of the People's Communes in China* (New York: Marzani and Munsell, 1960).
12. *Liberation Daily*, loc. cit.
13. Ibid.
14. *The Case of P'eng Te-huai: 1959-68* (Hong Kong: Union Research Institute, 1968); Chester Cheng, ed., *The Politics of the Chinese Red Army* (Stanford, Calif.: Hoover Institution, 1966).
15. *Liberation Daily*, loc. cit
16. See chapters 16, 22, and 23.
17. Kao Chu, "Open Fire On the Anti-Party, Anti-Socialist Black Line," *Liberation Army Daily*, May 8, 1966.
18. *People's Daily*, February 1, 1966
19. "Extracts from Kang Cho's Anti-Party, Anti-Socialist Materials," *Yang-cheng Wan Pao* (Canton), July 7, 1966.

20. *Asahi Shimbum* (Tokyo), July 2, 1964; *Chingkangshan*, May 27, 1967.
21. See chapter 18. Also see Richard H. Solomon, *Mao's Revolution and the Chinese Political Culture.*
22. See chapter 8.
23. *People's Daily*, May 11, 1967.
24. New China News Agency (NCNA), radio broadcasts; *People's Daily* and other Chinese sources (dates and pages are listed in the Selected Bibliography).
25. NCNA, June 28, 1967.
26. See note 24
27. NCNA, November 3, 1967.
28. Radio Nanchang, November 27, 1970.
29. Mao Tse-tung, "Women Have Gone to the Labor Front," introductory note, *The Socialist Upsurge in China's Countryside* (Peking, 1955), vol. 1.
30. *Hsinhua Daily*, March 8, 1971

CHAPTER 3

1. *Signal Fire on Tienshan*, January 24, 1968, and intelligence sources.
2. *Tungfanghung*, June 3, 1967.
3. *Signal Fire*, loc. cit.
4. See the Selected Bibliography.
5. *Signal Fire*, loc. cit.
6. *The Ninth National Congress of the Communist Party of China* (Peking, 1969).
7. Radio Peking, April 1, 1969; *Asahi Shimbun*, April 3, 1969.
8. Radio Peking, April 1, 1969.
9. NCNA, April 14, 1969
10. NCNA, April 25, 1969
11. NCNA, April 28, 1969
12. *The Ninth National Congress of the Communist Party of China* (Peking, 1969)
13. Ibid.

Reference Notes

14. Ibid.
15. Ibid.
16. Ibid.
17. NCNA, August 24, 28, and 30, 1974.

CHAPTER 4

1. *The Ninth National Congress of the Communist Party of China* (Peking, 1969). Also see additional information at the end of the chapter.
2. *Tungfanghung,* June 3, 1967
3. *Tzu-liao Chuan-chi,* November 17, 1967
4. Ibid.
5. *Chu-ying Tungfanghung,* April 1968
6. *Chingkangshan,* July 10, 1967
7. *Red Guards* (Peking), January 18, 1967; *Red Guard Rebels,* February 10, 1967
8. NCNA, August 24 to 29, 1973, and chapters 1, 2, and 10

CHAPTER 5

1. NCNA, October 3, 1966.
2. NCNA, May 1, 1967.
3. NCNA, May 2, 1967.
4. See NCNA reports of May 1, and September 30 of each year.
5. NCNA, October 1, 1971.
6. *Peking Review,* January 6, 1967.
7. Ibid.
8. Ibid.
9. NCNA, March 3, 1968
10. NCNA, April 13, 1968.
11. NCNA, January 11, 1972.
12. NCNA, March 30, 1972.
13. NCNA, July 13, September 5, and December 14, 1972; January 11 and 30, 1974

14. Ernest Barker, *Essays on Government* (Oxford: Clarendon Press, 1945), p. 6.

CHAPTER 6

1. *Red Flag:* 1970, vol. 5; 1969, vol. 12.
2. NCNA, January 11, 1967.
3. NCNA, January 15, 1967.
4. Ibid.
5. NCNA, June 20, 1967.
6. *People's Daily*, August 2, 1967.
7. NCNA, November 9, 1971.
8. NCNA, February 3, 1967; *People's Daily*, November 29, 1967.
9. *People's Daily*, October 6, 1967; NCNA, October 12 and 13, 1967; *China Reconstructs*, January 1968, p. 4.
10. NCNA, November 8, 1969; June 24, 1972.
11. NCNA, June 2, 1971
12. NCNA, June 4, 1971.
13. NCNA, June 9, 1971
14. NCNA, March 12, 1973
15. *People's Daily*, May 4, 1967
16. *People's Daily*, October 23, 1967.
17. NCNA, September 21, 1971.
18. NCNA, February 10 and December 8, 1973.
19. *People's Daily*, May 1, 1967.
20. NCNA, June 25, 1970.
21. *People's Daily*, June 28, 1970.
22. NCNA, June 29, 1970
23. NCNA, October 26, 1970
24. NCNA, December 5, 1971
25. NCNA, October 25, 1972; June 18 and 20, 1973.
26. *People's Daily*, July 5, 1970; NCNA, March 19, July 29, and October 29, 1972
27. NCNA, May 12, September 17, and November 24, 1971.
28. NCNA, November 22 and 26, 1971

Reference Notes

29. NCNA, May 12, September 18, and November 24, 1971.
30. NCNA, November 7, 1970.
31. *People's Daily*, December 20, 1966.
32. Radio Peking, March 19, 1968; NCNA, November 22, 1971.
33. NCNA, November 25, 1971.
34. NCNA, December 12, 1972; February 1 and 2 and June 7, 1973.
35. Radio Peking, February 11, 1967.
36. *The Current Digest of the Soviet Press*, vol. 20, p. 20.
37. *People's Daily*, November 7, 1967.
38. NCNA, August 5 and 10, 1968.
39. NCNA, September 19, 1972; December 8, 1973.
40. NCNA, July 22, 1968.
41. NCNA, February 21 and 27, 1974.
42. NCNA, April 17 and 22, 1972
43. *People's Daily*, August 13, 1968
44. NCNA, August 2 and 3, 1971
45. NCNA, September 3, 1971
46. NCNA, September 12 and December 7, 1973.
47. NCNA, January 1, 1971; October 11, 1972.
48. NCNA, December 23, 1971.
49. *People's Daily*, November 25, 1965.
50. *Peking Review*, April 3, 1970.
51. NCNA, February 16, 1972.
52. NCNA, February 19, 1972.
53. *People's Daily*, May 21, 1970.
54. NCNA, December 23, 1971.
55. NCNA, December 29, 1971.
56. NCNA, February 22, 1972.
57. NCNA, February 29, 1972.
58. NCNA, May 23, 1972.
59. NCNA, October 5 and 14, 1972.
60. NCNA, June 19, 1973
61. NCNA, July 17 and 19, 1973
62. NCNA, September 17, 1973
63. NCNA, October 19, 1973
64. *Peking Review*, June 9, 1967

65. NCNA, June 9, 1967.
66. NCNA, November 24, 1967
67. *Peking Review,* March 13, 1970.
68. *People's Daily,* March 18, 1968.
69. NCNA, December 23, 1969.
70. NCNA, November 16, 1971.
71. NCNA, August 25 and September 7, 1973.
72. *China Reconstructs,* April 1969.
73. Ibid.
74. *Peking Review,* January 1, 1967

CHAPTER 7

1. *Tungfanghung* (Shanghai), June 3, 1967.
2. Ibid.
3. *Great Victory for Chairman Mao's Revolutionary Line* (Peking, 1967), p. 16
4. *Tungfanghung,* June 3, 1967
5. Chiang Ch'ing, "Good Traditions of a Certain Company of the Red Army," *Chung-Kuo Chien-nien Pao* (Peking), August 26, 1961; *Fei-ching Studies* (Taiwan), November 1, 1963.
6. See note 5.
7. Radio Peking, April 20, 1967.
8. NCNA, April 20, 1967.
9. NCNA, September 16, 1967; *Peking Review,* September 13, 1968.
10. *East is Red* (Canton), September 21, 1967.
    This is explained and documented in subsequent chapters; see also the Selected Bibliography

CHAPTER 8

1. "Premier Chou En-lai Reports on the Work of the Government," *Peking Review,* January 1, 1965.
2. Ibid.

3. *Red Flag*, no. 9, 1967
4. NCNA, May 29, 1967.
5. NCNA, May 28, 1967.
6. Ibid.
7. NCNA, May 28, 1967.
8. Ibid.
9. Ibid.
10. Ibid.
11. Ibid.
12. NCNA, June 5, 1966.
13. NCNA, November 29, 1966.

CHAPTER 9

1. *Peking Review,* January 1, 1967.
2. *The Great Socialist Cultural Revolution in China* (Peking, 1968).
3. *Kuangming Daily* (Peking), March 27, 1967.
4. Ibid.
5. NCNA, March 2, 1967.
6. *Great Victory for Chairman Mao's Revolutionary Line* (Peking, 1967).
7. NCNA, April 22, 1967.
8. More details appear in chapters 10 to 13 and 18 to 20.

CHAPTER 10

1. *Tungfanghung,* June 3, 1967.
2. NCNA, July 22, 1967.
3. *Tungfanghung,* April, 1968.
4. Ibid.
5. "Towering Crimes of Ho Lung, Anti-Party Element and Army Usurper," *Peking Sports Front,* January 28, 1967.
6. *Collection of Documents Concerning the Great Proletarian Cultural Revolution* (Peking College of Chemical Engineering, May, 1967).

7. NCNA, January 12, 1967.
8. *Sankei* (morning edition, Tokyo), January 19, 1967.
9. AP Tokyo dispatch, quoted from Peking dispatch of *Keizai Shimbun*, September 6, 1967.
10. *The New York Times*, January 19, 1968.
11. *What's Happening on the Chinese Mainland?* (Taiwan, 1970), and intelligence sources.

CHAPTER 11

1. Minoru Shibata, *Sankei*, September 30, 1967.
2. *Chu Ying Tungfanghung*, April 1968.
3. Ibid.
4. Ibid.
5. *Chinese Communist Documents of the Great Proletarian Cultural Revolution* 1966-1967, pp. 410 ff.
6. NCNA, April 4, 1967; May 7, 1967.
7. *People's Daily*, July 23, 1967.
8. *People's Daily*, July 26, 1967.
9. *Public Security Combat News*, August 1, 1967.
10. Ibid.
11. Peking wall poster, December 25, 1966.
12. NCNA, December 17, 1967; *Chu Ying Tungfanghung*, April 1968.
13. NCNA, September 16, 1967
14. Ibid.
15. *Peking Daily*, September 17, 1967

CHAPTER 12

1. NCNA, March 9, 1968
2. French Presse Agence (Paris), April 9, 1968.
3. NCNA, August 7, 1967
4. Radio Shanghai, January 31, 1968
5. Radio Peking, January 31, 1968
6. Ibid.

Reference Notes

7. Radio Peking, January 31, 1968.
8. *Peking Review,* February 23, 1968.
9. Radio Peking, July 9, 1967.
10. NCNA, December 4, 1967.
11. Ibid.
12. NCNA, December 3, 1967.
13. *Wen-ko Tung-hsun* (Canton), no. 13, March 1968.
14. Radio Peking, January 25, 1969.
15. NCNA, December 3, 1967.
16. Radio Peking, August 12, 1968.
17. NCNA, December 5, 1967.
18. Radio Peking, August 12, 1968
19. NCNA, July 7, August 2, August 7, September 2, November 13, November 14, and December 3, all 1967; January 26, February 10, February 19, March 9, March 24, March 25, March 27, May 8, June 3, June 30, August 11, August 15, all 1968; and January 25, May 19, October 11, and October 14, 1969. *See also People's Daily* of February 20, August 8, and March 27, 1968; and *Peking Review* for March 15, and March 29, 1968.
20. *Current Scene* (Hong Kong), vol. 7, January 6, 1969.
21. *Tungfanghung,* April 12, 1967.
22. *Tungfanghung,* March 27, 1968.

CHAPTER 13

1. Radio Shanghai, January 31, 1968.
2. Radio Hofei, August 6, 1970.
3. Radio Nanking, November 28, 1970.
4. Radio Kunming, August 4, 1970.
5. Radio Canton, August 17, 1970.
6. Radio Nanking, October 29, 1970.
7. Radio Hofei, July 28, 1970.
8. NCNA, October 14, 1967.
9. NCNA, June 10, 1967.
10. Radio Foochow, December 1, 1970.

11. *Chinese Literature*, vol. 12, 1966, p. 127.
12. *Men Ho* (Peking, 1969).
13. Ibid.
14. NCNA, August 10, 1969.
15. Radio Hofei, August 12, 1970.
16. NCNA, October 29, 1970.
17. *Chinese Literature*, vol. 3, 1967, p. 8.
18. *The New York Times*, June 3, 1970.
19. May 10, 1970.
20. Radio Foochow, July 31, 1970.
21. Radio Nanching, July 31, 1970.
22. Radio Lhasa, August 13, 1970.
23. Radio Canton, October 29, 1970.
24. Radio Tsinan, August 14, 1970.
25. Radio Wuhan, October 8, 1970.
26. Radio Kunming, December 16, 1970.
27. NCNA, May 9, 1967.
28. Radio Changsha, May 25, 1968.
29. Radio Canton, August 18, 1970.
30. NCNA, July 31, 1967; June 30, 1968; July 1, 1968.
31. NCNA, July 31, 1972; September 15, 1973.
32. *People's Daily*, January 13, January 15, and February 4, 1967.
33. NCNA, January 12, January 15, February 3, and February 11, 1967; April 8, 1968; October 24, 1970.
34. NCNA, August 1, 1967.
35. NCNA, May 7, 1970.
36. *Red Flag*, December 1967.

CHAPTER 14

1. See *Selected Readings from the Works of Mao Tse-tung* (Peking, 1971); Chiang Ch'ing, *On The Revolution of Peking Opera* (Peking, 1968); and Mao Tse-tung, *On Literature and Art* (Peking, 1967)
2. Mao, *On Literature and Art*

Reference Notes

3. Ibid.
4. Ibid.

CHAPTER 15

1. Chiang Ch'ing, *On the Revolution of Peking Opera.*
2. *Literary Red Flag* (Peking, Ministry of Culture), November 13, 1967; also see sources listed in the Selected Bibliography.
3. *Kuangchou Hungchi,* December 29, 1967.
4. *Red Flag,* vols. 5 and 6, 1967; *People's Daily,* May 18, 1950.
5. *Quotations from Chairman Mao Tse-tung* (Peking, 1966).
6. *Red Flag,* vols. 5 and 6, 1967.
7. Ibid.
8. Ibid.
9. *Chinese Literature,* no. 7, 1967
10. Ibid.
11. May 20, 1951.
12. See Yao Wen-yüan, *On the Counterrevolutionary Double-Dealer, Chou Yang* (Peking, 1967).
13. *National Seminar on Communist China,* Ann Arbor, Michigan, October 30-November 1, 1964, pp. 1-6; and intelligence sources.
14. Intelligence sources; see also Selected Bibliography.
15. See chapter 16

CHAPTER 16

1. See sources for that period for which dates and pages are listed in the Selected Bibliography
2. "On the Counterrevolutionary Double-Dealer, Chou Yang," *Chinese Literature,* no. 3, 1967
3. *Cultural Revolution Bulletin,* no. 11, May 1967
4. *Chingkangshan,* May 15, 1967
5. See chapter 23 for a summary of the stories.
6. *People's Daily,* May 26, 1967

7. NCNA, June 1, 1967
8. *Chinese Literature*, vol. 11, 1967, and vol. 11, 1970.
9. See note 6.
10. "Chairman Mao's Talks at the Yenan Forum on Literature and Art is a Program for Building a Mighty Proletarian Cultural Army," by Chi Pen-yu, *People's Daily*, May 24, 1967.
11. Ibid.
12. *Chinese Communist Research Monthly Bulletin* (Taipei, Taiwan, 1968), vol. 2, issue 12
13. Ibid.
14. *People's Daily*, May 29, 1967
15. "Mao Tse-tung's Thought Illuminates the Revolutionary Line for Peking Opera," by the Revolutionary Commune of the Chinese Drama and Songs Research Institute, *Kuangming Daily*, June 5, 1967
16. *Chingkangshan*, May 25, 1967
17. Ibid.
18. Kung Chi, "History on Demonstrative Opera," *Wen Hui Pao* (Hong Kong), July 23, 1967.
19. *Asahi Evening News*, May 9, 1967
20. Kung Chi, loc. cit
21. *Chingkangshan*, May 25, 1967.
22. *People's Daily*, June 2, 1967; *Chinese Literature*, vol. 3, 1967.
23. See note 14.
24. *China Reconstructs*, January 1969; *Peking Review*, August 25, 1967.
25. *China Reconstructs*, September 1967
26. *Kuang-tung Wen-i Chan Pao*, July 5, 1967.
27. *People's Daily*, May 30, 1967; *Peking Review*, June 21, 1968.
28. "The Revolutionization of Peking Opera is a Great Victory for the Thought of Mao Tse-tung," *People's Daily*, May 24, 1967.
29. "Be a Pioneer in the Revolutionization of Peking Opera," *People's Daily*, May 11, 1967
30. "Make Revolution All My Life, Play Revolutionized Operas All My Life," *People's Daily*, May 11, 1967

31. "Long Live Chairman Mao's Brilliant Revolutionary Line on Literature and Art," *Red Flag*, May 27, 1967.
32. NCNA, June 5, 1967.
33. See note 26.
34. Kung Chi, loc. cit.
35. "Hail the Tremendous Victories in the Revolutionization of Peking Opera," *Red Flag*, no. 6, April 1967.
36. Chiang Ch'ing, *On the Revolution of Peking Opera* (Peking, 1967).

CHAPTER 17

1. *Peking Review*, no. 34, 1966.
2. *Liberation Army Daily*, December 10, 1966.
3. *People's Daily*, September 23, 1966.
4. *What's Happening on the Chinese Mainland* (Taiwan, 1970).
5. *Combat Bulletin of Doctrine of Mao Tse-tung*, no. 2, February 23, 1967.
6. See the Selected Bibliography.
7. Klaus Mehnert, *China Returns* (New York: E. P. Dutton & Co., 1972), p. 145.
8. Mehnert, op. cit., p. 138.
9. Mehnert, op. cit., pp. 144-45.
10. *Peking Review*, January 1, 1966.
11. Radio Shenyang (Liaoning), August 7, 1970.
12. "Bringing Socialist Culture to the Doorstep," *China Reconstructs*, July 1965, p. 20.
13. *Peking Review*, March 11, 1966; *Chinese Literature*, no. 11; Chou Kai, "Art Goes to the Villages," *Peking Review*, January 28, 1966.
14. See note 13.
15. Mehnert, op. cit., p. 143.
16. *China Reconstructs*, February 1968, p. 25.
17. Ibid.
18. *Chinese Literature*, 1970, p. 11.

CHAPTER 18

1. NCNA, June 6, 1966.
2. *Tungfanghung* (Shanghai), June 3, 1967.
3. Yao Wen-yüan, "On the New Historical Play *Hai Jui Dismissed from Office*," *People's Daily*, November 30, 1965; *Hungwei Chanpao*, December 29, 1965.
4. See note 3.
5. Wu Han, "Stories of Hai Jui," *Collected Works on Chinese History* (Peking, 1963), p. 15.
6. Yao Wen-yüan, loc. cit.
7. Wu Han, "Self-Criticism on Dismissal of Hai Jui," *People's Daily*, December 30, 1965.
8. NCNA, May 28, 1967.
9. *People's Daily*, May 9, 1966.
10. *Collection of Documents Concerning the Great Proletarian Cultural Revolution* (Peking, 1967).
11. Ibid.
12. *Liberation Daily*, May 10, 1966; *Wen Hui Pao*, May 10, 1966; *People's Daily*, May 9 and 11, 1966; *Wen Ke Tung Hsun*, May 18, 1966.
13. See note 12.
14. Neale Hunter, *Shanghai Journal* (New York: Praeger, 1969).
15. *Asahi Evening News*, May 9, 1967.
16. *People's Daily*, June 1, 1966; *Chingkangshan*, June 10, 1966; and intelligence sources.
17. *The Liberation Army Daily*, June 7, 1966; *Chingkangshan*, June 10, 1966; and intelligence sources.
18. *People's Daily*, June 8, 1966; *Chingkangshan*, June 11, 1966.
19. *China Reconstructs*, October 1966, pp. 6-10; *Peking Review*, August 19, 1966.

CHAPTER 19

1. *Current Background*, June 26, 1967, p. 3; see also the Selected Bibliography.

2. See note 1.
3. *Peking Review,* August 26, 1966.
4. NCNA, September 29 and 30, 1966.
5. NCNA, October 31, 1966.
6. A. Zhelokhovtsev, "The 'Cultural Revolution' Close Up (Notes by an Eyewitness)," Moscow, *Novy Mir (New World),* March 1968, pp. 181-213 (Translated from the Russian in *Joint Publications Research Service,* no. 45701, June 17, 1968, Washington, D.C.)
7. NCNA, December 3, 1966.
8. Anna Louise Strong, *Letter from China,* no. 41, September 20, 1966.
9. NCNA, December 3, 1966.
10. *People's Daily,* December 4, 1966.
11. In *Sankei,* October 6, 1967.
12. Ibid.
13. Peking wall poster, December 25, 1966.
14. *Peking Review,* January 1, 1967.
15. *People's Daily,* February 23, 1967.

CHAPTER 20

1. *Tungfanghung,* June 3, 1967.
2. *Sankei (Tokyo),* April 29, 1967; *Mainchi Shimbun,* February 6, 1967; *Chingkangshan,* January 23, 1967.
3. *Asahi Shimbun* (Tokyo), January 13, 1967; *Hung Tien Hsun,* March 27, 1968.
4. For examples, see NCNA for December 3, 1966, and *Sankei* for October 6, 1967.
5. *Kuang-chou Jih Pao,* December 27, 1966; *China Reconstructs,* vol. 16, March 1967, pp. 5-6; *Kuangming Daily,* March 27, 1967; NCNA, April 20 and September 16, 1967.
6. Mao Tse-tung Thought Workers Red Guards Corps Headquarters *Kuang-chou Jih Pao,* January 4, 1967.
7. "We Workers Will Not Be Deceived Again," *Red Guard Dispatch,* November 15, 1966.

8. Chiang Ch'ing's January 10 speech in *Red Guards* (Peking), January 18, 1967.
9. Ibid.
10. *Mainichi Shimbun*, February 6, 1967.
11. *Red Guards* (Peking), January 18, 1967.
12. *Mao Tse-tung's Doctrine Combat News*, February 3, 1967.
13. Ibid.
14. Ibid.
15. Ibid.
16. Ibid.
17. Ibid.
18. *Mainichi Shimbun*, February 6, 1967.
19. NCNA, January 20, 1967.
20. *People's Daily*, January 25, 1967.
21. *Truth Daily* (Hong Kong), January 21, 1967.
22. *People's Daily*, July 14, 1967.
23. NCNA, January 31, 1967.
24. NCNA, January 29, 1967.
25. NCNA, March 18, 1967.
26. NCNA, March 2, 1967.
27. French Press Agency, January 12, 1967.
28. Yao Wen-yüan, *Comments on Tao Chu's Two Books* (Peking, 1968).
29. NCNA, March 24, 1967.
30. *Collection of Documents Concerning the Great Proletarian Cultural Revolution* (Peking, 1967), pp. 163 ff.
31. *Collection of CCP Central Documents* (Peking, 1967).
32. *Red Rebel Journal* (Lhasa), June 11, 1967.
33. *Special Collection Materials* (Canton), July 1968.
34. *Tungfanghung* (Canton), September 21, 1967.
35. *People's Daily*, September 17, 1967.
36. Red Guard pamphlet, undated (photocopy seen in Hong Kong).
37. *Studies on Chinese Communism* (Taiwan), October, 1967, pp. 23 ff.
38. *Red Flag Correspondence*, January 11, 1968.
39. *Tokyo Shimbun*, August 3, 1967.

Reference Notes

40. *Hong Kong Tien Tien Daily*, February 18, 1968.
41. *Red Guard Guerrillas*, Bulletin no. 1, December 28, 1967.
42. *Asahi Shimbun*, January 13, 1967.
43. *Canton Cultural Revolution Bulletin*, March 1968.
44. Ibid.
45. Ibid.
46. Ibid.
47. *Newsweek*, April 1, 1968.
48. *Red Guard Rebel*, April 14, 1968.
49. *Hsing-Tao Jih Pao* (Hong Kong), September 3, 1968.
50. For other statistical data on casualties of the Cultural Revolution see: Charles Neuhauser, "The Impact of the Cultural Revolution in the Chinese Communist Party Machine," *Asian Survey*, vol. 8, no. 6, June 1968, pp. 466 ff.; Donald Klein, "The State Council and the Cultural Revolution," *The China Quarterly*, July-September, 1968, pp. 78-95; and Parris H. Chang, "Mao's Great Purge: A Political Balance Sheet," *Problems of Communism*, vol. 18, no. 2, March-April, 1969, pp. 1-10.
51. Ibid.
52. Peking Wall posters, March 1968 (photocopies seen in Hong Kong).
53. "Betrayal of Proletarian Dictatorship Is the Heart of the Book on 'Self-Cultivation,'" *Hungchi*, May 8, 1967.
54. Ibid.
55. "The Struggle Between the Two Roads in China's Countryside," *Hungchi* and *Liberation Army Daily*, November 23, 1967.
56. NCNA, May 28, 1967.
57. NCNA, May 3, 1967.
58. *Kuang-ming Jih Pao*, April 1967 and May 10, 1967; *People's Daily*, May 25, 1967.
59. Ibid.
60. Ibid.
61. *People's Daily*, May 8, 1967.

CHAPTER 21

1. See for example her September 7, 1968, speech in *Peking Review* for September 13, 1968.
2. NCNA, June 3, 1970.
3. Ibid.
4. January 15, 1971.
5. NCNA, June 9, July 1, October 11, and November 6, 1972.

CHAPTER 22

1. Chiang Ch'ing, *On The Revolution of Peking Opera* (Peking, 1968).
2. See Chiang Ch'ing's speeches in *China Reconstructs*, August 8, 1967 (entire issue); *Kuang-tung Wen-i Chan Pao*, July 5, 1967; NCNA, May 28, 1967; NCNA, December 3, 1966; *Kuang-Chou Jih Pao*, December 27, 1966; *Red Guards*, January 18, 1967; *Sing-tao Jih Pao*, March 26, 1967; *Kuangming Daily* (Peking), March 27, 1967; NCNA, April 20, 1967; *Great Preparatory Committee of People's Automobiles, Red Flag*, September 18, 1967; *Peking Review*, March 31, 1967, p. 11, and March 10, 1967, p. 5; *People's Daily*, April 21, 1967; NCNA, April 16, 1967; *Peking Review*, September 13, 1968, p. 8; *Peking Leaflet*, April 12, 1967; *China Reconstructs*, March, 1967, p. 5; NCNA, May 9, 1967; NCNA, September 16, 1967; *Hung Wei Ping*, December 6, 1966, p. 3; *Hung Wei Ping Pao*, December 22, 1966, p. 1; *Mao Tse-tung Doctrine Combat News*, February 23, 1967, pp. 1 and 3; *Hung Se Chih Kung*, January 29, 1967, p. 2; *Hung Pei Ying*, May 23, 1967, p. 2; *Hung I Chan Pao*, February 15, 1967, pp. 2-3; *Hsin Pei Ta*, January 20, 1967, p. 1, and January 24, 1967, p. 1; *Hsing Huo Liao Yuan*, January 27, 1967, p. 1; *Feng Lei*, May 22, 1967, pp. 1-2; *Hsi Chu Chan Pao*, May 21, 1967; *Chingkangshan*, February 11, 1967, p. 1; *Tungfanghung*, December 20, 1966, p. 1;

T'ieh Tao Hung Ch'i, January 20, 1967, p. 3; *Tsao Fan,* January 11, 1967, p. 4; *Tungfanghung,* December 17, 1967, p. 2; *Peking New Literary Gazette,* May 18, 1967; *Red Flag,* vol. 15, 1966, pp. 692-96; *Red Flag,* vol. 6, 1967, pp. 314-18. Also see her model works described in the next chapter and the notes for that chapter.

CHAPTER 23

1. *Taking Tiger Mountain by Strategy* (Peking, 1971). *China Reconstructs,* February 1970, pp. 38-44; March 1967, pp. 8-11. *Chinese Literature,* August 1967, pp. 129 ff.; June 1970, pp. 119-25; January 1971, pp. 58-59; and February 1971, pp. 86-94. *Peking Review,* January 15, 1971.
2. *People's Daily,* October 25, 1969.
3. *Chinese Literature,* January 1969, pp. 3-73. *Peking Review,* August 25, 1967, pp. 28-29. *China Reconstructs,* January 1969, pp. 40-44.
4. *Shachiapang* (Peking, 1972). *Chinese Literature,* November 1967, pp. 3-132; March, 1967, pp. 3-13; November 1970, pp. 63 ff. *Peking Review,* September 29, 1967, pp. 33 ff.
5. *Raid on the White Tiger Regiment,* Afro-Asian Writers' Bureau, 1967: *Chinese Literature,* October 1967, pp. 13 ff. and 59 ff. *Peking Review,* January 15, 1965, pp. 30 ff.; and June 21, 1968.
6. *The Red Lantern* (Peking, 1972). *China Reconstructs,* December 1965, pp. 35-38; October 1968, pp. 19-44; September, 1970, pp. 1-16. *Chinese Literature,* May 1968, pp. 98 ff. *Peking Review,* June 4, 1965, pp. 30-31; July 5, 1968, pp. 8-9; November 24, 1967, pp. 37 ff.; July 26, 1968, pp. 4-6; September 20, 1968, pp. 28-32; and February 12, 1971, pp. 20 ff.
7. "A True Portrait of the Chinese Working Class," *China Reconstructs,* September 1970.
8. *The Red Detachment of Women* (Peking, 1972). *Chinese Literature,* March 1967, pp. 9 ff.; January 1967, pp. 2 ff.

China Reconstructs, February 1965, pp. 20-24; October 1970, pp. 9 ff.; January 1970, pp. 2 ff. *Peking Review,* February 5, 1965, pp. 30-31; March 22, 1968, pp. 37 ff.; February 12, 1971, pp. 20 ff.
9. *The White-Haired Girl* (Peking, 1972). *Chinese Literature,* August, pp. 117-40. *China Reconstructs,* August 1966, pp. 28-50.
10. Jack Belden, *China Shakes the World* (New York: Monthly Review Press, 1970), pp. 210-11.
11. August 1966.

CHAPTER 24

1. See the Selected Bibliography.
2. NCNA, May 11, 1967.
3. Ibid.
4. October 24, 1967.
5. *Peking Review,* July 15, 1966.
6. *China Reconstructs,* September 1967.
7. *China Reconstructs,* January 1967.
8. Ibid.
9. Ibid.
10. Ibid.
11. Klaus Mehnert, *China Returns* (New York: E. P. Dutton & Co., 1972), p. 144.
12. Ibid., p. 141.
13. NCNA, June 16, 1967.
14. *Chinese Literature,* vol. 2, 1966.
15. *Chinese Literature,* vol. 4, 1967.
16. *China Reconstructs,* September 1967.
17. Mehnert, op. cit., p. 149.

Selected Bibliography

NOTE: Chinese language sources are listed in this bibliography under the title as it appears in the notes. Where the title is easy to translate into English, or was seen by the writer in English translation, it is listed under the English version of the title, unless it is widely known by its Chinese title. Where a Chinese language source is listed under its English translation, the notation "(c)" is added to indicate that the original is in Chinese. Where translation was difficult or inappropriate (as in the case of proper names), the title is listed under its original Chinese version in Wade-Giles romanization. In cases where the place of publication of a periodical neither forms part of its title nor is given afterward, it can be assumed that the place of publication does not appear on the copies of the periodicals that were consulted. The citations include sources containing direct quotations of Chiang Ch'ing's speeches and statements, even though they may not have been specifically annotated as such in this section.

PRIMARY SOURCES

1. Principal Newspapers, Broadcasts and Periodicals

Canton Kuang-chou Hung-szu. 1967. (c)
Chieh-fang-chun Wen-i (Liberation Army Literature and Art). Peking. (c)
China Pictorial. Peking.
   1966—vol. 1, pp. 43 ff.

1967—vol. 1, pp. 52-56; vol. 2, pp. 3-15, 35 ff.; vol. 3, pp. 22-27; vol. 7, pp. 4-25; vol. 9, pp. 14 ff.; vol. 11, pp. 32 ff.
1968—vol. 2, pp. 3-5; vol. 5, pp. 1 ff.; vol. 6, pp. 42-43; vol. 8, pp. 2-5; vol. 9, pp. 2-11; vol. 10, pp. 10-11; vol. 12, pp. 2-7.
1969—vol. 3, pp. 3-6; vol. 6, pp. 2-9; vol. 7, pp. 14-37.
1972—vol. 3-4, pp. 42-43.

China Reconstructs. Peking.

1965—February, pp. 20-24; July, pp. 20 ff.; August, pp. 20 ff.; December, pp. 35 ff.
1966—August, pp. 28-50; October, pp. 6-10, 11 ff., 26 ff.
1967—January; March, pp. 5 ff.; June, pp. 12 ff.; August, pp. 34 ff., 55 ff.; September, pp. 8-41; October, pp. 9-44; November, pp. 5 ff.; December, pp. 9 ff.
1968—January, pp. 41 ff.; February, pp. 18 ff.; April, pp. 27 ff.; June, pp. 35 ff.; July, pp. 1-5; November, pp. 5 ff.; December, pp. 9 ff.
1969—January, pp. 40-44 ff.; April; May, pp. 4 ff.
1970—February, pp. 38-44; September, pp. 1-16; October, pp. 9 ff.
1971—July, pp. 25 ff.; August, pp. 14 ff

China Youth (Chung-kuo Ching-nien Pao). May 1951; 1959. August 1961; 1967. (c)

Chinese Literature. Peking.

1965—vol. 2, pp. 127 ff.; vol. 5, pp. 3 ff., 98 ff.
1966—vol. 10, pp. 112 ff.
1967—vol. 3, pp. 3 ff.; vol.; 4, pp. 84-122; vol. 5 and 6, pp. 115 ff., 159 ff.; vol. 7, pp. 3 ff., 97 ff., 116-17, 118 ff.; vol. 8, pp. 118-25, 129 ff.; vol. 9, pp. 3-23; vol. 10, pp. 13 ff., 59 ff.; vol. 11, pp. 3-132.
1968—vol. 5, pp. 98 ff.; vol. 6, pp. 37 ff.; vol. 8, pp. 107 ff.; vol. 9, pp. 7 ff.; vol. 10, pp. 3 ff., 87 ff.; vol. 11, pp. 3-182; vol. 12, pp. 96 ff.
1969—vol. 1, pp. 73 ff.; vol. 2, pp. 99 ff.; vol. 3, pp. 85 ff.; vol. 4, pp. 75 ff.; vol. 10, pp. 59 ff
1970—vol. 1, pp. 3 ff. and 87; vol. 2, pp. 93 ff.; vol. 6, pp. 111-25; vol. 8, pp. 3 ff., 8 ff., 52 ff.; vol. 11, pp. 3 ff., 63 ff., 111 ff.

Selected Bibliography

1971—vol. 1, pp. 58-59, 81 ff.; vol. 2, pp. 86-94; vol. 9, pp. 99 ff.
Chinese Workers (Chung-kuo Kung-jen). 1958 (c)
Fukien Daily. July 31, 1970 (c)
Honan Daily. August 2, 1958. (c)
Hopeh Daily. August 25, 1958. (c)
Hopei Daily. August 2, 1954. (c)
Hsin Min Pao. 1950-53. (c)
Hsin Min Wan Pao. 1967. (c)
Hsinhua Daily (New China Daily). March 8, 1971. (c)
Hunan Daily. May 23, 1969. (c)
Kan Chin Pao. October 15, 1967. (c)
Kiangsi Jih Pao. 1967. (c)
Kuang-ming Jih Pao. April and May, 1967. (c)
Liberation Daily (Chieh-fang Jih Pao). Shanghai. May 10, 1966; May 8, 1966; June 7, 1966; December 10, 1966; November 23, 1967. (c)
Liberation Daily (Chieh-fang Jih Pao). Shanghai. May 10, 1966, December 27-29, 1967
Literary Gazette. April and May, 1951. (c)
New Anhwei Daily. May 29, 1968; July 28, 1970. (c)
New China News Agency (NCNA) (c)
  1966—June 5, 6; September 29, 30; October 31; December 3.
  1967—January 5, 9, 11, 12, 15, 16, 18, 20, 23, 24, 29, 30, 31; February 2, 3, 4, 11, 12, 21, 23; March 2, 20, 23, 24, 26; April 2, 4, 13, 14, 17, 18, 19, 20, 21, 22, 23, 25, 27, 28, 30; May 1, 2, 3, 5, 6, 9, 12, 14, 24, 28, 29; June 6, 9, 10, 11, 17, 21, 23; July 7, 8, 13, 22, 23, 26, 31; August 1, 2, 3, 5, 7, 8; September 1, 2, 3, 6, 16, 28; October 2, 13, 14, 24; November 2, 3, 7, 13, 14, 15, 25, 30; December 3, 4, 17.
  1968—January 26; February 10, 19, 20; March 3, 7, 8, 9, 12, 18, 19, 24, 25, 27; April 3, 4, 8, 9, 14; May 1, 2, 8, 9, 19, 21, 23, 29, 30; June 1, 3, 4, 22; July 1, 2, 11; August 6, 11, 12, 13, 14, 15, 16; September 10; October 1, 2, 3, 6, 28; December 4, 5, 8, 13
  1969—January 26; February 25; March 20; April 1, 3, 14, 25, 28; May 2, 19, 20, 23; July 29; October 7, 11, 12, 14, 15, 19, 26, 29; November 1, 2, 8; December 23.

1970—January 5, 10, 11, 15; February 8, 13; April 3, 8; May 2, 7, 8, 10, 11, 12, 21, 25; June 1, 3, 25, 28, 29; July 6, 7, 9, 28, 30; August 2, 7, 12; September 6; October 1, 2, 20, 24, 25, 26, 29, 30; November 7; December 16, 29.

1971—January 1; May 2, 12; June 2, 4, 9; August 1, 2, 4; September 4, 18, 21; October 2; November 9, 15, 16, 21, 22, 24, 25; December 5, 23, 29, 30.

1972—January 11; February 17, 20, 23; March 1, 20, 30; April 17, 22.

Peking Kuang Ming Jih Pao. 1950-53. (c)

Peking Review. Peking.

1965—January: 1, pp. 13 ff.; 15, pp. 30 ff. February: 5, pp. 30-31; 26, pp. 30 ff. March: 12, pp. 27-30; 19, pp. 23 ff. June 4, pp. 30-31. October: 1, pp. 30-31; 15, pp. 5-7.

1966—January 28, pp. 8 ff. March: 11, pp. 12-17, 31 ff.; 18, pp. 31 ff. May: 20, pp. 25-27; 26, pp. 3-42. June: 3, pp. 4-5; 9, pp. 17-23; 16, pp. 5-6, 15-18; 30, pp. 41 ff. July: 8, pp. 17 ff.; 15, pp. 3-15; 28, pp. 30-32. August: 5, pp. 7 ff.; 12, pp. 32-38; 19, pp. 4-8, 29-39; 26, pp. 3-22. September: 2, pp. 5-9, 17-26; 23, pp. 5-9. October: 7, pp. 3-9; 21, pp. 5-9. November: 11, pp. 6-9; 18, pp. 5-7. December: 2, pp. 6 ff.; 9, pp. 5-12; 23, pp. 19 ff.

1967—January: 1, pp. 4-32; 20, pp. 21-23; 27, pp. 7-9, 11-12. February 17, pp. 13 ff. March: 10, pp. 5-6; 24, pp. 6-9, 31, pp. 7-9, 11-14. April 28, pp. 5 ff., 10-21. May 5, pp. 6-9, 14-15, 29-30; 12, pp. 13-17, 28-29; 19, pp. 29 ff.; 26, pp. 18-20, 24-32, 37-41. June: 2, pp. 21-27; 9, pp. 16 ff.; 16, pp. 6-7; 23, pp. 5 ff.; 30, pp. 6 ff., 33-36. July: 7, pp. 33-35; 14, pp. 5-6. August: 11, pp. 11-13, 28-29; 25, pp. 28-29. September 29, pp. 32-33. October 6, pp. 5-8, 20-25; 27, pp. 6-7, 14 ff. November: 10, pp. 8-9; 17, pp. 5-6; 24, pp. 5-6, 36-37. December 8, pp. 5-6.

1968—January 3, pp. 7-8. February: 2, pp. 6-7; 9, pp. 5 ff. March: 15, pp. 6-8; 22, pp. 37-38; 29, pp. 5 ff. April 12, pp. 5 ff. May 3, pp. 5-8; 17, pp. 5-7; 24, pp. 5-7. June: 7, pp. 5-7; 21, pp. 5-6, 26-27; 26, 4-6; 28, pp. 3-4. July: 5, pp. 5-10; 25, pp. 10 ff., 32 ff.; 26, pp. 4-6. August: 9, pp.

Selected Bibliography

4 ff.; 16, pp. 5-8; 23, pp. 5-7. September: 13, pp. 5-8; 20, pp. 28-32. October: 4, pp. 7-19, 20 ff., 27 ff.; 11, pp. 3-4. November 1, pp. 11-14.

1969—January 31, pp. 5-7. April 30, pp. 47-49. May: 5, pp. 23-27; 16, pp. 9-12; 23, pp. 7-8. October 17, pp. 7-10. December 5, pp. 12 ff.

1970—March 13, pp. 12 ff. May: 8, pp. 5-7, 10-12, 29 ff.; 15, pp. 3-16; 23, pp. 10-14. June: 19, pp. 3-4; 26, pp. 3-4. July: 3, pp. 9 ff., 14-18; 10, pp. 5-6; 17, pp. 3-6; 24, pp. 3-4. August: 7, pp. 8-9; 21, pp. 3-4. September 30, pp. 4 ff. October 20, pp. 5-12. November 20, p. 5. December: 4, pp. 4-5; 25, pp. 6-9.

1971—January 15, pp. 19 ff. February 12, pp. 20 ff. March 26, pp. 9-11. May 7, pp. 6-9. July 2, pp. 27-28. October 8, pp. 3-5, 20 ff.

1972—February 25, pp. 6-9. March 14, pp. 4-8.

Peking Sports Front. January 28, 1967. (c)

People's Daily (Jen-min Jih Pao). Peking (c)

1949—November

1950—May 18.

1951—March 11. May: 16, p. 3; 20, pp. 1, 3, 5; 24, p. 1; 25, p. 3; 26, p. 3; 27, pp. 3-5; 29, p. 2; 30, p. 3; 31, pp. 2, 3. June: 1, pp. 2, 3; 3, pp. 5, 6; 4, p. 4; 5, pp. 1, 3; 6, pp. 2, 3; 8, p. 2; 10, p. 5; 14, p. 2; 15, pp. 2, 3; 16, p. 3; 17, p. 5; 18, pp. 2, 3; 19, p. 3; 20, p. 3; 21, p. 3. July: 23; 24; 25; 26; 27; 28.

1958—June 30. July 1.

1966—February 1; 6. April 24. May: 9; 16; 29. June: 1, 8; 15. August 19, p. 1. September: 1, p. 1; 12, p. 1; 16, p. 1; 23; 30, p. 1. October: 2, p. 3; 3, p. 2. November: 1, p. 1; 27, pp. 1, 3. December: 4, pp. 1, 2; 19, pp. 1, 2; 21, p. 1; 22, p. 6; 28, p. 6.

1967—January: 12, p. 4; 13; 15, pp. 1, 5; 16, p. 2; 25; 30, p. 6. February: 4, pp. 2, 3; 23, p. 1. March: 24, pp. 1, 3; 27, pp. 1, 3. April: 21, pp. 1, 2, 5; 25, p. 1; 27, pp. 1, 2; 28, p. 4. May: 1, p. 5; 2, pp. 1, 3-4; 5, p. 1; 8; 10, p. 1; 11, pp. 1, 2, 5; 12, p. 1; 13, p. 4; 24, pp. 1, 4; 25, 26; 29; 30.

June: 2; 11. July: 8, p. 1; 13, p. 1; 14; 22; 23, p. 1; 26, pp. 1, 13. August: 2; 3, p. 1; 5, p. 3; 8, p. 2. September: 3, p. 2; 10, p. 1; 17, p. 1; 18, p. 1; 19, p. 1; 28, pp. 1, 3. October: 2, p. 36; 14, p. 1; 23; 24, p. 1. November: 7; 14, p. 1; 15, p. 1; 25, p. 1; 26; 27; 29; 30, p. 1. December: 4, p. 1; 23.
1968—February: 1, p. 1; 20, pp. 1, 2. March: 18; 19, p. 1; 27, p. 1; April 14, p. 2. May: 2, pp. 1, 3; 9, pp. 1, 2; 21, pp. 1, 2. June 22, p. 1. August 6, pp. 1, 8; 12, pp. 1, 3; 14, p. 1; 16, pp. 1, 2. October: 1, p. 3; 2, pp. 1, 3, 5; 6, pp. 1, 2.
1969—January 26, p. 1. April 2, p. 2. May: 2, p. 2; 20, p. 1. October: 2, pp. 1, 3; 15, p. 1; 25. December 23, p. 1.
1970—April: 8, p. 1; 21. May 22, p. 1. June: 28, p. 2; 30, pp. 1, 5. July: 6, p. 1; 7, p. 1. October: 2, pp. 1, 3; 25; 30. November 7. December: 16; 29.
1971—January 15.

Radio Broadcasts. China. (c)

Radio Changsha. January 10, 1970.

Radio Chengchou, Honan. May 23, 1968.

Radio Foochow, Fukien. October 7, 1969; May 10, 1970.

Radio Hangchou, Chekiang. February 1, 1972.

Radio Harbin, Heilungkiang. September 6, 1970.

Radio Hofei, Anhwei, July 29, 1969; October 29, 1969; June 3, 1970.

Radio Kunming, Yunnan. July 6, 1970; December 16, 1970; March 2, 1971.

Radio Nanking. July 4, 1955.

Radio Peking. March 19, 1968; April 1, 1969; October 7, 1969; November 2, 1969; February 8, 1970; February 13, 1970; October 19, 1969; April 3, 1970; May 21, 1970; October 1, 1970.

Radio Shanghai. May 29, 1968; July 11, 1968; October 26, 1969; November 1, 1969; January 5, 1970; January 15, 1970; July 9, 1970; February 4, 1972.

Radio Shenyang, Liaoning. May 12, 1970; August 7, 1970.

Radio Tsinan, Shantung. December 29, 1970.

Radio Urumchi, Sinkiang. October 30, 1970.

Radio Wuhan, Hupeh. May 23, 1968; May 10, 1970; May 30, 1968.
Red Flag (Hung-chi). Peking. (c)
    1966—vol. 9; vol. 15, pp. 692-96.
    1967—vol. 5, pp. 239-53; vol. 6, pp. 314-22, 323-27, 692-96; vol. 8, pp. 428-33, 434-44, 448-55, 458-61, 468-72; vol. 9, pp. 531-37, 544-49, 553-59; vol. 11; vol. 12.
    1968—vol. 1, pp. 3 ff.; vol. 3, pp. 18 ff.
    1969—vol. 11, pp. 664-73; vol. 12.
    1970—vol. 5, pp. 393-402
Red Flag Correspondence. January 11, 1968. (c)
Shanghai Wen Hui Pao. May 21, 1951; May 29, 1968. (c)
Shanghai Ta Kung Pao. 1950-53. (c)
Special Reference Material Supplement. November 17, 1967. (c)
Ta Chung Tien Ying. 1950-53. (c)
Tien-ching Chinpu Jih Pao. 1950-53. (c)
Tien-ching Jih Pao. May 1951. (c)
Yang-cheng Wan Pao (Canton Evening Newspaper). Canton: July 7, 1966. (c)

2. Red Guard Sources (c)

Canton Cultural Revolution Bulletin. March 1968
Canton Hung-wei Pao. 1967.
Canton News in Brief (Kuangchou Chien Hsun). December 1967.
Canton Red Congress (Kuangchou Hung Tai Hui). April 15, 1968.
Canton Red Flag (Kuangchou Hung-chi). December 29, 1967.
Canton Red Guard Guerrilla Bulletin (Kuangchou Hungweiping Yeh Chan Pao). June 1, 1968.
Canton Red Guard Headquarters Reprint (Kuangchou Hungszu Fanyin). October 1967
Chan Pao (Combat Bulletin). March 1967
Cheng Fa Hungchi (Politics, Law Red Flag). October 17, 1967.
Chin Chun Pao. January 11, and May 1, 1967
Ching Chi Pi Pan. Peking: 1967

Chingkangshan. 1966: May 10; June 10, 11; December 20. 1967: January 7; February 11; May 15, 25, 27.

Chu Yin Tungfanghung (Chu Yin East is Red). October 1, 1967; April, 1968.

Combat Bulletin of Doctrine of Mao Tse-tung. February 23, 1967.

Collection of Documents Concerning the Great Proletarian Cultural Revolution. (Peking College of Chemical Engineering Collection). May 1967

Cultural Revolution Bulletin

Feng Lei. May 22, 1967

English Chinese Red Rebel Reprint Materials (Ying Chung Hung-she Tsao-fan-tuan Fan-yin Tsai-liao). April 14, 1968.

Film of Workers, Peasants, Soldiers (Kung, Nung, Ping, Tien Ying). April 13, 1967

Film Review (Tien Ying Pi Pan). May, 1967.

Film Revolution (Tien-ying Ke-ming). May 27, 1967

Great Preparatory Committee of People's Automobiles.

Hsi Chu Chan Pao (Hsi Chu Combat Bulletin). May 21, 1967.

Hsin Pei-ta (New Peking University). 1967: January 20, 24, 28.

Hsing Huo Liao Yuan. January 27, 1967.

Hung I Chan Pao. February 15, 1967.

Hung Pei Ying. May 23, 1967.

Hung Se Chih Kung. January 29, 1967.

Hung Tien Hsun (Red Cable Dispatch). March 27, 1968.

Hungwei Chan Pao (Red Guard Combat Bulletin). 1965: December 29. 1966: November 16; December 17, 19, 30. 1967: January 4, 8, 10; March 27

Hung-wei-ping (Red Guards). December 6, 1966.

Hung-wei-ping Pao (Red Guard News). December 22, 1966.

Huo Chu Tung Hsun (Fire Torch Dispatch). June 3, 1968.

Jen Ta San Hung. May 25 and May 27, 1967.

Ke-ming Kung Jen Pao (Revolutionary Workers' News). January 4, 1967.

Ke-ming Lou. March 10, 1967.

Ke-ming Tsao Fan Pao (Revolutionary Rebel Bulletin). May 15 and December 9, 1966.

Ko-ming Kung Jen Pao (Revolutionary Workers). January 4 and 12, 1967.
Kuangchou Hungchi (Kuangchou Red Flag). December 29, 1967.
Kuangchou Jih Pao (Kuangchou Daily). December 27, 1966; January 4, 1967.
Kuang Ming Daily (Kuang Ming Jih Pao). Peking: March 27 and June 5, 1967; March 20, 1969.
Kuang Yin Hungchi (Kuang Yin Red Flag). October 29, 1957.
Kung An Chan Pao (Public Security Combat Bulletin). August 1, 1967.
Kung Jen Tsao Fan Pao (Workers Rebel News). December 15, 1966; March 13, 1967.
Kuangtung Printing Red Flag. October 29, 1967.
Kuangtung Wen I Chan Pao (Kuangtung Literature and Art Combat Bulletin). July 5, 1967
Literature and Art Combat Bulletin (Wen Yi Chan Pao). March 9, 1968.
Literary Combat Bulletin (Wen Hsueh Chan Pao). March 23, 1967.
Literary Gazette.
Mao Tse-tung Doctrine Combat News
News Warrior. November 22, 1966.
Pei Hang Hungchi (Pei Hang Red Flag). January 20, 1967.
Peking Cheng Fa (Peking Politics and Law). 1967.
Peking Hung-wei-ping (Peking Red Guards). 1967.
Peking New Literature and Art (Peking Hsin Wen Yi). June 8, 1967.
Peking New Literary Gazette. May 18, 1967.
Peking Wall Posters. December 25, 1966.
Peking Workers (Peking Kung Jen). May 20, 1967.
Red Cable Dispatch (Hung Tien Hsun). March 27, 1968.
Red Guards. Peking: January 18, 1967.
Red Guard Dispatch. November 15 and 18, 1966.
Red Guard Guerrillas Bulletin. December 28, 1967.
Red Rebels. April 14 and 27, 1968
Red Guard Tsinghua University Chingkangshan. January 7 and May 18, 1967

Red Lantern Newspaper (Hung Teng Pao). September 22, 1964; May 20, 1967.
Red Rebel Journal. Lhasa: June 11, 1967.
Red Review (Hung Se Pi Pan Pao). May 24, 1967.
Signal Fire on Tienshan. January 24, 1968.
Special Collection Materials. Canton: July, 1968.
Tieh Tao Hungchi (Railroad Red Flag). January 20, 1967.
Ti-Yu Chien Shao (Sports Vanguard). March 27, 1967.
Ti-Yu Pao (Sports News). 1968.
Tsao Fan (Rebel). January 11, 1967
Tungfanghung (East is Red). Canton: May 23 and September 21, 1967.
Tungfanghung (East is Red). Peking: 1967: May 23, June 3, and December 17
Tungfanghung (East is Red). Shanghai: 1967: January 19; June 3, 13; September 19, 21.
Tzu-liao Chuan-chi (Special Collection of Materials). November 17, 1967.
Wen Hua Hsien Feng (Literary Vanguard). March 6, 1967
Wen Ke Tung Hsun. 1966-68.
Wen Yi Pao (Literature and Art News). 1967.
Wen Yi Hungchi (Literature and Art Red Flag). May 30, 1967; January 10, 1968.
Wen Yi Ke-ming (Literature and Art Revolution). June 2, 1967.
Wu Pa (Five-Eight). February, 1968.

3. Other Mainland Chinese Sources

NOTE: Except where otherwise indicated, the publisher is Jen-min Ch'u-pan She (People's Publishing House).

Chiang Ch'ing. *On the Revolution of Peking Opera*. Peking: 1967. (c)
Chen Chi-hua. *History of Chinese Films*. Peking: 1967. (c)
Collection of CCP Central Committee Documents. Peking: 1967. (c)
Collection of Documents Concerning the Great Proletarian Cultural Revolution. Peking: 1967. (c)

Selected Bibliography

The Great Proletarian Cultural Revolution. Peking: 1967. (c)
Great Victory for Chairman Mao's Revolutionary Line. Peking: 1967. (c)
Mao Tse-tung. *On Literature and Art.* Peking: 1967. (c)
Men Ho. Peking: 1969. (c)
The Ninth National Congress of the Communist Party of China. Peking: 1969. (c)
Popular Motion Pictures. Peking: 1961. (c)
Quotations from Chairman Mao Tse-tung. Peking: 1966. (c)
Raid on the White Tiger Regiment. Afro-Asian Writers' Bureau: 1967.
Red Detachment of Women. Peking: 1972. (c)
Red Lantern. Peking: Foreign Languages Press, 1972.
Selected Readings from the Works of Mao Tse-tung (Mao Tse-tung Hsüan Chi). Peking: 1971. (c)
Shachiapang. Peking: Foreign Languages Press, 1972.
Taking Tiger Mountain by Strategy. Peking: Foreign Languages Press, 1971.
The White-Haired Girl. Peking: Foreign Languages Press, 1972.
Wu Han. "Stories of Hai Jui." *Collected Works on Chinese History.* Peking: 1963. (c)
Yao Wen-yüan. *Comments on Tao Chu's Two Books.* Peking: 1968. (c)
Yao Wen-yüan. *On the Counter-Revolutionary Double-Dealer Chou Yang.* Peking: 1967. (c)
Translations of Mainland Publications
Current Background. Hong Kong: American Consulate General.
Joint Publications Research Service. Washington, D.C.
Selections from China Mainland Magazines. Hong Kong: American Consulate General.
Survey of China Mainland Press. Hong Kong: American Consulate General

SECONDARY SOURCES

4. Non-Mainland Chinese Newspapers and Periodicals

Central Daily. Taiwan. (c)

Fei-ching Studies. Taiwan. (c)
Hong Kong Kuai Pao. (c)
Hong Kong Chen Pao. March 13, 1967; February 9, 1968. (c)
Hong Kong Hsin Pao. January 10, 1969. (c)
Hong Kong Hsing Tao Jih Pao. 1968: January 15, 19, 20, 28; March 22; May 6; September 3, 26. (c)
Hong Kong Hsing Tao Wan Pao. 1967: January 12; June 27; July 14. 1968: September 26.
Hong Kong Ming Pao. May 15, 1967. January 27, 1968. February 5, 1969. (c)
Hong Kong Tien Tien Daily. February 11, 1967. 1968: February 13, 18; September 12. (c)
Hong Kong Times. 1967: May 24; July 4. 1968: January 19, 20-29; September 15. 1969: April 10. (c)
Hong Kong Wen Hui Pao. (c)
Hsin Sheng Pao. Taiwan. (c)
Issues and Studies. Taiwan. (c)
Mainland Today. Taiwan: July 1, 1966. 1969: April and May. (c)
New Kwangsi Daily. Manila: May 20, 1968. (c)
Overseas Daily. Hong Kong: August 20, 1967. (c)
Republic of China Research Institute. *Chinese Communist Research Monthly Bulletin.* Taiwan: Republic of China Research Institute. (c)
Sing-tao Wan Pao. Hong Kong: March 26, 1967. (c)
Studies on Chinese Communism. Taiwan. (c)
Ta Kung Pao. Hong Kong. November 1, 1951. (c)
Truth Daily. Hong Kong: January 21, 1967. (c)
Tsu Kuo (China Monthly). Hong Kong. (c)

5. Other Newspapers and Periodicals

Asahi Evening News. Tokyo: May 9, 1967.
Asahi Shimbun. Tokyo: July 2, 1964. 1967: January 13; April 18, 26; July 24. April 3, 1969
Asian Survey. Berkeley, California
Chin News Analysis. Hong Kong
China Mainland Review. Hong Kong

Selected Bibliography

China Quarterly. London. July-September 1968.
Current Scene. Hong Kong.
Far Eastern Economic Review. Hong Kong.
Foreign Press Digest. November 7, 1967.
French Press Agency. April 9, 1958. 1967: January 12, May 14. August 12, 1970.
Keizai Shimbun. Tokyo: September 6, 1967. April 8, 1968.
Kyodo Japanese Press Agency. Tokyo: April 6, and June 12, 1967.
Mainichi Shimbun. Tokyo: January 21, 22; February 6, 1967.
Newsweek. U.S.: April 1, 1968; February 18, and March 4, 1974.
The New York Times.
  1966: September 11; December 5, 6, 11, 27.
  1967: January 13, 16, 21, 22, 24, 27; February 3, 16; March 16, 28; April 19; May 10, 11, 30; June 2, 8; July 24; September 1, 18, 22; December 16
  1968: March 27; April 19, 26; May 3, 7, 9; June 3, 25; July 2, 3; September 11, 22; October 6
  1969: April 2, 13, 25; July 2, 13; September 21, 25; October 1, 6, 16, 19
  1970: February 8; June 3, 26; September 8
Nihon Keizai. Tokyo: 1967: January 10; April 20, 23.
Problems of Communism. Washington, D. C.: March-April, 1969.
Radio-Japan. January 23, 1967
Sankei. Tokyo: 1967: January 19; April 29; May 18; September 2, 3; October 6
Strong, Anna Louise. *Letters From China.* Peking: September 20, 1966.
Tokyo Shimbun. 1967: May 23; August 3, 6.
The Washington Post. Washington, D.C.
Yomiuri. Tokyo: February 4, 1967

6. Books and Monographs

Asia Research Centre. *The Great Cultural Revolution in China.* Tokyo: Charles E. Tuttle Co., 1968.
Barnett, A. Doak. *China After Mao.* Princeton, N.J.: Princeton University Press, 1967

Baum, Richard and Bennett, Louise B., eds. *China in Ferment.* Englewood Cliffs, New Jersey: Prentice Hall, 1971.

Belden, Jack. *China Shakes the World.* New York: Monthly Review Press, 1970

Bulletin of the Atomic Scientists. "China After the Cultural Revolution." New York: Random House, 1969.

The Case of P'eng Te-huai, 1959-68. Hong Kong: Union Research Institute, 1968. (c)

Chang, Parris H. *Radicals and Radical Ideology in China's Cultural Revolution.* New York: Columbia University Press, 1973.

Cheng, Chester, ed. *The Politics of the Chinese Red Army.* Stanford, Calif.: Hoover Institute, 1966.

Chiang, Kan Pin. *Chiang Ching Te Chou Shih Yu Yen Wen.* Hong Kong: Yu Chou Chu Pan She. (c)

Chung, Hua-min, and Miller, Arthur. *Madame Mao, A Profile of Chiang Ching.* Hong Kong: Union Research Institute, 1968.

Hinton, Harold C. *China's Turbulent Quest.* New York: Macmillan Company, 1970.

Hinton, Harold C. *Communist China in World Politics.* New York: Houghton Mifflin Company, 1966.

Hsiung, James Chieh. *Ideology and Practice: The Evolution of Chinese Communism.* New York: Praeger Publishers, 1970.

Hunter, Neale. *Shanghai Journal: An Eyewitness Account of the Cultural Revolution.* New York: Frederick A. Praeger, 1969.

Mehnert, Klaus. *China Returns.* New York: E. P. Dutton & Co., 1972.

Robinson, Thomas W., Baum, Richard, et al *The Cultural Revolution in China.* Berkeley and Los Angeles: University of California Press, 1971.

Sidel, Ruth. *Women and Child Care in China.* New York: Hill and Wang, 1972,

Snow, Helen Foster. *Women in Modern China.* Paris: Mouton and Co., 1967

Solomon, Richard H. *Mao's Revolution and the Chinese Political*

Selected Bibliography

Culture. Berkeley and Los Angeles: University of California Press, 1971.

Strong, Anna Louise. *The Rise of the People's Communes in China*. New York: Marzani and Munsell, 1960.

Ting, Wang. *Chiang Ching Chien Chuan*. Hong Kong: Contemporary Chinese Research Institute, 1967. (c)

What's Happening on the Chinese Mainland. Taiwan: 1970.

Wilson, Dick. *The Long March, 1935*. New York: The Viking Press, 1971

Index

Africa, 41, 43, 117, 153
Afro-Asian Table Tennis Friendship Invitational Tournament, 46
Afro-Asian Writers' Bureau, 44
Ah Chia, 100, 135
Air Force (Chinese), 66, 76
Aishwarya, Queen (Nepal), 41
Albania, 34, 37-38, 46
Algeria, 41
All-China Students Federation, 140
All-China Youth Federation, 140
All-PLA Cultural Revolution Committee, 17, 65, 69, 73-75, 83, 133, 175-76
American Progressive Students Delegation, 43
Anhwei, 71
Anhwei Revolutionary Committee, 17
Anti-Chemical Corps, 76
Armed Forces (Chinese). *See* People's Liberation Army
Armored Force, 66, 76
Artillery Corps, 66, 76
Asia, 37-38, 43, 117, 153
Australia, 45-46
Australian Communist Party, 45
Autumn Export Commodities Fair (Canton), 46
Awakening of a Farmer, 6

Belden, Jack, 163
Birch, Reginald, 42
Birenda, King (Nepal), 41
Blood Flowing on Lang Shan, 5

Borrowing a Wife, 139
Boumediene, President Houari (Algeria), 41
Boxer Rebellion, 92
British Communist Party, 42
Burma, 34, 46

CCP. *See* Chinese Communist Party
Cambodia, 39-40, 46
Cambodian Order of Independence, 39
Canton, 18, 46, 51, 82, 132, 135
Ceausescu, President Nicolae (Romania), 38
Central Cultural Revolution Group, 20, 22, 35-37, 65-66, 69, 133-35, 175-76
Central Nationalities Music Ensemble, 108
Central Philharmonic Society, 60
Central Song and Dance Ensemble, 60
Chang Ch'un-ch'iao, 17, 21, 27, 29, 55, 113, 176
Chang Jih-ching, 73
Chang Keng, 97, 100-1
Chang Szu-teh, 34
Chang Tung-chuan, 135
Changsha, 82
Chao Chen-ti, 165
Chao Yang Ditch, 100
Chao Yung-fu, 132
Chaochou County Revolutionary Committee, 74
Chekiang, 18, 136

Ch'en I, 35, 129
Ch'en Pai-hsin, 128
Chen Po, 130
Ch'en Po-ta, 4, 124
Ch'en Tsai-tao, 69-70
Chen Yung-kuei, 166
Ch'eng Ch'ien, 35
Cheng Ming-yuan, 71
Chengtu, 131
Chi Pen-yu, 118
Chi Village, 18
Chi Yen-ming, 97
Chia-ch'ing, Emperor, 56
Chiang Kai-shek, 90, 149
Chien-hsien, 116
Chile, 46
China, People's Republic of, 3, 6, 11-14, 20, 27, 32-34, 37-38, 41-47, 65-66, 91, 94, 97, 100, 107-8, 114, 119, 137, 140, 146, 152-53, 167, 174, 176. *See also* Chinese Communist Government
China Peking Opera Institute, 100
China Reconstructs, 164
Chinese Communist Government. *See also* China, People's Republic of
  Ministry of Culture, 10, 59, 95, 125
  National Defense Council, 35, 66
  Standing Commitee of the National People's Congress, 35
  State Council, 70, 119, 133, 136
  Supreme People's Court, 70, 136
  Supreme State Conference (1957), 13
Chinese Communist Party (CCP), 4, 6, 9-10, 14, 17, 23, 28, 31, 35, 39, 55-56, 83, 106, 126, 133, 136, 169, 173-74, 176
  Central Committee, 12, 20-22, 30, 35-36, 42, 55, 59, 72, 95, 106, 113, 116, 118-20, 122, 133, 135-36

Constitution, 12, 20-23, 174
Eighth Congress, 12
Eleventh Plenary Session of the Eighth Central Committee, 116, 120
Military Affairs Committee, 35, 66-67, 70, 83, 113, 133
Military Commission, 14, 20, 51, 64, 81
Ninth Congress, 20-22, 27, 84, 174
Politburo, 12, 23, 28, 30, 36, 47, 64, 84, 136
Presidium, 21, 23
Propaganda Department, 59, 92, 106, 120, 125
Secretariat, 12, 20, 37, 135
Tenth Congress, 23, 30, 84, 174
Tenth Plenum of the Eighth Central Committee, 15, 55
Chinese Delegation to the UN, 42
Chinese Embassy (Moscow), 41
Chinese-Japanese War
  1894, 91, 167
  1937, 6, 8
Chinese People's Volunteers, in Korean War, 39, 157-59
Chinese Stage Songs Research Institute, 100
Chinese Writers Association, 139
Ch'ing Dynasty, 147
Ching-kang-shan, 94
Chou En-lai, 4, 8, 27, 29-30, 35, 39, 42-45, 51, 53, 55, 62, 65-66, 68, 70-71, 79, 84, 97, 102, 125, 135-36
Chou T'ai-mo, 3, 4
Chou Yang, 16, 92-93, 97, 100-2, 106, 120, 139
Ch'u Ch'iu-pai, 4
Chu Yu-sung, 109
Chucheng, 3
Chun Ching, 81
Chunking, 6
Columbia, 46

Index

Comic Marriage, A, 139
Communist Party. *See* individual listings
Communist Youth League, 140
Confucius, 3
Congo, Republic of, 34, 46
Cultural Revolution. *See* Central Cultural Revolution Group; Great Proletarian Cultural Revolution

Doll's House, A, 3
Downtrodden People, The, 6

Early Spring in February, 94
East China People's Art Theatre, 139
East China Sea Fleet, 76
Egypt (United Arab Republic), 46
Emperor and the Waitress, The, 91
Europe, 43
Experimental Drama League, 101

Fang Ming, 75
Fang Pei-fu, 168
Farah, Empress (Iran), 41
Festival of Peking Opera, 104-5
Fighting on the Plains, 34, 40
Foochow, 131
Forum on Literature and Art in the Armed Forces, 17, 33, 56, 115
Forum on Short Novels, 16
France, 46
French Communists, 42
Frontline, 96
Fukien, 131

Gobi Desert, 61
Great Hall of the People, 37, 79
Great Leap Forward, 13, 15-16, 19, 96, 109, 114, 117, 173
Great Proletarian Cultural Revolution (GPCR), 13, 16, 18, 22, 28-30, 36, 52-78, 84, 105-6, 113-22, 124, 126, 128, 135-36, 140-41, 173, 175
Group of Five in Charge of the Cultural Revolution, 113, 115, 118
Guinea, 46

Hadden, Richard and Frances, 44
Haguruma Theatre (Japan), 39
Hai Jui Dismissed from Office, 15-16, 55-56, 96, 113
Hai Yen, 81
Hainan Island, 101, 161
Han and Yen, 5
Hanoi, 37
Harbin Municipal Revolutionary Committee, 74
Heilungkiang, 18, 132
Hill, Cheryl, 43
Hill, E. F., 45
Ho Chi Minh, 40
Ho Hsiang-ning, 35
Honan, 13, 18, 100
Hong Kong, 28, 102
Hopei, 13, 80
How to Be a Good Communist, 137
Hsi Shun-ta, 169
Hsia Yen, 93, 106, 139
Hsiao Hua, 66
Hsieh Chang-hou, 59
Hsieh Fu-chih, 35, 69, 135
Hsinhua News Agency. *See* New China News Agency
Hsu Hsiang-chien, 66
Hsu Kuang-ping, 35
Hu Ch'iao-mu, 92
Hu Shih, 87
Hu Tsung-nan, General, 8
Huang Pei-yuan, 165
Huang Yung-sheng, 66
Hunan, 18, 76
Hunan Revolutionary Committee, 71
Hundred Flowers Movement, 13, 173
Hung Wen, 81

Hupei, 18

Ibsen, Henrik, 3
Ideals, Integrity and Spiritual Life, 132
India, 41, 76
Indochina, 43
Indonesia, 34, 39, 46
Inner Mongolia, 108
Inside Story of the Ch'ing Court, 10, 91-92
Iran, 41
Italian Communist Party, 42
Ivens, Joris, 42

January Revolution, 126, 128
Japan, 6, 8, 38-39, 46, 51, 99
Japan-China Friendship Association, 38
Japanese, 4-6, 8, 37-39, 69, 90, 97, 100, 125, 149, 155, 159-61
Japanese Communist Party, 39
Jerquet, Jacques, 42
Journal l'Humanite Rouge, 42

K'ang Sheng, 4, 6, 30, 124, 176
Kaunda, President Kenneth (Zambia), 41
Kiangsi, 19, 131
Kiangsu, 12, 18
K'o Ching-shih, 152
Korea, 39, 46, 104, 158
Korean War, 39, 104, 157
Khrushchev, Nikita, 12, 137
Kuan Feng, 118
Kuang-hsu, Emperor, 91-92
Kunming, 82
Kunshun, 12
Kuo Mo-jo, 44, 93
Kuomintang, 149
Kwangsi, 18, 79
Kwangtung, 18, 168
Kweichow, 18, 131
Kweiyang, 82

Lan P'ing, 5
Laos, 46
Latin America, 43, 117, 153
Le Duc Tho, 40
Lhasa (Tibet), 82
Li Cheng-tao, 44
Li Chin, 93
Li Hsien-nien, 27, 30
Li Hsueh-feng, 59, 124
Li Pao-hua, 71
Li Shao-chun, 135
Li Ta, 118
Li Ta-chang, 4, 51
Li Teh-sheng, 17, 30, 51, 53, 66, 176
Li Yu-ho, 100
Liao Mo-sha, 116
Liaoning Daily, 108
Liberation Army Daily, 57, 78, 116, 118-19
Lien Wah Film Company, 4
Life of Wu Hsun, 10, 92-93
Lin Mo-han, 97, 100-2, 106
Lin Piao, 14, 23, 29-30, 33-34, 45, 56, 59, 62, 66-67, 70, 84, 136
Lin's Shop, 94
Little Heroic Sisters on the Grassland, 104
Liu, Chih-chien, 59, 65, 129
Liu Hsiu-shan, 71
Liu Shao-ch'i, 11-12, 14-15, 91-92, 95-96, 101, 116, 119-20, 126, 130, 132, 136-39
Liu Shao-wen, 62
Liu-teng, 68
Liuchung Commune, 19
Lo Jui-ch'ing, 65, 125
Long March, 62
  Detachments, 126
Loridan, Merceline, 42
Lu Cheng-ts'ao, 129
Lu Hsun, 39, 124
Lu Hsun Academy of Arts, 6, 163
Lu P'ing, 118
Lu Ting-yi, 65, 92, 104, 125

Index

Lu Yen-hua, 109
Lushan Conference, 14

Mali, 34
Mansudae Troupe (Japan), 39
Mao Hsiao-li, 57, 78, 115
Mao Tse-tung, 6-16, 21-22, 28, 30, 33-36, 41-47, 51, 56-62, 67, 77, 82, 84, 87, 89-90, 92-93, 95-96, 99, 102, 108, 113, 115, 120, 123-24, 130, 134, 136, 138-39, 157-59, 169, 173, 176
Maoist influence, 9, 14-21, 30, 32, 46-47, 55, 57-59, 62, 64, 68-71, 73, 75-78, 84, 87-88, 90, 106, 108-9, 115, 118-20, 127-29, 131-41, 147, 149-50, 153, 155, 157-59, 164, 169, 173-74, 176
Marxism-Leninism, 4, 42, 45, 58, 65, 89
Matsuyama, Makiko, 39
Mauritius, 46
May Day, 32-34, 175
Mehnert, Klaus, 107, 109, 167, 169
Mei Lan-fang, 10, 91
Men Ho, 80
Mencius, 3
Mexico, 46
Ming Dynasty, 114-15
Money Is the Thing, 139
Museum of Chinese Art, 109

Nanchang, 82, 131
Nanking, 6, 79
National Day, 32-34, 175
National Liberation Front of South Vietnam, 40
National Peking Opera Theatre, 60
National Salvation Theatrical Troupes, 6
Navy (Chinese), 66, 76
Nepal, 41, 46
New China News Agency (NCNA), 59-60, 62, 72, 74, 76, 81, 140
New York Times, 66, 81
New Zealand, 34
New Zealand Communist Party, 45
Nouyen Duy Trinh, 40
Nieh Yuan-tzu, 118
Nigeria, 46
Nightless City, 94
Nixon, President Richard M. and Mrs., 43-44
North Korea (Democratic People's Republic of Korea), 39, 46, 158
North Vietnam (Democratic Republic of Vietnam), 40
Nyerere, President Julius K., 41

Oceania, 43
October Socialist Revolution, 41
Ode to Imeng, 34, 42
Ode to the Dragon River, 34
On the Docks, 102-3, 151-54, 168
"One Million Heroes," 65, 69
Opium War, 104

Pakistan, 34, 41
Palestine, 46
Pei-ching Jih-pao, 116
Pei-ching Wan-pao, 116
Pei-kuo Chiang-nan, 94
Peking, 9, 11, 15-16, 30, 32, 34, 37-46, 59, 61, 69-70, 73, 79, 90, 93, 104, 109, 118, 123, 125-28, 132-33, 139, 141, 165
Peking Ballet Company, 101
Peking Daily, 56, 59, 96
Peking Municipal Party Committee, 59, 99, 125
Peking Opera, 3, 7-8, 10, 15, 17, 34, 46, 55, 57, 91, 95-108, 149-61, 165-69
  Company Number One, 60, 97, 103
  Festival of, 104-5

Peking Physical Culture Institute, 43
Peking Revolutionary Committee, 17, 35, 59
Peking University, 59, 118, 123
Peking Weekly, 92
Peking Workers Stadium, 61, 123
P'eng Chen, 55-56, 59, 65, 96-99, 104, 106, 113, 115-18, 125, 129
P'eng Te-huai, 14-15, 56, 96, 113-14
People's Daily, 41, 84, 92-94, 115-19, 126, 137, 141, 165
People's Liberation Army (PLA), 14, 17, 20, 25, 30, 33, 51-52, 56-79, 83, 104, 115, 122-23, 131, 149, 162, 174-75. *See also* Air Force; Armored Force; Artillery Force; Navy; Railway Corps; Signal Corps
People's Live Action Army, 80
People's Republic of China. *See* China, People's Republic of; Chinese Communist Government
Peru, 42
Phan Van Dong, Premier, 40
Philadelphia Symphony Orchestra, 44
Physical Culture and Sports Commission, 40, 43
Picking Up a Jade Bracelet, 91
Pinghsing Pass, 7, 90
Pompidou, President Georges, (France), 42
Prairie Fire, 139
Press Ganging, 94
Proletarian Educational Revolution, 134
Pyongyang National Opera Troupe of Korea, 39

Quotations from Lin Piao, 67

Radio Shanghai, 73
Radio Wuhan, 81-82
Raid on the White Tiger Regiment, 103-4, 157-59
Railway Corps, 66, 76
Red Detachment of Women, The, 38, 41-44, 52, 101, 161-64, 167
Red Flag, 84, 137
Red Guards, 29-30, 34, 41, 59-62, 118, 120, 123-39
Red Lantern, The, 33-34, 36-37, 46, 81-84, 100, 108, 159-61, 165, 168
Red Sun, 94
Red Vanguards of Air Force Headquarters, 62
Revisionists, 17, 19, 45, 52, 57, 59-60, 68-69, 89, 106-7, 114, 116, 118-19, 126-27, 130-31, 136, 139, 175
Revolutionary Committees, 18, 21, 68, 72, 78, 108, 121, 127, 174
Romania, 37-38
Russia. *See* Soviet entries

Sea of Blood, 39
Self-Cultivation, 132
Shachiapang, 33-34, 37, 79, 81, 99-100, 103, 154-57, 168
Shanghai, 3-6, 16, 18, 30, 34, 44, 55-56, 102, 105, 113, 126-29, 152-53, 165
Shanghai Ballet Troupe, 101
Shanghai Committee, 128
Shanghai People's Art Theatre, 139
Shanghai People's Opera Troupe, 98
Shanghai Revolutionary Committee, 17
Shantung, 3, 6, 13, 93, 132
Shantung Experimental Drama Academy, 3
Shansi, 18, 131, 166, 169
Shansi Provincial Revolutionary

Index

Committee, 18, 73
Shen Chi-lan, 169
Shibata,, Minoru, 69, 125
Shimizu, Masao, 39
Signal Corps (Chinese Army), 76
Sihanouk, Prince Norodom, 39, 40
Sinkiang Autonomous Region, 108, 130, 132
Sino-Japanese War. *See also* Chinese-Japanese war of 1894, 91, 167
Sisters of the Stage, 94
"Sixteen Points," 116, 120-22
Snow, Edgar, 43-44
Snow, Helen Foster, 43-44
Socialist Education Movement, 13, 15, 55, 122, 173
Sons and Daughters of China, 6
South Vietnam, 34, 40
Southeast Asia, 38
Soviet Communist Party Secretariat, 22
Soviet Twentieth Party Congress, 12
Soviet Union. *See* Union of Soviet Socialist Republics
Sparks Amid the Reeds, 97-98, 154
Ssu-t'u Hui-min, 4
Stalin, Josef, 22
Stories of Hai Jui, 114
Strong, Anna Louise, 14, 42-43, 125
Study of the Dream of the Red Chamber, 94
Sukarno, 39
Sung Ching-chih, 10, 94
Sung Yu-ch'ing, 104
Swan Lake, 102
Swaziland, 47
Switzerland, 43
Szechuan, 18, 69, 100, 137
Szechuan Revolutionary Committee, 18

Tachung Daily, 82

Taiwan, 28
Taking the Bandit's Stronghold, 45, 52-53, 79, 82, 103
Taking Tiger Mountain by Strategy, 82, 103, 108, 149-51, 155
"Talks at the Yenan Forum on Literature and Art," 7, 44, 82, 84, 87, 90
T'an Chen-lin, 68-69, 136
Tan Fu-ying, 17
Tanzania, 34, 41
T'ao Chu, 99, 130, 132, 136
Teng Hsiao-p'ing, 12, 22, 96, 99-100, 129-30
T'eng T'o, 16, 116-17
Teng Tzu-hui, 35
Teng Wan-tien, 166
Thinking, Feeling, and Literary Talent, 132
Third World, 41
"Three-Family Village," 15, 115-17
"Three-Famous" Principle, 138
Three-in-One Revolutionary Committee, 132
Tibet, 82
T'ien Han, 8, 16, 139
Tienanmen Square (Peking), 43, 70
Tientsin, 70, 136
Tonozaki, Yoshiaki, 39
Ts'ao Ti-ch'iu, 128
Tsinan, 3, 4
Tsinghai, 18, 132
Tsingtao, 4
Tsingtao University, 4
Tsui Wei, 135
Tu Chin-fang, 103
Tuchuan Mountains, 34
Tung, Jerry, 43
Tunisia, 46
Twenty Cents, 5
Tz'u-hsi, Dowager Empress, 91

USSR. *See* Union of Soviet Socialist Republics

Union of Chinese Drama Workers, 16
Union of Soviet Socialist Republics (USSR), 12-25, 22, 34, 37-41, 83, 137
Union of Working Youths of Albania, 38
United Action Committee, 129, 131
United Action Red Guards, 65
United Nations, 36, 43
United Press International (UPI), 132
United States of America, 37, 39, 43-44

Vanguard, 45
Vietnam. *See also* National Liberation Front of South Vietnam; North Vietnam; South Vietnam War, 37
Vietnam Workers' Party, 40

Wan Shih, 167
Wanchow Shan, 16, 118
Wang Chi-fan, 35
Wang Chia-hsiang, 35
Wang Hung-wen, 30, 42, 176
Wang Lao Wu, 5, 20
Wang Li, 69
Wang Meng-yun, 103
Wang Ming, 90
Wang Shu-sheng, 35
Wang Tsu-chieh, 166
Wang Tung-hsing, 176
Wang Yin-o, 18
Wang Yu-chang, 53
Wen Hui Pao, 55, 97, 114, 116

White Haired Girl, The, 33, 40, 47, 52, 101, 161-66
Wilcox, V. G., 45
With Troops under the Walls of the City, 94
World of Money, The, 139
Wu Han, 15, 55-56, 113-16
Wu Hsun, 10, 92-93
Wu Shu-yang, 165
Wu Te, 59
Wuhan, 69-70, 82
Wuhan University, 118

Yang Hsiu-fang, 136
Yang Shang-k'un, 125
Yang Tsu-jung, 52-53, 149-51, 155
Yang Yu-hsi, 166
Yang Yung, 65
Yangtze River, 69, 99
Yao Wen-yüan, 16-17, 21, 27, 29, 38, 55, 113, 116-18, 132, 176
Yeh Chien-ying, 27, 30, 51, 53, 84, 129
Yellow River, 34, 36
Yenan, 6-8, 28-29, 34, 51-52, 62, 87-90, 137, 163
Yenan Peking Opera Theatre, 8
Yin Wei-chen, 166
Young Pioneers, 140
Yu Hui-yung, 103
Yu Ping-po, 95
Yu Yen-hua, 168
Yuan Mu-chi, 92
Yuan Shih-hai, 136

Zambia, 41
Zhelokhovtsev, A., 124